CW00358296

Become an
NLP PRACTITIONER
with NLP Principles.

The Essential
Neuro Linguistic Programming Practitioner
Handbook, Guide & Reference Book.

Written by
Lee Groombridge

INLPTA NLP Trainer & NLP Master Practitioner

First published in Great Britain in 2022 by
Groombridge Group Limited.

Written and Illustrated by Lee Groombridge.

The right of Lee Groombridge to be identified as the Author of
this Work has been asserted by him in accordance with the
Copyright, Design and Patent Act, 1998.

Cover artwork by Lee Groombridge.
Cover image © Bestmoose, Dreamstime.com, ID14400210
Cover image Extended Print License Groombridge Group Limited

INLPTA refers to International NLP Trainers Association.
INLPTA.org

ANLP refers to ANLP International CIC.
ANLP.org

First Edition –
Version 1.0.0 – 27th March 2022 – Original Edit
Version 1.1.0 – 31st March 2024 - Minor edits & additional book
recommendations

ISBN: 9798441713467
Imprint: Independently published

This book contains all the information and knowledge required to become a certified Neuro Linguistic Programming Practitioner.

For more information about our internationally accredited Neuro-Linguistic Programming certification training courses visit,

www.nlpprinciples.com

P.S.

Don't tell anyone but if you have purchased this book, you'll be eligible for a discount on certification training. Check out *Getting Certified* at the end.

EPIGRAPH

A quote to set a theme for what you are about to
read, learn and experience.

*"Everything we hear is an opinion,
everything we see is a perspective,
not the truth."*

Marcus Aurelius

ACKNOWLEDGEMENTS

For bringing Neuro Linguistic Programming to us all.

The first acknowledgements have to go to the people who co-created NLP; Richard Bandler, John Grinder and Frank Pucelik. Their curiosity and talents enabled them to elicit and in turn document the models from world-class therapists, sharing with the world the initial techniques that formed the basis of a discipline that has gone on to make such an impact around the world to so many people.

Beyond these three co-founders are the people who helped develop the change technology and extended the library of models and techniques. Although I have not yet met all of these people in person, I would like to extend gratitude for their talents and for their generosity in sharing their incredible work and content. Thank you to; Steve Andreas, Connirae Andreas, Robert Dilts, Judith DeLozier, Stephen Gilligan, Shelle Rose Charvet, Michael Hall, Judith Lowe, Tad James, Wyatt Woodsmall, John Overdurf and Julie Silverthorn to name just a few! You can learn more about some of their contributions in this book.

Throughout this book, where I am able to, I have attributed the original source (book and page number) of the NLP Practitioner material to allow you to further your education and research on particular topics and subjects that interest you. I have genuinely referenced to the best of my ability and knowledge, and yet with that being said if I have mis-referenced or omitted a reference I would very much welcome and be grateful for any feedback so that I can amend or add appropriate references for future revisions and editions.

You will also find an extensive *bibliography* at the back of this book, if after reading this book you are serious about becoming an NLP Practitioner, and hopefully following the journey to becoming a Master Practitioner and Trainer like myself, I highly recommend that you become familiar with these original works. You will learn throughout this book and in particular the *NLP Communication Model* the closer you can get to the original source for your knowledge and models the better! More of that later...

For my Neuro Linguistic Programming journey.

Thank you to my NLP Master Trainers Reb Veale, Dr Henrie Lidiard, the original Master Trainer and Master Modeller himself Wyatt Woodsmall and to the first European NLP Master Trainer Bert Feustel, for a period of time together that will be remembered for a lifetime. I'm grateful for having the opportunity and experience to become a certified international NLP Trainer with world-class trainers not to mention some of the true pioneers of NLP.

An extra special thank you goes to Bert Feustel, co-founder of INLPTA. Without your generosity in sharing your extensive knowledge with me, spending hours reviewing the content and our one-to-one calls to ensure the quality of this book is as high as possible and correct to know history, this book as it exists now would not be possible. I am truly privileged and grateful for having the opportunity to gain your input and insights.

Thank you to Chris Menlove-Platt and Sam Dyer for setting me up and off into the world of NLP. I will always be grateful for your generosity and openness to share your knowledge with me on my road to becoming an NLP Master Practitioner and Humanistic Neuro-Linguistic Psychology Coach.

On my very own journey to becoming an NLP Trainer, I was also extremely fortunate to share time with some incredible people that I can now proudly call friends; Mark Deacon, Aliyah Mohyeddin, Andy Coley, Iain Adenis, Katalin Marton, Jayne Rolls, Bo Goeran Peterson, Lou Laggan, Francis Petot, Chris Bell and also Cara, Sarah, Dean, Helen, Emma, Michelle and Lorraine, I truly appreciate and cherish the fun and on occasion challenging times we spent together. I'm grateful for the positive impact each and every one of you had on my learning. Thank you for your support and ongoing alliance.

For my personal journey.

Thank you to my wife Clare for your love and unwavering support.

To my parents, thank you for your unconditional love and positive influence on my life.

And then there is my daughter Millie, thank you for all the things you have no idea you have taught me. I love you and am so very proud to be your dad.

HOW TO USE THIS BOOK.

Based on my own experience of learning and studying NLP, a lot of consideration has been put into how this book has been designed and written. The aim was to provide you, the reader and learner the maximum flexibility for how you wish to access, reference and process the content.

A Reference Book. Extended Contents & Index to support learning.
The contents section is larger than most books by design. The intent is to enable you to quickly pinpoint and access topics, models, methodology and techniques from the front of this book. It also provides an overview of the content you will be learning in a logical order. In addition, the index at the back is alphabetically sorted for quick reference and cross-referencing.

A Coursebook. Learn by reading the syllabus from front to back.
The content and sections are presented in a way that enables you to build up your knowledge in a linear sequential fashion. Each section builds on the previous sections, taking you logically through the NLP syllabus.

A Revision Guide. Use this as a perfect reference and revision book.
The content is distilled and presented in a way that allows each section to be stand-alone making it an ideal resource for revision on route to becoming a certified NLP Practitioner, Master Practitioner or NLP Trainer.

An NLP Dictionary. Use this book as an NLP glossary of terms.
If you are looking for quick reference definitions of NLP terms you will find an extensive glossary of NLP terms at the back of this book presented in alphabetical order. These distilled NLP definitions are perfect to help communicate terms to clients, use in presentations or assist in training.

A Companion Book. Use this book as an ultimate reference handbook.
Whether you are starting your journey into NLP or you are already certified, you undoubtedly from time to time find yourself in a place where you need to look up and refresh your memory on a particular topic. The best effort has gone into not only providing you with content but also providing direct page references to the original books where the content was sourced from. These references enable you to access the creators' material giving you the opportunity to go further and deeper to enhance your learning. These references are my way of paying full respect to the amazing work done by those individuals who created this discipline and the techniques and models shared within.

CONTENTS

SPECIAL MENTION DUE TO CONTRIBUTION

BERT FEUSTEL
NLP MASTER TRAINER | CO-FOUNDER INPLTA

Before I travelled to the beautiful village of Cancon, in France to complete my NLP Trainers training, I had already written 300 or so pages of the book you are reading right now. My intention was to complete the content after the training and publish it on my return. One particular day in the middle of our 5-week training experience, a small group of us had an opportunity to sit with Bert Feustel one of the co-founders of INLPTA. We discussed, amongst many things, how we could help contribute in a positive and meaningful way to the world of NLP. It was during this conversation I presented Bert with a draft copy of this book. After a short flick through he jumped to the back of the book to see what sources and references I had used to create the content. It was only then he happened to mention that he knew and had worked with almost everyone that was referenced on those pages – unsurprising really due to the fact he had been a pioneer in bringing NLP to Germany and Europe for that matter! At this point, I asked if he would like to read through the draft to ensure that the quality of the content was up to scratch and ensure the accuracy of the references and NLP history - which due to my research differs from some books. Much to my delight he agreed!

After providing Bert with a digital copy to review and comment on, what followed was more than I could have ever expected. Extensive feedback, additions, enhancements to definitions, and suggestions on content order, all to make this book purposeful and unique to the NLP books that already exist. With Bert witnessing my enthusiasm to put all the feedback into practice and in place he then offered to have multiple one-on-one calls to ensure that my desire to produce a quality book was achieved. Bert's influence and knowledge is peppered throughout this book and is why this dedication page is written so that I can properly acknowledge his contribution and also extend an immense amount of gratitude to Bert for helping me produce this book. I hope and trust this book is welcomed by the NLP community for providing some new information and extensive direct source references. For any up-and-coming NLP enthusiasts wanting to jump in a learn about the subject, I hope this sets you off with great momentum. To accompany this special mention, I'm honoured to present to you the foreword to this book by the man himself, over to you Bert…

FOREWORD

NLP is now about 50 years old, and in those years, after the dozen or so original NLP sourcebooks written by the first generation of authors, hundreds of additional books have been written all over the world. A few have become classics, and many of them were just summaries and interpretations of what the next generation of authors thought NLP was. It took about 25 years for some NLP Trainers in different countries to attempt to create an encyclopaedia or dictionary of NLP terms and definitions. Today we still have a lot of work to do - because the language of NLP definitions is vague, there are multiple versions, and different interpretations of how NLP techniques, presuppositions or models are used.

INLPTA was founded in 1993 primarily for three reasons:

1. to create a higher quality of training and precision in the use of NLP models and definitions.
2. to unite the various factions of NLP schools that had separated in the first 10 years to re-establish a complete picture of what NLP has to offer.
3. to provide a framework for ethics, professionalism and quality in training.

This book for the first time includes the 2022 published unified code of ethics that the four leading international NLP associations have established.

Originally, NLP was created as a psychotherapeutic model to treat people who have psychological difficulties. However, over time, other contexts have been found and NLP is now used and taught not only in coaching and sales but also in advertising, team development, leadership or more generally to improve communication. So today you can actually learn NLP without having the need or desire to treat anyone.

This book by Lee Groombridge is a great way for anyone who wants to learn NLP to understand how modern NLP can be taught. In saying that, if you are someone doing any NLP training and you want to deal more intensively with the content, this book will also be a great help to see the connections and many possible applications.

Bert Feustel, *NLP Master Trainer & INLPTA Co-Founder*

INTRODUCTION

As I sit facing the front of the room with six other people, little did I know I was about to begin an experience that would change my life forever. I had set off the night before, travelling for three hours down dark country lanes, alone in my car to start a new chapter. The previous week, I had resigned as CEO and left a business that I had co-founded and built up over 10 years. After many great years and an acquisition, the tide had turned and the business had evolved into something that I no longer felt connected to.

Being the CEO means that you are the leader of a business and the leader of the company's people, therefore being disconnected is somewhat of an issue if you are an ethical and authentic leader. Although the easy option was to stay, I knew deep down I could no longer lead with my previous passion and excitement, and that this misalignment would eventually be to the detriment of the business, the people involved, let alone me. We had done so well to get to where we were and I did not want to hinder or obstruct their future, so it was time for me to get out of their way. With a heavy heart, I went separate ways with my co-founders to get back on a path right for me.

So, why did I like feel this? Why was the push so strong? What was I going to do next? All great questions, and honestly, I had no idea how to answer any of them. Firstly, I looked at business coaching, with a credible and tangible track record for being involved and starting a number of businesses, most of which had scaled to a more than reasonable size and seen financial success. I had extensive practical real-world experience and advice that could help people either start businesses or scale ones they were already in. My style of running a business focuses towards operations, people and financial analysis, so I knew I could help businesses get clarity, pivot and navigate through the many issues that come from running a business. However, as I investigated providing people and businesses with this kind of help, something still felt missing to me, there was still a piece to this puzzle to find!

I'm fortunate to live close to the beach on the south coast of England and when I have a question that I'm pondering on I have a routine of taking a long walk along the seafront to have a good think. On one sunny yet crisp morning, as I looked out at the sea, the missing piece fell into place. Sure, I could help *businesses* with all the knowledge I had but what I was really inspired me was to help the *person* or *people* that run the businesses! A position that can be highly pressured and isolating in the good times as well as the low times. This was something I had direct experience and empathy with as well as a desire to positively contribute towards solutions to help. So, with this newfound perspective, I started to research high-performance personal development, mentoring and psychology coaching. The doors flung open to information and content that immediately resonated with me. I had found what I was going to focus my attention on. Let the studying commence!

Research repeatedly led me to something that I had been intrigued about in past years and yet never really pursued beyond reading a few books and watching a few videos. This, which as you are reading this book will come as no surprise, was Neuro-Linguistic Programming. I knew it was powerful with regards to influencing behaviour and yet beyond that, I knew very little. So, with some excitement and a passion to learn I signed up for an in-person NLP Practitioner and Humanistic Psychology Coaching course. It was quite some distance from home, but this didn't matter. I had not only found what I needed to learn but also found someone who could start my learning journey.

So, did this course provide me with what I thought it would? Absolutely not! It gave me so, so much more. I do not want to extend this introduction onto another ten pages as we have important information to cover, so let me just say this, you are now reading a book based on the fact that I not only completed that course to become an NLP Practitioner, I went on to become an NLP Master Practitioner and then ventured even further to become an internationally certified NLP trainer. I think that says enough really!

As it stands today, you are reading a book published by my new company that provides businesses with exactly what they need to thrive and grow as well as providing the people behind businesses with all the support they need to perform at their highest level to succeed. In addition, for those people like you interested in the discipline of NLP for personal growth or maybe to become a coach, we provide internationally accredited NLP certification.

Whatever the reason you are reading this book, as we say in our courses, I promise you one thing, whatever you think NLP is, it is way, way more than you can ever imagine! I'm extremely happy and privileged to be a part of your learning journey having the opportunity to provide you with information that could most probably impact, or course correct your life, as it did for me. I do not take your investment with me for granted, I have done my very best to provide you with the most thorough knowledge that I possess right now. And right now, you are reading a complete handbook containing all you need to *become an NLP Practitioner*. Please do enjoy…

WHY NLP?

I'm often asked the question "Why did you specifically choose Neuro-Linguistic Programming?" I love this question. I genuinely see it as a great opportunity to share and give people a newfound understanding of what NLP actually is. Although asked through curiosity of my own personal circumstances, it would be amiss to not acknowledge there is often a subtle undertone of scepticism with the discipline of NLP. So, let's deal with this right off the bat!

I am what you might call a very logical practical person, so initially, I thought NLP would offer me an opportunity to challenge myself to learn something that, let's say exists in the more intangible holistic side of life; psychology and emotional intelligence. However, what you quickly learn is that even though the things you can achieve with NLP techniques appear to be completely illogical and intangible, the theories behind these techniques are founded on extremely logical strategies. This for me was enough of an olive branch to spark intrigue to learn more. As you will also grow to learn, NLP *has* to be based on logic or the results could not be repeated nor trained to anyone.

It's not magic – despite the confusion caused by the original books written sharing this discipline being called *The Structure of Magic*. Although some outcomes achieved using the techniques may appear to be to the untrained eye. Which leads us on to the fact that NLP is *not* the techniques themselves either. Another common misconception is that some unqualified people will have you believe. NLP is the code that gives us the capability to model desirable human behaviour that creates excellent results, enabling the creation of repeatable models, processes and techniques so that others can achieve that same excellence. All this will become clearer as you learn more.

NLP also focuses on positive future-focused principles, giving you the mindset and tools to define where you want to go in life and help you get there. The NLP Practitioner course itself is a great route to learn soft skills that last a lifetime, skills that are transferable to anything you decide to put your mind to and do in the future. It is for this reason I say that, no matter the context, the time spent learning NLP will not be and is not time wasted.

Now, my question to you is, "Why are *you* choosing NLP?". As you work through this NLP Practitioner book, I trust that in some way you will find your own answer and eventually feel the same level of positivity and gratitude towards it.

A SERIOUS WORD OF WARNING!

Before you read another page of this book, I would like to warn you of something. That is, that you will be unable to unsee or unlearn the things you are about to learn and experience from the content in this book. Progress knowing the content *will* change your perception of how you see your world, not to mention what others say and how others behave.

The metaphor I use for my own personal experience of learning NLP is that I had been unaware that I had been living only seeing the world in black and white and understanding NLP immediately switched on all the colours.

I am grateful that you are reading *this* book right now and that I have somehow managed to cut through the noise of all the NLP training material that is out there. I have come to find that there is unfortunately such a large variance of skill level, knowledge and sadly integrity with regards to sharing the body of work that NLP has to offer. I take the responsibility of training NLP very seriously as I know first-hand that it can have such a profound positive impact on you. With this know that ethics, professionalism and high quality are fundamentally important and the NLP Practitioner syllabus content presented to you here has all of those values front of mind.

Similarly, the insights, 'a-ha' moments, or light bulbs this book will give you may inspire you to help others. With this knowledge and your new capabilities comes great power and responsibility, please use it wisely, use it ethically and use it to make positive change for yourself and others.

If after finishing or during this book you wish to convert and progress your learnings to an *in-person* experience and become a certified NLP Practitioner, whether for personal achievement or maybe to become a better coach, manager or leader, it would be a privilege to be a continued part of your NLP journey. Our internationally accredited certification courses meet the highest professional standards of NLP training delivered by high-quality, professional and ethical trainers. Visit *nlpprinciples.com* or see the certification section towards the back of this book for more information. It would be a pleasure to hear from you and to meet you in person one day.

Now, with all that said, let the learning begin!

SO, WHAT CAN YOU USE NLP FOR?

This book is written very much in a way that adheres and tips its hat to the origins of Neuro-Linguistic Programming. It focuses on providing you with how the NLP Practitioner syllabus was shared back in the 1970s, 80's and 90's. Sharing the content in this way does tend to steer you towards therapy and coaching. However, please don't be fooled, NLP has many more use cases than just these fields. In an attempt to share with you how you can benefit and utilise this information let me take you for a little walk along the timeline of NLP.

1960's & 70's – Therapy and treating of others.

Due to the origins of the NLP, in that the focus was on learning how outlier therapists and clinical hypnotists gained their results, a lot of the original models discovered and in turn techniques created had a focus on psychoanalysis, psychotherapy and behavioural therapy. Although these techniques worked and the co-creators were seeing incredible results for patients, treating issues such as phobias and PTSD (Post Traumatic Stress Disorder), the co-creators were not professional therapists nor clinical hypnotherapists, they were expert modellers. As expert modellers, they were able to reproduce in practice the most effective strategies. This steer towards action however led to a lack of academic rigour and data collection in their work, so despite clearly achieving results, the professional bodies put actions in place to hinder or halt the use of techniques that had been discovered via NLP. Still to this day even though some proven techniques such as Double Dissociation and Fast Phobia Cure exist even as an NLP Master Practitioner you need a professional clinical therapist license to perform these techniques. It is for this reason some specific techniques around curing Phobias are removed from this book – to protect us both!

1980's – Self-Therapy and Personal Growth

As NLP gathered some momentum, people also began to realise that the models and techniques being discovered were at their core about managing emotions, behaviour and state control. With this realisation, people began to utilise NLP knowledge to enhance their own performance with self-therapy or as we would call it today personal development or personal growth. With a focus on personal insights, people used NLP techniques to manage issues like anger or anxiety. There was also attention put on defining and reaching personal goals and achieving success more efficiently and effectively. This in turn gave birth to the category of self-help books in bookstores. This category shared previously complicated academic knowledge in a much more obtainable, readable and practical way, which unsurprisingly flew off the shelves a faster than the previous heavy reads on these therapy-based topics.

1980's & 1990's – Transferable Communication Skills

Coupled with the self-help movement bringing this knowledge to a wider audience, people started connecting the dots on a broader series of use cases for the skills NLP was sharing and developing. As people began to realise that a superior therapist was someone who was; an excellent listener, an advanced observer, a good communicator, a master of asking the right questions, and a talented problem solver, all being transferable skills useful in being a top performer in a number of other professions and aspects of life. This dawned the arrival of using NLP to enhance professional skills; being a better teacher, a more empathic police officer and in the context of business, a more effective salesperson and a much cleverer marketer!

1990's – Leadership and Social Skills

Once NLP had hit the business world it drew a lot of attention. Then, in the late 90s, with the introduction of the term Emotional Intelligence invented by Daniel Goleman (someone who had written about NLP in the 80s in Psychology Today), NLP was being referenced as something that could train emotional intelligence due to the fact that you were learning about human behaviour in yourself and others. This was when NLP became associated with building social skills and leadership abilities. When this happened the original therapy-based techniques that appeared in the original syllabus fell by the wayside and more practical niche trainings arrived. Still, to this day people are training content that is influenced by NLP and yet they are probably unaware! With the lack of official policing of NLP content due to the lack of academic rigour or an official centralised association, NLP landed in a place where although providing some incredible personal growth and effective results, it is fragmented and somewhat watered down from the original modelling techniques and learnings – hence the purpose for the references in this book to help you source and learn from this material.

To summarise the original question, 'What can you use NLP for?'. Well, it can in fact be used as a layer to advance and enhance performance and efficacy in pretty much most things that involve people or achievement, whether that is in your personal or professional life.

AN OVERVIEW OF YOUR
NLP PRACTITIONER HANDBOOK.

The purpose of this book is to provide you with all the knowledge you need to take the next step in becoming a certified NLP Practitioner. For this reason, you can read this book purely for the purpose of personal development or you can use it as a fundamental workbook to prepare yourself for any credible NLP Practitioner certification.

The intention of an NLP Practitioner certification is to provide you with thorough knowledge of NLP as well as some practical implementations to be able to make a positive and ethical impact on yourself and the world around you. Although the core knowledge and teachings of all credible NLP Practitioner certifications will hold the same or similar knowledge and terminology, for clarity and transparency the contents in this book align specifically with the **INPLTA (The International Neuro-Linguistic Programming Trainers Association)** and **ANLP (The Association of Neuro-Linguistic Programming).** These are the two associations as the author of this book I align with, stand by, respect and proudly represent.

In addition, and following on from INLPTA guidelines, the content is also heavily influenced by, and where possible makes direct reference to, the original teachings presented by the NLP co-creators and other inspiring people that influenced the early development of NLP. There is an extensive bibliography at the end of this book that allows you to further research topics or techniques directly from the original material in these phenomenal books. At this point you are invited to, if you haven't already, take a look at the acknowledgements in this book for the author's own direct line to some of the original, most influential people, trainers and mentors in NLP.

With all that being said the reason for this book being written is that I wanted to contribute to the INLPTA mission statement;

"The purpose of INLPTA is to facilitate the alignment of professional NLP trainers around the world in the ethical and professional use of NLP throughout the standardisation and continual improvement of the NLP accreditation process"

With this, the intention is that this book will be updated as time passes with new information as it is discovered and yet always have references to the origins so that continuity can be maintained with the original works.

This book is split into 15 sections, presenting the information in such a way that each section builds on the last supporting your learning as if you are working through the content of the book front-to-back.

1 Foundations & Fundamentals	2 Communication Model	3 Values & Beliefs
4 Understanding States	5 Outcomes	6 Representational Systems
7 Rapport	8 Coaching with NLP	9 Anchoring
10 Language	11 Strategies	12 Sub-Modalities
13 Framing	14 Reframing	15 Learning

PART 1. FOUNDATION & FUNDAMENTALS

Where did NLP originate from and what are the core fundamentals?
You will learn about the history of NLP, the co-creators, how NLP came to be and how it is defined by the founders. Section one also shares some fundamental concepts that underpin most NLP content.

PART 2. COMMUNICATION MODEL

How do we create our perception of the world?
In this section, we will cover how we sense events that occur outside of us. We'll also cover how we process the data that we receive through our senses to create our very own bespoke perspectives and meanings of what happens in the world. You will also learn about what actually impacts our behaviour.

PART 3. VALUES & BELIEFS

What are the things that drive our behaviour?
Here you learn about the things that are most important to you and how values and beliefs drive your behaviour. Learn how these values were formed and how they can change depending on what aspect of life you are operating in at any given moment of time.

PART 4. UNDERSTANDING STATES

What are states and why are they important for effective NLP?
In this section, you will not only learn what a State is but also the different states you can find yourself or others in. You'll find out how these states can be positive or negative for you and how you can increase or remove your feelings and emotions associated with a particular experience.

PART 5. OUTCOMES

How can you structure an outcome using NLP to achieve success?
Here you will review why setting an outcome is important and specifically why setting a well-formed outcome with specific conditions is essential for you to be able to progress towards what you want and be successful.

PART 6. REPRESENTATIONAL SYSTEMS

How do we prefer to make sense of the world?
In this section, we will cover the different ways in which a person can create meaning, access past experiences and prefer to communicate. You will learn about how our eyes can give huge clues away to what and how we are thinking, processing and accessing information.

PART 7. RAPPORT

How do we build trusted relationships with others?
In this section, we will cover the art of rapport and building quality relationships. You'll become acutely aware of the observation skills required to understand the body language and verbal communication people are offering you constantly. You learn to know that we cannot not communicate.

PART 8. COACHING

What is coaching and what is your role if you are one?
In this section, we will learn about the future-focused, present-state to desired-state model where resourcefulness is the centre of all work done with NLP. You will also get a fundamental awareness of the roles and responsibilities of coaching compared to other frequently associated roles such as mentoring.

PART 9. ANCHORING

How can you manage and change states?
Learn what an anchor is and how you can create and apply one to optimally change how you are feeling at any moment of time. In this section, you will also gain knowledge about reflex reactions and how you can use NLP techniques to overcome situations where these reactions are not serving you.

PART 10. LANGUAGE

How what we say means much more than what we say!
Here you'll discover the language models and patterns of NLP; Meta Model and Milton Model. With these models, you will be able to use language in an elegant artful way to work out what someone is communicating to you and how, once you know this, you can help them be more resourceful.

PART 11. STRATEGIES

How do you sequence thinking to achieve a desired outcome?
Strategies are a core component of NLP modelling and therefore are important to understand for an NLP Practitioner. In this section, you will learn how to elicit and document the series of conscious and unconscious behaviours a person runs through to achieve predictable outcomes.

PART 12. SUB-MODALITIES

How do we actually attach meaning to experiences?
Find out about the finer details behind how we distinguish between different events and how we differentiate meaning from multiple events using our senses. Understanding this will also give you the power to be able to change how you perceive events from the past as well as in the future.

PART 13. FRAMING

How you form your perspective on things.
This section gives you the opportunity to build awareness, perspective and in turn understanding of the meaning you associate to any given situation. Within this section, you will also learn how framing can be done on both a conscious and unconscious level.

PART 14. REFRAMING

How can you gain insight into a situation from multiple perspectives?
Learn how to understand a situation from different perspectives and perceptions. See how to elicit multiple people's perceptions of the same situation to give you a more rounded awareness of any given situation to resolve conflict or find creative solutions for any project in the future.

PART 15. LEARNING

What is learning?
Learn what learning is and the cycle that we all take when gaining a new capability. You will also discover the theory and methodology of the Feedback model used within NLP which is essential for growth and movement towards a well-formed outcome.

EXTENDED EDITION:
MASTER PRACTITIONER BONUS CONTENT

Although this book is focused on you becoming an NLP Practitioner by presenting a full NLP Practitioner syllabus, I believe there are a few topics that can add extra depth a value to your learning right now. So as a bonus and a way to give you an insight into what is beyond the Practitioner level, this book contains three bonus chapters to introduce you to the Master Practitioner syllabus. This also allows this book to be an even more useful reference book for those of you already at the NLP Practitioner level.

1	2	3
Meta-Programs	Utilising Values	Disney Strategy

BONUS 1. META-PROGRAMS
What ready-made programs are we all running that impact our decisions?
We are all running a number of decision processes that impact how we react to what we see, hear and feel every second of the day. This section will present all of the main meta-programs enabling you to identify these preferences in yourself and also in others.

BONUS 2. UTILISING VALUES
How can we become more resourceful using Values?
Learn that not all values are equal and that with this knowledge you can use NLP techniques to move them around in a hierarchy to work for you better providing you more flexibility in achieving desired outcomes.

BONUS 3. DISNEY STRATEGY
What are the secrets behind genius?
Learn the strategy behind consistent creative output. You will see an example of how one of the early contributors to NLP, Robert Dilts, elicited a strategy from the genius Walt Disney, and how he utilised different capabilities, preferences and perceptions to reliably produce creative solutions.

PART ONE:

FOUNDATION
& FUNDAMENTALS

NLP DEFINITION

As you begin to learn more about NLP you will no doubt be enthused to share your knowledge. I myself experienced this after a few 'light-bulb' moments. Although people listened with interest to what I enthusiastically had to say, the same questions came up again and again,

"That's great but what actually is NLP?"
"Isn't all this about manipulation?"
"So, can you control people's minds now?"

I'll be honest, on my path to becoming an NLP Practitioner, I went into my initial training session with most, if not all, of the same questions in mind.

Here's the thing, once you have finished this book or taken a credible certification course, you realise that all of these questions are extremely good signals that the person asking has not experienced NLP before, giving you a great opportunity to share what you know and potentially excite someone enough to learn more. I truly believe the information within an NLP Diploma and Practitioner should appear somewhere in the national curriculum at schools because the things you learn within this NLP syllabus literally apply to every human on the planet. Interestingly, every single NLP Practitioner (or level above) I have ever had a conversation with agrees with this also!

By the end of this syllabus, you will develop your own responses to inquisitive questions regarding NLP even if they are critical or negative. However, for now, let's jump into what NLP technically is so that you, as a person who is about to enthusiastically share what you learn with others, have an answer to the main core question, 'What is NLP?'.

Based on the fact you are reading a book about learning to be an NLP Practitioner and making an assumption about your level of current knowledge, I'm curious to know what you would say *right now* if you were asked. What will be interesting for you is how your answer will most probably change after reading just this section. Although some official definitions are shared here, you will also come to learn that it is highly possible that you will arrive at your very own interpretation and definition of what NLP means to you once you become an NLP Practitioner.

Let's begin with the term *NLP* itself and the meaning of the words behind this acronym; Neuro, Linguistic and Programming.

Neuro
How we think and how our mind takes information in.

In this instance, *Neuro* refers to our neurological systems, in particular the way in which we take in information and data. It is based on the principle that we all experience the world through our own senses and then translate this sensory information into thoughts. It is important to note that this is not just about the brain in our head, it refers to our complete nervous system. It is also fundamental to acknowledge that we process sensory data both at a conscious and an unconscious level. To simplify *Neuro,* think of it as *Data In.*

Linguistic
How we outwardly communicate with words and how language affects us.

Linguistic refers to how we communicate the meaning of our experiences to the outside world. It is easy to understand how *linguistics* is often assumed to mean just the words we use. However, it is important to acknowledge that within NLP, linguistics refers to both our verbal and non-verbal language (also commonly known as body language). To simplify *Linguistics*, think of it as *Communication Out*

Programming
The processes, patterns and strategies behind our thoughts and actions.

Programming in the context of NLP can be broken down into two parts; Firstly, the strategies we use to notice the data coming in via our senses and the processes we use to translate this information into our own personal understanding of an experience, situation or event. Secondly, with your own personal understanding of an experience, programming refers to the processes leading to thoughts that cause you to react to this information or in some cases cause unconscious behaviour to achieve a particular result. To simplify Programming think of it as *Processing Within.*

With these brief explanations of the three elements, and by embracing the fact that everyone has their own unique understanding of experiences, it is easy to consider that due to a person's own focus or perspective, definitions of NLP can vary and a single definitive definition of NLP is not exactly possible. This also explains how NLP as a subject matter, discipline or field of study, is so open to so much interpretation.

Now all this aside, let's not omit the fact that you are reading this section to learn and gain a definition of NLP that you can use. So, below are a number of common definitions. Some will make more sense to you as you work through the NLP Practitioner material and yet for now, they will give you a good understanding of the variety of angles people come at NLP from even though there are only three fundamental words behind what is being described. To pay respect to the co-creators and initial developers of NLP, their definitions have these highlighted, which also provides an interesting insight into how they personally define NLP.

Definitions of NLP

NLP is;

- the art and science of human excellence.
- an instruction manual for the mind.
- the study of subjective experience.
- a way that allows us to defrag our human computers.
- the 'how-to' manual of subjective excellence and modelling it.
- the systemic study of human communication.
- the influence of language on our mind and subsequent behaviour.
- a highly effective technology for accelerating personal and professional development.
- the 'how-to' of Emotional Intelligence where you can study the strategies of excellence and pass these on to yourself or others.
- a technical approach to let you understand more about the inter-relationship between the way you think, what you say, how you feel and what you do.
- whatever works. (*Robert Dilts*)

The Co-Creators' Definitions of NLP

- "NLP is an attitude and a methodology, which leaves behind a trail of techniques." (*Richard Bandler*)

- "NLP is an accelerated learning strategy for the detection and utilisation of patterns in the world" (*John Grinder*)

It is always interesting to notice which one you like, prefer or resonates with you right now, and then after becoming an NLP Practitioner, if and how that has changed. In fact, on becoming an NLP Practitioner you are asked to create and share your very own personal definition of what NLP is and means to you. As the author of this book I will share mine;

NLP is,

- a discipline of communication allowing us to understand, document and repeat the detailed mechanics of people's patterns enabling effective change." (*Lee Groombridge*)

As previously mentioned, the content of this book is in alignment with the INLPTA NLP Practitioner standards for the purpose of providing a level of standardisation to the syllabus. Therefore, with this front of mind, we will look into and break down the definition provided by the co-creator Richard Bandler.

Richard Bandler states that NLP is,

"An attitude and a methodology, which leaves behind a trail of techniques."

Let's look at each part of this separately;

- Attitude
- Methodology
- Trail of Techniques

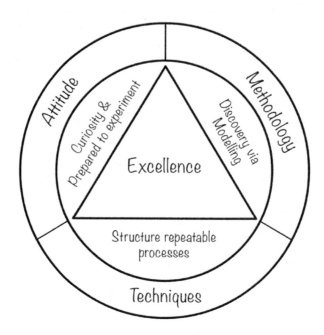

Attitude

A state of mind to allows us to be curious and prepared to experiment to discover excellence.

Attitude brings immediate attention towards looking at a desired mindset or state of mind. It sets the foundation for getting you prepared to learn, change and grow which explains why some feel this is the key behind understanding human excellence. Here is a list of NLP attitudes;

- Be purposeful and act from intention
- Professionalism gets results
- Wed competence and confidence
- Flexibility: be outrageous or crazy
- View life as a challenge
- Use common sense: take only calculated risks
- Always act from integrity
- Be fascinated and curious:
  - ask how
  - be wide-eyed
  - be in awe and radical amazement

To enrich and extend your understanding of an NLP attitude further here is a list of words that can be associated to it courtesy of INPLTA co-founder Wyatt Woodsmall.

The 12 C's, the 12 E's and the 4 I's.

12 C's	12 E's	4 I's
Congruency	Excellence	Integrity
Competence	Excitement	Impeccability
Confidence	Envision	Integration
Creativity	Energise	Intentionality
Concern	Enable	
Care	Ecology	
Commitment	Entertain	
Curiosity	Enlightenment	
Choice	Expectation	
Challenge	Experiment	
Clarity	Ecstasy	
Consequences	Eliminate seriousness	

Methodology
Modelling a behaviour to discover excellence.

Methodology is the next most impactful element, if not on equal par to Attitude. Using your readiness to experiment you must try things that are new to you, things you may consider to be beyond your competence and outside of your comfort zone. Within the field of NLP, *methodology* relates directly to something called *modelling*.

Modelling describes the elicitation and understanding of the patterns, processes and strategies a person is running to produce or achieve an outcome you are either curious about or wish to be able to do.

Modelling allows you to determine and document what it is that makes a person so effective, therefore the resulting model enables the training of their methods to other people. In essence, it is about *how* they are achieving excellence.

Trail of Techniques
The structure and repeatable processes to produce excellence

Lastly, let's look at *trail of techniques*. This refers to the repeatable steps that you can follow to predictably create the same desired outcome that you have modelled. Interestingly, due to the fact that the *techniques* are what people see and hear NLP Practitioners do, it is not hard to understand that these techniques often influence how people incorrectly identify what NLP is.

People are generally unaware that NLP is about identifying excellent behaviour, eliciting this excellence as a model and then creating and running a model using custom communication to create predictable change towards a desired outcome. It is not just the technique they see, hear or experience.

So, before we move on to the next section let's remind ourselves of the original question, 'What is NLP?'. I wonder how your answer has now evolved after reading just this section, especially as you now know it is about;

- your state of mind,
- your communication,
- how you run strategies,
- learning from other people,
- study excellence.

Whatever your answer, we know one thing. It will evolve and change again!

Section Source Material & Further Learning on What NLP is.
(1979) Frog into Princes, Bandler & Grinder: Page i
(1980) NLP Vol I, Dilts, Grinder, Bandler, Bandler, De Lozier: Page 3
(1985) Using Your Brain for Change, Bandler: Page 7
(1987) Turtles All the Way Down, De Lozier & Grinder: Page 9

PILLARS OF NLP

Before we move on to a more in-depth look at the history and origins of NLP, let's cover the six basic principles or '*the 6 Pillars of NLP*'.

The point of presenting these at this early stage is to enable you to have an even richer explanation of what NLP is as well as give you an understanding as to why the co-creators started doing what they were doing in the first place.

Rather than just presenting these pillars as a definitive list of six, I want to take you on a little journey from the;

- *3 Legs of NLP*, through the evolution to the
- *4 Legs of NLP,* onto the
- *5 Principles of Success* and then finishing on the
- *6 Pillars of NLP.*

Remembering back to my early years of learning NLP, I can relate to the confusion that can be caused due to the overlapping and common cross-references of these four models and definitions. So, in order for this to not happen to you, I will present them in a logical order where each one builds on the previous, eventually allowing us to arrive at an understanding of what the 6 Pillars of NLP are and where they came from.

3 LEGS OF NLP

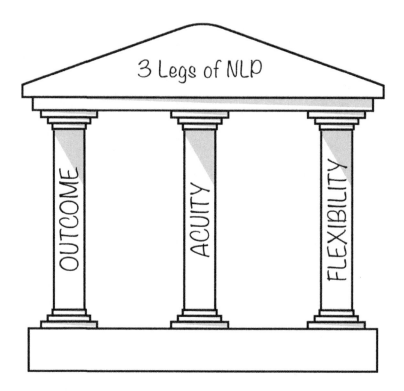

The 3 Legs of NLP are actually the three principles or elements required to achieve success. By success, we are referring to the achievement of a *desired outcome*. This desired outcome is sometimes assumed and defined as a 'successful life' and yet we can refine success to be literally anything that a person actually wants to achieve at any time.

- Outcome
- Acuity
- Flexibility

1) Outcome

Know what outcome you want to achieve.

Until Milton Erickson came along (someone you will become very familiar with by the end of this book) most therapists did not have defined outcomes for their sessions or work with clients. Milton Erickson, an American psychiatrist and psychologist specialising in medical hypnosis and family therapy, believed an outcome was required to enable success to be possible for his patients. As he was one of the first subjects to be modelled by the co-creators of NLP, *Outcome* became a part of the success model.

2) Sensory Acuity

Have sufficient sensory acuity to know if you are moving towards or away from your desired outcome.

There is an entire section in this book about Sensory Acuity but for the purpose of understanding this principle now it effectively means that you need to be alert and have awareness of the change that is happening, the results and feedback you are getting, whether that is in yourself or others. Then as you notice this change, be able to know if this is getting you closer or further away from your desired outcome.

3) Flexibility

Have sufficient flexibility of behaviour so that you can vary your behaviour until you get your outcome.

With continuous awareness and calibration of results to see whether the desired outcome is getting closer or further away, this next element of the model is for you to have the ability to vary your behaviour. Simply put, if what you are doing is not working, change what you are doing. Or, said another way, if what I am doing isn't getting me closer to my desired outcome, what can you do differently to get closer? Ultimately, this brings to light that the more choice you have leads to the more flexibility of behaviour you have which results in a greater chance of success.

4 LEGS OF NLP

The 4 Legs of NLP is also a model of how to be successful in achieving a goal. It is actually an evolution of the 3 Legs in that it contains all of the elements contained within the 3 Legs with the addition of a fourth *action-orientated* leg.

- Outcome
- Acuity
- Flexibility
- Take Action

1) Outcome.

Know what outcome you want to achieve.

2) Sensory Acuity

Have sufficient sensory acuity to know if you are moving toward or away from your desired outcome.

3) Flexibility

Have sufficient flexibility of behaviour so that you can vary your behaviour until you get your outcome.

4) Take Action

Change your behaviour to achieve your outcome.

There is no real need for an extensive explanation as to why *take action* is required to achieve something, however, a good way to distil and articulate this is to know that nothing ever happens until someone actually takes the initiative to act.

As a quick aside, this additional part of the model was added by Anthony Robbins, who was trained in part by Wyatt Woodsmall, a co-founder of INLPTA, a person I also have the privilege of calling one of my trainers and mentors!

5 PILLARS OF SUCCESS

With the 5 Pillars of Success, we evolve this model further with another addition from Anthony Robbins. He noticed and documented that in the doing of something it was not just *what* you did that contributed to success it was *how* you did it.

- Outcome
- Acuity
- Flexibility
- Take Action
- Physiology and psychology of excellence (P.O.E)

1) Outcome

Know what outcome you want to achieve.

2) Sensory Acuity

Have sufficient sensory acuity to know if you are moving toward or away from your desired outcome.

3) Flexibility

Have sufficient flexibility of behaviour so that you can vary your behaviour until you get your outcome.

4) Take Action

Change your behaviour to achieve your outcome.

5) Physiology and psychology of excellence (P.O.E)

Manage your physical and mental state to match that of the model of excellence you are using to achieve your outcome.

To improve your chances of success even further the addition of the fifth element opens up your action to not only be flexible but also to introduce the type of behaviour that is needed to produce the outcome you desire.

Although it is only a single point, it brings the entire concept and modelling of human excellence into the pillars of success.

6 PILLARS OF NLP

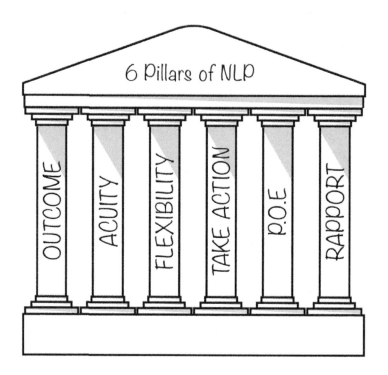

The last evolution, being the 6 Pillars of NLP, introduces a factor of awareness. Awareness of the influence of good relationships and how that contributes to achieving success.

- Know your Outcome
- Sensory Acuity for Feedback
- Flexibility of Behaviour
- Take Action
- Operate from a physiology and psychology of excellence (P.O.E)
- Rapport with yourself and others

1) Outcome

Know what outcome you want to achieve.

2) Sensory Acuity

Have sufficient sensory acuity to know if you are moving toward or away from your desired outcome.

3) Flexibility

Have sufficient flexibility of behaviour so that you can vary your behaviour until you get your outcome.

4) Take Action

Change your behaviour to achieve your outcome.

5) Physiology and psychology of excellence (P.O.E)

Manage your physical and mental state to match that of the model of excellence you are using to achieve your outcome.

6) Rapport

Gain and maintain mutual trust, high-quality relationships and communication by respecting the way others perceive the world.

Being in rapport with others builds good trustworthy relationships and these are an important factor in achieving outcomes. It enables opportunities to be presented increasing choice and flexibility. In addition, when extra resources are required, rapport enables the ability to lead and motivate others, and yourself, towards achievement.

It is only right of me to note that in some models of the 6 pillars of NLP *'Presuppositions of NLP'* replace the 'Take Action' or the 'Physiology and psychology of excellence' pillars. For the purpose of standardisation, I prefer to see a pure evolution from the *3 legs of NLP* to *6 pillars of NLP* which is why I have presented all the models as I have. We have an entire section on the Presuppositions NLP, which for ease of explaining at this stage are the guidelines of beliefs and ideas that are to be assumed as true with regards to

NLP. Once you have finished that section you can make your own mind up about their relevancy for inclusion in the 6 pillars yourself.

So, there you have it, the pillars of NLP.

Ultimately it summarises NLP to be about;

- being conscious of what you are thinking about,
- being vigilant and aware,
- ensuring you are actually doing the things to get you what you want out of life.

Section Source Material & Further Learning
(1979) Frog into Princes, Bandler & Grinder: Page 54 (1986) Unlimited Power, Anthony Robbins Page 11

BRIEF HISTORY & FOUNDERS OF NLP

When I started learning about NLP, maybe much like the stage you are at now, I'm not going to lie, I was more interested and focused on what I was going to learn and how I could use what I learned as opposed to knowing about the origins of NLP. It wasn't until I neared the end of my NLP Practitioner certification course, the moment when it was time to complete the written integration paper, that I looped back to review the history of co-creators and where NLP originated from in more depth. In all honesty, I wish I had done it sooner – which is exactly why I'm putting this section at the start of this NLP handbook, manual or reference book (depending on how you are using it). Understanding the origins of Neuro-Linguistic Programming, who started it and what they were doing with whom, made so much of the content within the syllabus click into place. So, whether you follow my recommendation of learning about this now or you are indeed looping back yourself, this information will help reinforce the knowledge, techniques and practical applications of being an NLP Practitioner.

Richard Bandler

In the early 1970's Richard Bandler was a computer scientist and mathematician at the University of Santa Cruz in California (UCSC). He was also a Gestalt therapist, which is an important thing to note as Gestalt therapy heavily influenced NLP coming to fruition as well as providing some of the core principles used within NLP. His interest in Gestalt therapy is also the reason why some of the original and most famous NLP techniques are based on therapy. As a psychotherapy, Gestalt is client-centred, helping them focus on the present and understand what is really *actually* happening in their lives right now as opposed to what they may perceive to be happening based on the distortions they are using due to previous experiences. By working through the Gestalt process a client will learn to become more self-aware of how their own thought patterns and behaviours are blocking them, enabling them to then work through unblocking themselves to move towards what they want. This is an extremely over-simplified explanation and yet for now that is enough knowledge to understand a little bit more about the origins of some of the techniques you will learn later.

Frank Pucelik

Around the same time, Richard met another Gestalt therapist at UCSC called Frank Pucelik. At that time Frank was actually helping addicts at UCSC, using Gestalt therapy, the common ground for which they came to meet.

Dr. John Grinder

During this time at UCSC, there was also a professor of linguistics called John Grinder. His linguistic work was well-known and he had published a number of books on the subject. Richard and Frank met John during this time due to common interests but also because Richard Bandler had a book project that he thought John Grinder would be perfect for.

These three men were fascinated not only by the highly positive and practical integrative therapeutic approach of Gestalt but also by what enabled certain outliers to surpass the results that others could achieve. This resulted in them forming a cohort of students to enable the study of three of the world's greatest therapists and to determine what it was these outliers were doing that made them so effective. The intention was not merely to understand and document but also to be able to train others to replicate their methods and results. This is when Bandler with Pucelik invented and developed a process called *modelling*. A process that enabled them to investigate and study these outliers.

The three people they would initially focus their modelling on consisted of;

- **Fritz Perls** the creator of Gestalt therapy,
- **Virginia Satir** the mother of modern-day family therapy,
- **Dr. Milton Erickson** the father of modern hypnotherapy,

The project that started all this was a book Richard Bandler was writing with Fritz Perls to document and publish his methodology. Unfortunately, Fritz Perls died before this book was completed and the project looked like it was going to remain unfinished and unpublished. However, during the creation of the content Bandler had been recording the therapy sessions Fritz was having with his clients and he approached the publishing house to say that he could try and complete the work using this footage as a resource. They agreed and the project continued.

This was one of the key moments that combined the knowledge and skills of Bandler, Pucelik and Grinder as they began to notice that *what* Fritz Perls explained he was doing did not align with what he was actually doing. It was the moment they discovered that an expert producing excellence was unaware (or unconscious) of some of their behaviour that goes into producing their results. So, with the help of the modelling process they had created, which now contained a linguistic element provided by Grinder, they began to create models of Fritz Perl's behaviour.

After creating these initial models, replicating the process with other experts and experimenting with their cohort, the moment arrived when they knew they were onto something extremely powerful.

At this moment and with this information fresh in your mind it is a poignant time to emphasise and revisit exactly what NLP is. NLP is the modelling process. These models then contain processes and strategies which in themselves contain the knowledge and content of what is being modelled. NLP is *not* the techniques being modelled; these techniques are the product of using NLP. With this layer of history, you can now understand that the things commonly marketed commercially as NLP are in fact the *product* of this NLP modelling process and are not NLP itself.

From Fritz Perls, the NLP Practitioner syllabus contains models and techniques related to the humanistic style of coaching, from Milton Erickson the NLP syllabus contains models and techniques related to trance and hypnosis, and from Virginia Satir, the NLP syllabus contains models and techniques related to questioning that discovers first principles or as some like to say initial root causes.

Before we continue, I would also like to give a special mention to a book called *The Origins of Neuro-Linguistic Programming*. Even though you now have a very brief history of how NLP came to be it would be amiss of me not to acknowledge that there are a few versions of what actually happened. For a period of around 20 years, Frank Pucelik vanished from the NLP scene leading to some confusion, something only compounded by the distance that has grown, physically and relationship-wise, between Richard Bandler and John Grinder. In some instances, Frank Pucelik is completely missing from some people's description of the origin of NLP not to mention some of the other extremely significant people such as; David Gordon, Robert Dilts, Judith DeLozier, and Stephen Gilligan to name just four! So, Frank Pucelik and John Grinder put together 'The Origins of Neuro-Linguistic Programming' with a collection of the others from that original cohort to clear up some myths. As Wyatt Woodsmall perfectly puts it,

"Finally! Forty-two years later the true origins of NLP are revealed which up to now have only been the subject of mystery and legend. This is a must-read book for any student of NLP. In it we learn what actually happened during the first nine years of NLP and which set the stage for everything that has followed."

From this information, you can begin to piece together the beginnings of NLP and for the purpose of being an NLP Practitioner, this provides more than enough depth of knowledge. When you move on to be an NLP Master Practitioner the history is investigated further.

To supplement this chronological knowledge, I feel it is of additional benefit at this stage of your learning to provide you with a brief background on the names responsible for specific developments that have found their way onto the NLP Practitioner syllabus. This will serve you in two ways; firstly, to provide some context of what you are about to learn and secondly to provide you with some reference for avenues to investigate certain areas of the syllabus that particularly interest you as you work towards becoming an NLP Practitioner.

Fritz Perls

Fritz Perls provided some of the principles of NLP as well as the introduction of sensory awareness and Representational Systems. Fritz Perls was modelled to create techniques such as Fast Phobia Cure. He was also responsible for parts of the Meta Model, a structure of questioning that focuses on getting to the root cause of an issue. Specifically, Fritz Perls liked to investigate things called Modal Operators of Necessity.

Virginia Satir

Virginia Satir was modelled for her language patterns. They gave her the ability to continually question people to uncover more and more specific information. Her methodology is responsible for the majority of the section called Meta Model. Interestingly before NLP was called *NLP* it has been mentioned that *Meta* was the first name given to what Richard Bandler, John Grinder and Frank Pucelik were creating.

Milton Erickson

While all the initial focus was on questioning people to get more and more detailed information, eventually Richard Bandler and John Grinder were introduced to a doctor who was achieving incredible results without using the Meta Model. This doctor was Milton Erickson. Intrigued, they began to study and model his behaviour. What they found was that he was artfully creating language patterns that were deliberately vague and ambiguous. This is what we come to know as hypnotic language or within the NLP syllabus the Milton Model. This is also the beginning of understanding and theory of the conscious and unconscious mind.

Although a more extensive history of NLP at this stage would see us go back further to the contributions from Alfred Korzybski, Ivan Pavlov, George Miller and Gregory Bateson, their content will show up throughout this book.

There are people such as; Wyatt Woodsmall, Tad James, Shelle Rose Charvet, Michael Hall, Judith Lowe, John Overdurf and Julie Silverthorn to name just a few who all deserve a mention in this section as their work and content will also make an appearance in this book.

This leads me on nicely to make a reference to the *bibliography* and *recommended reading* at the back of this book. I want to acknowledge that this NLP Practitioner book summarises the great work of the people who have developed NLP and yet I acknowledge this is created from *my* perspective and what I have heard and researched.

With all this said, this concludes enough history for what is required at this stage of your journey to becoming an NLP Practitioner. What I hope it has done is serve you enough evidence to warrant that there is an incredible level of depth to NLP, not only in the number of contributors but also in the range of topics that have been uncovered using NLP modelling. It also reveals that although NLP is already possibly more than you originally thought it was, it also brings to your awareness that NLP is an ongoing and ever-growing discipline.

Section Source Material & Further Learning
(2013) Origins of Neuro Linguistic Programming, Pucelik & Grinder

PRESUPPOSITIONS OF NLP

As we now know, NLP is not just a bunch of techniques, it is a philosophy and an attitude that is extremely useful when you are in the pursuit of excellence in any field, skill or achievement of a goal.

So, before we learn anything specific about NLP it is only wise to first cover the principles that form the foundation for what NLP is built upon. These principles are called *"The Presuppositions of NLP"*.

These principles originate from some of the outliers initially studied with NLP, those people who consistently produced extraordinary results. In addition, some principles are based on systems theory and natural laws.

Firstly, 'What is a presupposition and why are we starting with them?'

Before starting any kind of learning, decision making or action it helps to know what assumptions are being made on what is believed to be true. This leads us to the definition of a presupposition;

"a thing that is assumed beforehand at the beginning of a course of action."

With regards to NLP, the things that are presupposed are in relation to effective communication.

Please note that although the presuppositions are numbered and listed in this section, this is done for ease of reference and in no way means they have a hierarchy or that some have more importance than others.

Quick Reference:

Summary of the 13 Presuppositions of NLP:

1. The meaning of your communication is the response you get.

2. The map is not the territory.

3. Language is a secondary representation of experience.

4. Mind and body are parts of the same system and affect each other.

5. Ashby's Law of Requisite Variety: The person with the most flexibility will control the system.

6. Behaviour is geared towards adaptation.

7. Present behaviour represents the best choice available.

8. Behaviour is to be evaluated and appreciated or changed as appropriate in the context presented.

9. People have all the resources they need to make the changes they want.

10. Possible in the world and possible for me is only a matter of how.

11. The highest quality information about other people is behavioural.

12. It is useful to make a distinction between behaviour and self.

13. There is no such thing as failure, there is only feedback.

Source Material & Further Learning
(1975) Thorsons Way of NLP. O'Conner & McDermott: Page 165

1. The meaning of your communication is the response you get.

It is easy to navigate through life assuming that communication is the transfer of information from the person communicating to the person receiving the information.

What we know is that the person communicating wants the other person to comprehend and understand the information in the way that they intended. The common misunderstanding is that the communication is over once the information has been passed to the recipient.

For effective communication, we must understand that this first pass of information is just the beginning of transferring what is intended. Simply put the communication continues well passed the moment when the first person finishes communicating. At this moment all that is present is that the recipient thinks they know what was intended to be said. Often *what* was said and what they *think* was said are two different things. The moment when the communicator finishes is when they need to pay attention to the response they are getting. If the response is not what they want then they need to communicate again varying the transmission of the information being communicated. This must be repeated until they get the response they desire.

There are a number of reasons misunderstandings can take place. From a language perspective, it could be that life experience has attached a different meaning to some of the words being communicated. In addition, there may be some misunderstanding about the tone of voice being used. Other non-verbal (body language) communication such as facial expressions or gestures could similarly be the source of some misunderstanding.

Source Material & Further Learning
(1979) Frog into Princes, Bandler & Grinder: Page 30

2. The map is not the territory.

As events happen in the world we see, hear and feel them with our senses. We then process what we sense through filters that we have built up over a lifetime in order to create representations of these events. It is from these representations that we create meaning and comprehension.

It is important to consider that our filters are unique to us as well as the meanings we place on these representations therefore explaining that each and every one of us experiences the world from our own unique perspective.

In addition to this, we can also consider that what we experience and process is different to what the actual event in the world was. Within NLP we use the term *territory* to refer to the actual world events that happen outside of us and we use the term *map* (or *model of the world*) to describe what our internal representation of these events is after our filters. This now allows us to make sense of 'the map is not the territory'.

With this considered you can understand that each and every one of us creates our own unique 'model of the world' and therefore we live in somewhat different realities from one another. It is our reality that we operate from and determine what choices you feel you have available to you which then creates our behaviour.

Source Material & Further Learning
(1975) The Structure of Magic, Vol I. Bandler & Grinder: Page 7

3. Language is a secondary representation of experience.

First comes the stimulus from the world (*the territory*), second is your representation after your filters or experience of that stimulus (*the map*), and third is your description of that experience via *language*. Considering this allows us to understand that language is not an experience, it is instead a tool that we use to communicate our internal representations of experience.

Words themselves are arbitrary in that they are just used to represent things we see, hear, feel, smell or taste. People who speak other languages use different words to represent the same things that English speakers see, hear, feel, taste or smell. Since each of us has a unique *map* or *model of the world*, our words therefore have different meanings attached to each of them.

Chapter Source Material & Further Learning
(1975) Turtles all the way Down, DeLozier & Grinder: Page 14

4. Mind and body are parts of the same system and affect each other.

The *mind* and *body* are not separate, they are words to describe aspects of the same *whole system*. As there is no separation, anything that happens in one part of a cybernetic system will affect all other parts of the system. To that end both mind and body act as one and therefore influence each other.

This means that how you think impacts how you feel and your physiology can impact how you think. With this, a person's comprehension of an experience, their internal thought process, their emotional process, state and behaviour, all occur both simultaneously and through time.

Source Material & Further Learning
(1988) The New Peoplemaking, Satir: Page 10 (2001) Modeling with NLP, Dilts: Page 8

5. Ashby's Law of Requisite Variety: The person with the most flexibility will control the system.

W. Ross Ashby was a British psychologist and a cyberneticist, that studied the science of communications and automatic control systems in both machines and living things. During the 1960's he proposed a law, now known as the First Law of Cybernetics:
"When the variety or complexity of the environment exceeds the capacity of a system (natural or artificial) the environment will dominate and ultimately destroy that system."

By *variety*, Ashby is referring to the number of possible states within a system. This in turn allows the Law of Requisite Variety within NLP to be translated and have an adopted meaning to be:
"The person with the most flexibility will control the system"

Flexibility is referring to the variability of behaviour. Said another way, having the choice of the widest range of behaviours,

System can be referring to the *mind and body* (see presupposition 4) or it could mean an interaction with another person.

Control in a system refers to the ability to influence the quality of an experience. That could be an internal experience or other people's experience in the moment and through time.

The third pillar of success (see Pillars of NLP) tells us to '*vary your behaviour until you get your desired outcome*'. Effectively saying that, if what you are doing is not working then try something else as literally anything else is better than what does not work.

This presupposition can also be directly related to having *choice*. Choice is always preferable to no choice and more choice is always preferable to having less choice. The person with the most choices has the most flexibility in behaviour and will therefore control over the system.

Source Material & Further Learning

(1956) Introduction to Cybernetics, W.R. Ashby: Page 206 & Page 245
(1979) Frog into Princes, Bandler & Grinder: Page 74

---

6. Behaviour is geared toward adaptation.

A person's behaviour is determined by the context which the person is currently uniquely experiencing. Whether the behaviour is perceived to be good or bad, positive or negative, resourceful or unresourceful, it is an act or a process of change with the desired outcome to better suit the situation. This desired outcome will either be to survive or function better in that situation. This is why this presupposition is sometimes referred to as *'all behaviour has a positive intention'*. We must also consider that behaviour is contextual and it exists to be useful in the context in which it is appearing. Certain behaviours may or may not have use or be appropriate in another context and therefore must be adapted or changed. All this being said we can understand that a person's behaviour is appropriate to their reality (*model of the world*).

Source Material & Further Learning
(1975) The Structure of Magic, Vol I. Bandler & Grinder: Page 45

7. Present behaviour represents the best choice available.

Every person will have a varying degree of awareness of behaviour available to them based on and limited to their collection of life experiences. As 'every behaviour has a positive intent', a person's behaviour illustrates their best choice of behaviour available to them at any moment in time based on what they are aware of and what their desired outcome in that context is. If a person is given a perceived better choice, they will take it. Therefore, providing a person with more choice is the way to enable someone to change inappropriate or unresourceful behaviour. It is important to know that Neuro-Linguistic Programming techniques will *never* take choice away from someone, they should result in only ever providing the person with additional choices and in turn more flexibility of behaviour.

Source Material & Further Learning
(1975) The Structure of Magic, Vol I. Bandler & Grinder: Page 14

8. Behaviour is to be evaluated and appreciated, or changed as appropriate in the context presented.

We must strive to be the most capable that we can possibly be in any context.

When evaluating behaviour either in ourselves or others it is important to make this analysis not only in the associated single context but also against what that person is capable of becoming.

Source Material & Further Learning
(1975) The Structure of Magic, Vol I. Bandler & Grinder: Page 7

9. People have all the resources they need to make the changes they want.

A person does not need to spend time trying to gain retrospective insight into their problems or in developing resources to deal with their issues, as even though they may not be consciously aware, they have access to all the resources they need to make the changes they want.

Neuro-Linguistic Programming provides techniques to locate or access those resources, transfer them to the current time frame and make them available in the appropriate context.

Source Material & Further Learning
(1975) Frogs into Princes, Bandler & Grinder: Page 92

10. Possible in the world and possible for me is only a matter of how.

As we are all human cybernetic systems, if any other human being is capable of performing some behaviour, then it is possible for another human being to also perform it.

Via the process of modelling (see Modelling) Neuro-Linguistic Programming is focused on determining and documenting *how* a human performs excellent behaviour.

All NLP techniques are a result of modelling.

Source Material & Further Learning
(1975) Frogs into Princes, Bandler & Grinder: Page 36

11. The highest quality information about other people is behavioural.

Taking into account that 'language is a secondary representation of an experience' (*Presupposition 3*), we know that words and phrases are used to communicate our own unique representation of experience.

With this in mind, we can listen to what people say and yet it is far more important to pay more attention to what they do, how they behave and any other non-verbal communication. This is also related to 'the meaning of your communication is the response you get' (*Presupposition 1*).

If there is any contradiction between verbal and non-verbal communication, then rely on the behaviour as feedback. It is also therefore significant to look for behavioural evidence of change in someone and not to just rely on people's words.

Source Material & Further Learning
(1975) Frogs into Princes, Bandler & Grinder: Page 30

12. It is useful to make a distinction between behaviour and self.

Behaviour is a process of what a person says, does or feels at any moment in time. Knowing this allows us to understand that behaviour is what happens in the system of one's self and therefore behaviour is not the person.

Said another way, a person's self is greater than their behaviours. For example, a person is not *a smoker*, they are a *person* that smokes.

Source Material & Further Learning
(1975) Frogs into Princes, Bandler & Grinder: Page 13

13. There is no such thing as failure, there is only feedback.

If we take into account that we always want to be looking to be flexible with our behaviour in order to achieve a desired outcome, failure is merely feedback on the route to the goal allowing us to make changes and try something else.

It is so much more valuable to look at our experiences as learning experiences and use a learning frame as opposed to a failure frame. If you view experiences like this then a person can never definitively fail. At the very least they have found a way to not succeed yet and can adjust their behaviour accordingly.

Source Material & Further Learning
(1975) Frogs into Princes, Bandler & Grinder: Page 30

Other Presuppositions of NLP

For the purpose of standardisation, the thirteen presuppositions that have just been explained are the core presuppositions included within this INLPTA NLP Practitioner syllabus and body of knowledge.

There are variances of these presuppositions and many more presuppositions that appear in other NLP trainings. In no way are we suggesting that they are wrong and we acknowledge that some add even more understanding of the attitude and mindset you need when using NLP for yourself.

The list below shares some of the additional presuppositions that you may discover when doing further research and learning.

- *You cannot not communicate*
- *If what you are doing isn't working, do anything else*
- *Experience in and of itself has no meaning*
- *Have respect for the other person's map of the world*
- *People are much more than their behaviour*
- *Accept the person, change the behaviour*
- *Having choice is better than not having choice*
- *The unconscious mind is benevolent*
- *There are no resistant clients, only inflexible communicators.*
- *All procedures should increase choice and develop personal flexibility.*

THE CONSCIOUS & UNCONSCIOUS MIND

In NLP we consider that we have both a conscious and unconscious mind.

CONSCIOUS MIND

The conscious mind is what holds our current awareness at any moment in time. It uses words as its language and is capable of reasoning, setting targets and goals as well as planning a path to achieving them. The conscious mind excels at processing sequentially, working logically and working linearly (also see Conscious Awareness).

UNCONSCIOUS MIND

The unconscious mind holds on to everything the conscious mind does not. It could be described as all the things that are *not conscious*. You would be right in thinking this is a huge amount of information! A common metaphor, that originates from Sigmund Freud, is that of an iceberg, the conscious mind being what is visible above the water line, whilst the unconscious mind is what we cannot see under the surface and yet it is the majority of the iceberg. It is worth mentioning that this does not refer to Freud's model of psychoanalytic personality theory where he states there are three parts of a human personality; ID, ego and super ego. This is not compatible with the presuppositions of NLP nor the prime directives of the unconscious mind. (Also see Prime Directives of the Unconscious Mind).

The unconscious mind uses pictures, sounds, feelings, tastes and smells as it's language and has a primary function to serve your conscious mind by helping achieve goals with automated actions and behaviour that may be outside of your conscious control, such as breathing or blinking. It is important to note that, unlike other psychology systems, NLP views the unconscious as a repository of repressed and disruptive content and considers the unconscious to be benevolent. NLP views the unconscious mind as having all the experiences and feedback that we need and can use to gain wisdom. This is all very relevant as we get deeper into NLP due to the fact that our emotions drive our decisions (unconscious mind) and we then validate them with our logic (conscious mind).

Conscious vs Unconscious vs Sub-conscious/Pre-conscious

There are a few terms related to consciousness that you may hear that are incorrectly interchanged within the field of NLP. The most common probably being *sub-conscious* and another being *pre-conscious*. Although other psychologies, such as Fruedian, may have differing definitions of the terms within NLP we follow Milton Erickson's notions in that;

Conscious
Having mindful *awareness* which can be observed or controlled

Unconscious
Having *no awareness*, even though the unconscious can do everything the conscious mind can do and more (see Conscious vs Unconscious reference table).

Sub-conscious & Pre-conscious
These would suggest that there is a hierarchy of consciousness, which is not the case and therefore are not terms that are relevant within NLP.

Reference Table: Conscious vs Unconscious

Conscious Mind	Unconscious Mind
• 7±2 (See Miller's Law)	• Everything not in the Conscious Mind (The list opposite)
• Logic	• Intuitive
• Linear	• Cybernetics
• Thinking	• Feeling
• Sequential	• Simultaneous
• Voluntary Movements	• Involuntary Movements
• Aware of the present/now	• Stores Memories
• Deliberate	• Automatic
• Verbal	• Non-Verbal

Source Material & Further Learning

(1975) Frogs into Princes, Bandler & Grinder: Page 37
(1981) Trance-formations, Bandler & Grinder: Page 58
(1975) Patterns of The Hypnotic Techniques of Milton H. Erickson, Bandler & Grinder: Page 13

PRIME DIRECTIVES OF THE UNCONSCIOUS MIND

A *prime directive* is a guiding principle or the chief objective, so the prime directives of the unconscious mind collectively are a list of twenty guiding hard-wired principles that provide a framework and model for how the unconscious mind works. NLP considers the unconscious mind to be benevolent, in that it is well-meaning and kind, meaning the prime directives are not only how the unconscious mind works but it is how it works *for* us to try and benefit and help us.

Quick Reference:
Summary of the Prime Directives of the Unconscious Mind.

1. To Store Memories
2. To Organise Memories
3. To be the Domain of our Emotions
4. To repress memories with unresolved negative emotion
5. To present repressed memories in order to release emotion
6. To protect you by keeping repressed emotions repressed.
7. To run the system
8. To preserve the system
9. To ensure you are a highly moral being.
10. To take direction and follow orders
11. To control and maintain all perceptions
12. To generate, store, distribute and transmit energy.
13. To generate and maintain instinct and habit in order to respond
14. To build habits after experiencing repetition
15. To continually seek more and more
16. To seek optimum functioning with minimal parts
17. To comprehend and communicate in a symbolic way
18. To follow the principle of least effort
19. To take everything personally
20. To have the inability to process a negative

Let's take a look at the twenty prime directives of the unconscious mind in more detail.

1. To Store Memories

In 1960, following on from a study in the Penfield Study 1957, Carl Pribram won the Nobel Prize for work that concluded that the unconscious mind was able to and was responsible for coordinating the recording, storage and access of memories. He stated that memories were in fact stored in the whole of our body's nervous system and not just our head-brain.

2. To Organise Memories

Not only does the unconscious mind store our memories in our nervous system, but it also organises them. With the use of indexes, the unconscious can store, archive and retrieve memories. One such index is the perception of time which can be broken into two types; one that relates to past, present and future which we call *Temporal*, and one that is unaffected by time or independent from time which we call *Atemporal*.

3. To be the Domain of our Emotions

Despite often being felt consciously, it is actually the responsibility of the unconscious mind to store, maintain, recall and generate our emotions.

4. To repress memories with unresolved negative emotion

With a focus on the word *unresolved*, as long as a memory has a negative emotion connected to it, it is the responsibility of the unconscious mind to store and also repress this memory. This therefore means that repressed negative memories are trapped inside our nervous system until it is resolved, which unsurprisingly can cause hindrance to the flow of communication through our nervous system, especially when other prime directives are taken into account. Interestingly repressed memories are visible in temporal storage (time-based storage of memories) as dark or missing memories.

5. To present repressed memories in order to release emotion

It is the responsibility of the unconscious mind to present repressed memories to the conscious mind to enable the resolution and release of trapped negative emotions. If the conscious mind can rationalise the memory and preserve positive learning from it, the memory can then be cleared of the stored and trapped negative emotion. It must be known that there are times when the directive for repressing a memory with a negative emotion attached overrides the directive to present a repressed memory with a negative emotion in order for it to be resolved (Prime Directive 6).

6. To protect you by keeping repressed emotions repressed.
Taking into account the preservation of your body (Prime Directive 8) there are times that the unconscious mind, at least in the short-term, will reserve its option to keep a memory with a negative emotion attached repressed. However, in the long-term, the unconscious mind will eventually present the memories with negative emotions attached so they can be attempted to be resolved by the rationality of the conscious mind.

7. To run the system
The unconscious mind has the function of consciousness and provides the direction for running the body as a whole (system). This accounts for around 90% of everyday behaviour such as; breathing, blinking, and catching. The unconscious mind is effectively the mind for the body which is why it is sometimes known or referred to as the 'body-mind'.

8. To preserve the system
In the face of danger, you can witness how the unconscious mind is responsible for the preservation of your body as a whole by experiencing action to avoid the danger. In some cases, this action to avoid danger can be almost instantaneous with the conscious mind being completely omitted from the process. When sleeping the unconscious is working on the action of sleeping itself as well as other actions such as movement or lack of, to stop you from falling out of bed or waking you up when there is a particular noise.

9. To ensure you are a highly moral being.
As it progresses through time the unconscious mind will learn morals. For the purpose of healing, by instinct, our unconscious mind will enforce any of these built-in moral beliefs that it believes to be true. In a strange turn of events, for the purpose of self-preservation (Prime Directive 8) and learning, the unconscious mind may provide punishment to you as feedback for a broken moral. Morality (or a particular morality) is sometimes an important thing to be aware of if we are seeking to heal as it can identify the source of what you are trying to heal.

10. To take direction and follow orders

The unconscious mind likes to have and follow directions from the conscious mind. However, the unconscious mind will only take direction from the conscious mind if it is in sync (see Congruence) with it. If there is incongruence the unconscious mind will not follow the direction from the conscious mind. If congruent, our conscious mind can influence our unconscious mind. Based on the unconscious mind wanting to run the system (Prime Directive 7) you can understand why rapport between the conscious and unconscious is so important for us.

11. To control and maintain all perceptions

Our conscious sensory perceptions, or map (see the 2nd Presupposition of NLP) are a result of taking in data from outside of us (the world) and passing them unconsciously through certain filters. Of all the billions of bytes of information happening every second, our senses can only collectively sense around 11 million of these bytes of information. When you then take into account that our conscious mind can only process around 128 bytes (See NLP Communication Model) you can understand the extent to which these unconscious filters filter out the information that reaches our conscious mind. Said another way, the unconscious mind has the responsibility of refining massive amounts of data into manageable chunks of information so that our conscious mind can understand and make perceptions. With all this taken into account, we can also consider that we are unable to consciously process everything that our senses unconsciously pick up.

12. To generate, store, distribute and transmit energy.

With regards to running and preserving the body, our unconscious mind also has biological responsibilities. To be more exact, it is in charge of the management of energy sources. This is predominantly related to the chemical processing and distribution of energy that comes from oxygen and glucose. It is possible for the unconscious mind to be directed by the conscious mind (Prime Directive 10) in the redistribution of energy for running or preserving the body. It also explains why sometimes sleeping for a short period of time can re-energise you and yet other times even when fully rested we can experience and lack energy.

13. To generate and maintain instinct and habit in order to respond
When we start to learn something new, it is done by being conscious of the new actions and behaviours. Over time it is the responsibility of the unconscious mind to generate habits from these successful behaviours and actions. This allows us to have unconscious habits that enable appropriate timely use of these capabilities and instincts with regards to running and preserving the body. Some unconscious habits and instincts, such as 'fight or flight' are built in from birth.

14. To build habits after experiencing repetition
In order for the unconscious mind to generate and take control of a habit it requires the repetition of conscious behaviours and actions. As the unconscious mind is operating from a present 'now' place, it can mean that a large number of repetitions are required before a habit is formed and installed.

15. To continually seek more and more
The unconscious mind has a serious case of the 'shiny new object'. It is programmed to never settle and continually seek for more and more. You can imagine the unconscious mind saying continually, "Great, what next?" This can be visible in decisions people make throughout the course of their lives due to not having enough, not being enough or just wanting more.

16. To seek optimum functioning with minimal parts
Consider the unconscious mind working on the basis that the fewer parts there are the fewer things there are to break. With fewer parts, there is less chance of inner conflict. This takes into account that the unconscious mind will function perfectly by disregarding unrequired parts and distilling the process down, with the ultimate objective being to have a perfectly functioning wholly integrated single-functioning unit.

17. To comprehend and communicate in a symbolic way

The unconscious mind creates and responds to symbols and therefore much of what our unconscious provides us is symbolic by nature. Symbolic messages are a way of our unconscious mind communicating, so we must be aware of them as they will hold meaning. They are not to be disregarded if our conscious mind cannot at first interpret them rationally, quite the contrary, they should at least have some conscious focus and attention put on them.

18. To follow the principle of least effort

In order to preserve energy, the unconscious mind will take the path of least resistance in order to put in as little effort as possible.

19. To take everything personally

What your unconscious mind sees it believes that of itself. It understands that in order for you to understand or perceive something then it must be or have been present in you for you to understand what it is. It is for this reason the unconscious mind takes everything personally. What it sees is what it is and in turn what it believes you to be. This is perfectly summed up by the saying "Perception is projection" in that if you see something good in someone then you also possess that. Be aware that the opposite is also true, so if you see something bad in someone that is also you. A great visual metaphor for this is if you point at someone with your forefinger, one finger points at them and yet three fingers are pointing at you.

20. To have the inability to process a negative

The unconscious mind can only process what *to do* and therefore telling it to not do something is still *doing* something as an alternative to the thing you are not doing. What this actually means is that we should focus our conscious mind and in turn give direction to our unconscious mind (Primary Directive 10) on what we need to do, to think or to be.

CONSCIOUS AWARENESS (MILLER'S LAW OF 7 ± 2)

On review of the reference table for *Conscious Mind vs Unconscious Mind*, you will notice the numbers 7 ± 2 appear on the conscious mind list, which may have seemed a bit out of place within a list of words. 7 ± 2 is spoken as 'Seven Plus or Minus Two', and refers to a mathematical number range between 5 and 9 (e.g. $7+2=9$ and $7-2=5$). 7 ± 2 is also known as The Magic Number referring to a classic research paper about the conscious mind written and published by Professor George Miller in 1956. So why is this relevant? In George Miller's study, he observed how much information (referred to as *chunks* of information) someone's conscious mind could simultaneously deal with at any given moment in time. His initial research uncovered that a conscious mind could process about 7 chunks of information. Any more than this amount of information the conscious mind would protect itself from overload by ignoring or dropping awareness of certain things. He also concluded that a person's state directly impacted the number of chunks of information they could deal with. According to his research, a person in a resourceful state (see Understanding States) can hold more chunks of information (up to 9), than someone in an unresourceful state (as low as 5), hence 7 ± 2 became known as the Magic Number and referred to as Miller's Law. You can actually see this concept in action for yourself if you look up the 'Invisible Gorilla Experient' which won the creators Christopher Chabris and Daniel Simons the LG Nobel Prize. The experiment reveals that a person focused on one thing can easily overlook something else. You will also see 7 ± 2 appear in the Milton Model where overloading the conscious mind is deliberately induced to access the unconscious mind. Beyond awareness, chunking information into bite-sized chunks is also a mnemonic device to aid short-term memorisation. Miller's research suggested that chunking may be connected to long-term memory functions, therefore chunking patterns of information allows us to utilise our long-term memory to aid our short-term memory. If you were to try and remember a number sequence beyond 9 numbers it would be a challenge. We can witness this through common examples such as grouping numbers together to remember a telephone number or the way a 16-digit credit card number is grouped into four groups of four numbers.

Source Material & Further Learning
(1981) Trance-formations, Bandler & Grinder: Page 80

PATTERNS

Understanding what *patterns* are is fundamental to learning about what NLP actually is. You could even say that NLP is all about patterns. In fact, one of the early books published by an early contributor to NLP, Steve Andreas, was called *'The Patterns of Her Magic'* referring to Virginia Satir the family therapist that the co-creators modelled to create some of their original Meta Model language patterns, before utilising modelling to find patterns in other areas of genius.

So, what fundamentally are patterns? Patterns are repeating sequences of behaviour, of reactions, of feelings, of thinking, of problem-solving, and communication.

As mentioned, the first NLP project was related to language patterns, specifically what questions work and what questions do not work. Then came the discovery of thinking patterns. These revealed how people utilised what they see, hear and feel (Visual, Auditory, Kinesthetic). Then came patterns that revealed how people have a preference to react (see Meta Programmes). With just these categories you can begin to consider that our whole life is basically a set of 100's of thousands of patterns; communication patterns, problem-solving patterns, observation patterns and so on...

With a quick shift to this neurological perspective, know that when the brain witnesses a pattern that works it connects neurons together. Then, due to the fact that the pattern worked you are more likely to do it again and therefore the brain witnesses the pattern being repeated. This repetition enhances the connection or neuropathways to be stronger. Then due to the fact the pathway is stronger, they become more frequently used. In simple terms this is the creation of a pattern. We could even go as far as to say that the brain actually only works with patterns, having a basic function to find and then generate them.

So, the next question is why does biology evolution create patterns? The answer to this is related to energy. Having automated sequences means you do not have to make choices or decisions. This lack of thinking results in much faster and more efficient processing which in turn saves you a lot of energy and as we know in biology and physics, saving energy is the main objective of all living beings. So, in summary, the stronger the pattern, the less energy is used. Strong patterns can even become automated with little awareness that they are even running. With this explanation, it becomes easy to understand how patterns can also be described as habits as it is possible to have habits that you are not aware of because they happen automatically.

There are times when patterns or habits can become permanent and actually create a lack of flexibility for a person, something that as we know from the Presuppositions of NLP is undesirable. However, all is not lost as this leads us to have the ability to change patterns. This is possible and yet you can only change a pattern if you first have awareness of it. With this awareness, in order to change, you must also have to identify another option which will create more resourcefulness and flexibility. Then lastly to change you need to focus your effort on breaking the habit by consciously doing the other option.

This also leads us nicely to distilling what NLP does. Simply put NLP figures out what people's patterns are, looking for patterns that work and patterns that provide better results in others. Throughout this book, you will learn about patterns that the co-creators of NLP discovered. This will also enable you to begin to learn about the fundamentals behind your very own patterns and maybe, just maybe, by the end of this book you'll be thinking about how you can learn more about NLP to investigate and discover patterns that intrigue you that others possess and you would like to model to duplicate their results.

PATTERN INTERRUPT

A pattern interrupt does exactly what it says, it interrupts patterns with the desired outcome being that it causes a change. Before being able to perform a pattern interrupt a rigid *pattern* (See Pattern) must first be identified. A pattern can be referred to as a collection of behaviours that are being considered as a single unit of behaviour and this can present in an individual as well as part of a group of people.

Using the simple pattern example of a handshake where one person extends their arm with their hand open and the other person then follows the pattern and extends their arm to shake hands. A pattern interrupt in this case would be to grab the other person's wrist when they extend it rather than shake their hand. Effectively, you are beginning the pattern and then abruptly interrupting it, surprising the person with your action and causing a reaction.

From a more technical perspective when people engage in a pattern of behaviour, which could be occurring as one single unit of unconscious behaviour, if this pattern is interrupted mid-flow, it causes a state of confusion where they are stuck momentary. This is due to the fact that as the person sees the pattern as a single unit a break means there is no 'next step' to perform.

LEVERAGE

Leverage is connected to a Pattern Interrupt on the basis that when a person is in a state of confusion or stuck with no experience or knowledge of what to do next, due to the fact you have intercepted a single unit of behaviour, you can lead a person towards a more resourceful state with a suggestion of what the next step can be.

Source Material & Further Learning
(1981) Trance-Formations, Bandler & Grinder: Page 70 (19875) Patterns of The Hypnotic Techniques of Milton H. Erickson, M.D. Vol 1, Bandler & Grinder: Page 137

PART TWO:
COMMUNICATION MODEL

THE NLP COMMUNICATION MODEL

The model below illustrates how we process external stimuli or events in the world *outside of us*. It ultimately shows exactly how much goes on before the behaviour we see is created and also that our behaviour is due to how we process this external stimulus through our many filters.

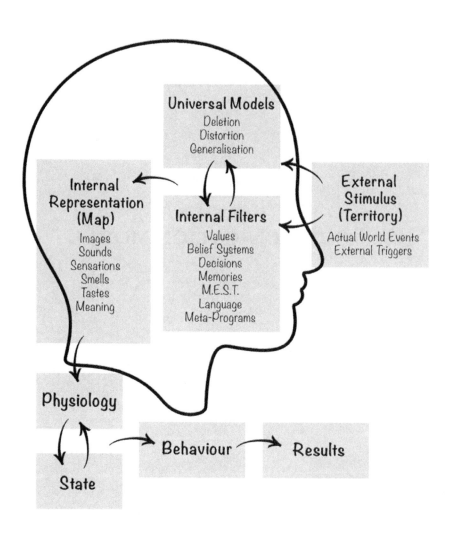

Let's focus on one of the NLP presuppositions,

"The map is not the territory"

and extend it slightly to,

"People respond to their map of reality, not reality itself"

The diagram shows that we each have a number of filters running that impact how we perceive an external event to be. Think of the *map* being your own version of events after all of your filters have processed the information you initially experienced.

Acknowledging that you have these filters and that you can only make sense of or meaning of an event after the data has passed through these filters, you can begin to understand that your perception of an event is extremely personal to you. This should also make it clear that your *model of the world* really cannot be the *territory*.

Also knowing the filters are unique to you, creating a very unique model of the world, we can also consider that each of us lives in somewhat different realities from each other. This is especially poignant when studying behaviour as we can only operate from our perceived map of the territory and not the actual events themselves.

With all this said, we need to take something else into account. We are still assuming at this stage our *map* is created by consciously taking in all the information we are experiencing. However, it is actually impossible as we have somewhat of a bottleneck in our conscious brain.

Based on research undertaken by Mihaly Csikszentmihalyi and later Robert Lucky from Bell Labs, they found that our conscious mind has a processing capacity of 128 bits per second. Sounds pretty good right? Well, when you consider the combination of all our senses; seeing, hearing, feeling, smelling, and tasting, can collectively sense around 11 million bits of information you can see that 128 bits is quite some reduction!

Sensory System	Bits per second
Eyes	10,000,000
Skin	1,000,000
Ears	100,000
Smell	100,000
Taste	1000
Total	**11,201,000**

That however is not it! Now if you also realise that there are billions of pieces of information being passed to your senses, and of those billions only 11 million are being sensed, and then in turn only 128 bits are being consciously used to create your *map*, you begin to realise the impact these filters have on your perception of the world that actually exists around you and that you really can never actually respond without any personal bias.

Billions (External) > 11 million (Our Senses) > 128 (Conscious Mind / Map)

So, how is all this information being refined and it being processed from 11 million down to 128 bits? Firstly, the information is passed through one or more of our three universal model filters or modelling processes;

- Deletion
- Distortion
- Generalisation.

Let's take a look at each one in detail and explain what they do.

UNIVERSAL MODELS

DELETION

What we leave out

This is actually an essential filter as without it we would be in a constant state of overload and overwhelmed by our experience of the world. Deletion could be referred to as what we ignore or shut out.

In itself Deletion is unbiased, meaning it has no positive or negative reasoning on what is deleted. However, what it deletes can then be interpreted as good or bad for you. Deletion can be referred to as the blind spots in our experiences. For example, deleting background noise while you work in a busy coffee shop so you can concentrate on work could be seen to be working for you and yet, if by deleting the background noise it causes you to miss the person calling your name to pick you up, this could be seen to be as working against you. Either way though, the same information, in this case sound, was being deleted.

DISTORTION

What information we give more weight to over other information.

Distortion is the way we misrepresent reality and change an experience. A common phrase attached to distortion is that of 'blowing something out of proportion'. Distortion also refers to how we can change the order of events, or based on assumptions add things to a sequence of events that were not even there. Our understanding of someone's behaviour towards us is a common source of misinterpretation (see Mind Reading).

Much like the other universal processes, Distortion in itself is neither good nor bad. We can see examples of the positive effects of distortion when we look at artists who find patterns in what they observe to create beautiful paintings or leaders who find creative solutions for problems that others just cannot see. On the other side, distortion can lead to exaggerating a situation leading to unresourceful beliefs or negative emotions that do not serve us well (see Unresourceful States).

GENERALISATION

How we represent a group of experiences and take them as one experience.

Generalisation creates global representations of things and experiences. In an experience where we may have witnessed things with minor variations, similar patterns or coding, we will see these things as the same thing putting them into a single heading for ease of interpretation and in order to reduce the level of data required to process.

One of the major benefits of Generalisation is that it helps us live and navigate through experiences in the world without having to constantly learn everything about every experience from scratch on each and every occurrence. A great example of this is a door with a door handle. Even in the absence of a push or pull sign on the door (meaning you may pull or push incorrectly - we've all done it!) you did at least know;

i)   it was a door,
ii)   how to open the door based on your generalisation of how to use the handle and which side of the door has hinges.

Just imagine having to learn how to use a door handle for every single door you face!

Beyond not having to repeatedly learn, generalisations can also be very useful to us to help us in situations that are completely new experiences to us. They enable us to look for patterns from past experience to help us create the best choice to deal with the new unknown situation. That being said, someone who over-generalises may inadvertently go into a situation with way too much confidence, unintentionally leading them to ironically be inflexible with their behaviour. (See Law of Requisite Variety)

INTERNAL FILTERS

In addition to the three universal models; Deletion, Distortions and Generalisation, we also have our very own set of *internal filters* that run before we finally create an internal representation (or perception) of the experience we have taken in from the outside world. These internal filters are:

Language
A filter that attaches meaning to the verbal language or symbols.

Meta-programs
A filter that takes our behavioural preferences into account.

Values
A filter that evaluates against what is important to us.

Belief Systems
A filter that generalises based on what we assume to be true in the world.

Decisions
A filter that utilises actions taken in past experiences and situations.

Memories
A filter that utilises our past experiences and emotions attached to them.

M.E.S.T (Matter, Energy, Space, Time)
A filter that takes into account the component parts of the physical universe.

So, there you have it, the three universal processes combined with your internal filters, all running after being triggered by an external stimulus or *external trigger*, combining to create our internal representation (*map*) of the world (*territory*), which in turn impacts our internal state, possibly our physiology, all causing us to react (*change our behaviour*), which ultimately affects the results we are able to achieve.

Source Material & Further Learning
(1975) The Structure of Magic, Vol I. Bandler & Grinder: Page 14+

INTERNAL REPRESENTATIONS

With regards to our internal representations, let's look at some relevant terms and concepts: *perception, model of the world* and *hallucination*, to cover how they are defined within NLP and how they refer to our sensory experience.

PERCEPTION

Our *perception* is our own internal sensory representation (map) of events that happen in the world (territory) after the data has passed through the universal model processes of deletion, distortion and generalisation and the internal filters; meta-programs, language, values, beliefs, decision, memories and M.E.S.T.

MODEL OF THE WORLD

Your very own *model of the world* acknowledges that we can only create a perception and recognise a sensory experience, either consciously or unconsciously, if we recognise that experience within ourselves. We are unable to perceive or label something that we have no experience of (or related experience) to construct a sensory experience from. So, if we know our map is based on what we create, we can also know that we create our perception of someone's behaviour towards us, meaning people are behaving in our perception as we choose them to be! A powerful realisation and concept once fully grasped, as it means we can effectively create the world we live in. So, be sure to create a resourceful world!

HALLUCINATION

Hallucinations from an NLP perspective are sensory experiences that do not exist in the territory. With this understanding hallucinations are closely related to mind reading (see Mind Read) in that they are a guess. Common hallucinations are our descriptions of emotions, such as 'he is *sad*' or 'he is *scared*' as there is no sensory evidence for sad or happy. To avoid creating a hallucination, we could describe the sensory experience for 'he is scared' as; his skin tone was white, and his eyes were wide open with pupils dilated.

Source Material & Further Learning
(1975) Frogs into Princes, Bandler & Grinder: Page 50 (1988) Time Line Therapy & Basis of Personality, James & Woodsmall Page 182

NLP: A PROCESS MODEL

With an understanding of the Communication Model and Internal Representations, it becomes easier for us to explain that NLP is a *Process Model* and not a *Content Model*.

Let's look at some terms to help explain what this actually means.

- Content
- Process
- Pattern

If we make reference to common objections or concerns that people have about NLP, such as manipulation or 'changing' someone, the knowledge that NLP is a *Process Model* is essential to comprehend in order to explain to people this is not the case with NLP. At no point should an NLP technique create or tell a person; what they are experiencing, what they need or want to have or be, what they should or should not work towards.

A clear demonstration of a poorly trained NLP Practitioner, NLP Coach or NLP Trainer is that they will offer up their own *Content* as a desired outcome for a client. As NLP is *not* a Content Model this should never be the case!

CONTENT
The What or What happens.

Content is the story or event itself as it happens, from the world (or territory).

With reference to the NLP Communication Model, *Content* is therefore what happens before your universal processes and internal filters create your perception (map) of what the *Content* is.

Content can also be an idea or communication from another person before we process and filter our interpretation of that what they are communicating.

You can increase your ability to obtain *Content* by consciously putting yourself in an Uptime state (see Uptime).

PROCESS

The How or How we represent 'Content'.

Process is how we create our perception (map) of a story or event as it happens, from the world (territory).

With reference to the NLP Communication Model, *Process* is therefore what our universal processes (Deletion, Distortion, Generalisation) and filters (Language, Meta-programs, Values, Beliefs, Decisions, Memories, M.E.S.T.) create. Said another way they create our perceptions of what the *Content* is.

From this explanation, you can understand that;

- *Process* is not *Content*
- *Process* is how we deal with *Content*.

This leads us to know that NLP is a *Process Model* not a Content Model.

To explain this further, let's use the example of 'Beliefs and Values'. NLP has techniques that help you discover what your Values and Beliefs are and yet these NLP techniques do not tell you what you should have or need to have as Values and Beliefs. At no point is NLP prescriptive of Content.

NLP provides us with the following;

- *Processes* (or techniques) to uncover *Content*
- Offers *Processes* (or techniques) to change your meaning of *Content*.

Said another way an NLP Practitioner will never tell you *what* you should think or do, instead an NLP Practitioner will offer ways of *how* you can think about what you think about or do.

A PATTERN

How the 'Content' is repeated. An aggregate to improve prediction.

As you know from the previous section Patterns are fundamental and core to NLP (see Patterns). In this particular section, we are *only* comparing what a *Pattern* is to *Content* and *Process* from a technical perspective to provide clarity towards NLP being a Process Model.

With this in mind a *Pattern* in this context can be described as an aggregate of *Content* or *Process* that can be divided into individual parts and yet when aggregated the observer can guess with better than random success the next event, object or occurrence, thus reducing the probability of guessing wrong.

A pattern can therefore in this context be a sequence or a situation that contains a cause-effect reaction for example,

- if '*X*' happens, then '*Y*' happens in the sequence,

or more accurately,

- if '*X*' happens, then with greater than random probability we can predict that '*Y*' will happen.

Source Material & Further Learning
(1975) The Structure of Magic, Vol I. Bandler & Grinder: Page 6 (1975) Frogs into Princes, Bandler & Grinder: Page 6

PART THREE:
VALUES & BELIEFS

DEFINING VALUES & BELIEFS

With reference to the Communication Model, a Value is one of the internal filters we use to create our internal representational (perception) of the world (territory), filters that can influence our state, physiology and behaviour. The definition being:

- **Value:** A filter that evaluates against what is important to us.

In this section, we will take a closer look at this specific filter as well as the interconnected *beliefs* we associate and hold with values.

- **Belief:** Something we know to be true in relation to a Value

All of our decisions both conscious and unconscious are based on Values and Beliefs, and these decisions are what we use to justify our behaviour and actions. This behaviour being to either move towards our values or move away from values.

Values and beliefs are also contextual. This means that depending on the context of life (see Life Context: Wheel of Life) you are operating from within, a person will hold a unique set of values and beliefs for which they are referring to, to make decisions and justify actions. With the knowledge of how we all have our own internal filters, it is easy to understand that no two people can have all the same values and beliefs nor meanings connected to these. In addition, this also allows us to consider that no value can be right or wrong, nor can a person's collective list of values be right or wrong.

VALUE

As you now know these are the internal filters that are responsible for; what we move towards or away from and how we define good or bad, right and wrong. Values mostly operate at an unconscious level, defining the positive intent behind all our behaviour and driving our actions. You can generally identify a value as it will be described as a Nominalisation (a verb has been turned into a noun);

- o **Growth** is the value and nominalisation of the verb *grow*
- o **Action** is the value and nominalisation of the verb *act*
- o **Leadership** is the value and nominalisation of the verb *lead*

BELIEF

Beliefs of values are the generalised statements a person holds that they believe to be true about a value. These therefore guide our judgement and behaviour. Beliefs are more conscious than values, although that being said, the link (or hook) between a belief and value is often unconscious.

CORE BELIEFS AND VALUES

These are values and beliefs that cross over multiple life contexts and have the most impact on our behaviour. They operate at an unconscious level, which is why they are closely linked to a person's identity and the basis of a person's personality (see Neurological Level).

As you progress with the NLP syllabus it can be easy to confuse Values with Beliefs and Values with Emotions so for future reference when you come to these aspects, here are some simple summaries to help your understanding.

VALUES AND BELIEFS

Values are the things (nouns) that we use to label what is important to us. These then determine our attitudes, judgements, behaviour and in turn our communication. *Beliefs* are the statements that contain the ideas of what we understand to be true about our values. A belief is also capable of determining judgements and states.

VALUES AND EMOTIONS

Values are demonstrated via our behaviour. *Emotions* are the feelings connected to those behaviours.

ORIGIN OF VALUES

Now we have Values defined, the next question is 'Where does a person get their values and beliefs from?'. Drawing upon the independent research conducted by the sociologist Morris Massey and psychologist William James, we understand that values are developed during four periods;

- The Imprint Period (Ages 0-7)
- The Modelling Period (Ages 8-13)
- The Socialisation Period (Ages 14-21)
- Business Persona Period (Ages 22-35)

THE IMPRINT PERIOD:
BIRTH TO AGE 7

This is a period of time when we have few experiences and little meaning connected to our internal filters. During this time, we act as a sponge picking up and storing as much from experiences as possible. Interestingly by the age of around 4 years old, most of our basic programming has occurred. Based on our lack of ability to consciously recall events from this period, this results in the creation and existence of some values (and in some instances phobias) being completely unconscious. Naturally, parents or guardians are generally the most influential people during this period.

MODELLING PERIOD:
AGE 8 TO 13

It is between these ages a child will start to develop a strategy for modelling behaviour. This can occur at an unconscious level and yet also be a very conscious act by the child. You may see this show up as mimicking mannerisms of key people or influential people (for example teachers or grandparents) within their environment. This also coincides with a development of awareness that there is a world outside of themselves. The research also showed that around the age of 10 is when a child becomes increasingly aware of what is happening in the world and where they are, resulting in some strong and critical values about life being formed.

SOCIALISATION PERIOD:
AGE 14 TO 21

These are the ages where independence commences. A child develops into a young adult and experiences situations in isolation from parents and key influencers. It is during these socialisations a young adult will build behaviours based on human interaction with peers and alike. This is why values in the context of relationships and friendship are most likely to be formed during this period. In fact, by the age of 21 most values in most contexts have been formed. Any development of values beyond this period will be the result of significant emotional events (S.E.E.) or change work.

With core values being formed around the age of 10 and others locked in by 21 you can understand why transformational coaching regarding values and beliefs using NLP techniques that utilise Timeline and Sub-Modalities initially focus on a person's history between birth and the age of 21.

BUSINESS PERSONA:
AGE 22 TO 35

There is one additional period that has been defined beyond these periods by a psychologist called William James. His research revealed that between the ages of 22 and up to around 33 years age a person will build values and beliefs about work. This could be about how we go about doing work or also our beliefs about work itself.

Source Material & Further Learning
(1980) Time Line Therapy & Basis of Personality, James & Woodsmall: Page 155 (1988) Change Your Mind and Keep the Change, Andreas & Andreas: Page 70 (1990) Introducing Neuro-linguistic Programming. O'Conner & Seymour: Page 147

NEUROLOGICAL LEVELS

Values and beliefs are only a part of the model that impacts our states. In this section, we will take a look at the Neurological Levels model, a concept created by Robert Dilts in 1988.

Taking the research conducted by Gregory Bateson on the logical levels of learning, Dilts proposed that we have varying degrees of commitment depending on what level a person is being challenged on. At a basic level we can comprehend that from a neurology perspective, the motive that drives behaviour when our identity or values are being challenged is somewhat different from the motive that drives us when we just pick something up off the floor.

The following illustration provides the model that Robert Dilts created. As you review the model understand that a change created on any level of the model will impact all the levels below the level the change was made on. This means a change in Values would not change your Identity or Purpose and yet a change in Identity can change Values, Beliefs, Capabilities, Behaviour and Environment.

NEUROLOGICAL LEVELS MODEL

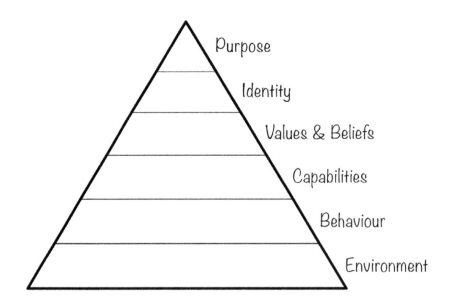

Environment
Where and When?

Environment refers to external settings and conditions that surround an individual. We perceive our environment via our sensory representational systems. Knowing this allows us to understand that Environment is responsible for our external kinesthetic sensations which can result in the unconscious creation of a feeling to match the environment being experienced.

Here are some questions that can be used to elicit Environment;

- Where is your location?
- What is the weather like?
- What kind of people do you like to be around?
- What time?

Behaviour
What?

Behaviour refers to what a person is doing, and what physical actions and physiology a person has within a particular environment (place, time, conditions, people).

Here are some questions that can be used to elicit Behaviour;

- What are you doing?
- What is your breathing like?
- How do you react?
- What habits do you have?

Capability
How?

Capabilities refer to the strategies, internal processes and mental maps that people develop that influence and direct their specific behaviour in a variety of environments. Capabilities are formed by past experiences over a wide range of situations. By recalling these external situations, capabilities are able to and can hold a stronger influence on selecting, altering and adapting behaviour than our sensory perception of a current environment.

Here are some questions that can be used to elicit Capability;

- What skills are you competent in?
- What is your knowledge and level of training like?
- What subjects would you consider yourself to be an expert in?
- What do you need to learn?

Beliefs & Values
Why?

Beliefs and Values are things that influence the evaluation and judgement of not only the external world but also of ourselves. They are responsible for the processing of meaning and impact the level of energy focused on capabilities and behaviours. The question 'Why?' is one that directs us immediately to what we believe to be true and is therefore rightly associated with obtaining information about a value and belief.

Here are some questions that can be used to elicit Beliefs and Values;

- Why did you do that?
- Why is that important to you?
- Why would that make a difference?
- Why must you do that?

Identity
Who?

Identity relates to how we identify with who we are. This is an internal perception that organises our values beliefs, capabilities and behaviours into a single whole system. We use this single system to then perceive how we relate to a larger system, whether that is a company, community or family. This then helps us to define a role within a larger system.

Here are some questions that can be used to elicit Identity;

- What kind of person are you?
- How would you describe yourself?
- Who are you in respect to the others?
- What do you like to identify as?

Spiritual
What else?

Spirituality relates to our sense of being in existence as part of something beyond ourselves. It brings awareness to the pattern that, as individuals, we are sub-systems of a larger system that connects individuals beyond their identities. This level is where we see people consider their purpose or their mission in life.

Here are some questions that can be used to elicit Spirituality;

- What is it all for?
- What purpose do you have?
- What would you like to be remembered for?
- What contribution to the world would you like to make?

Source Material & Further Learning
(1973) Steps to an Ecology of Mind, Bateson (2003) From Coach to Awakener, Robert Dilts. Page xxi

UNDERSTANDING CONTEXT

Something that can assist our understanding and processing of a situation or behaviour is knowing the context of what we notice. It is very tangible to notice that you can see, hear or feel the same thing but in a different context your internal and external reaction or behaviour can differ. We can summarise this by saying *'All meaning is dependent on context'*. You will see context appear multiple times throughout the NLP syllabus as it is a fundamental element of processing information and defining well-formed outcomes. Here is a breakdown of the different contexts we can find ourselves and others in.

SITUATION CONTEXT
Where, when and with whom?

Let's quickly look at the example of a grown man shouting and ask 'In what context is the man shouting?'. As we review each one of the following contexts notice how your own reaction differs internally;

a) *The man is shouting* in the football stands with 50,000 other fans celebrating because his team has just scored a goal.

b) *The man is shouting* for help in pain while he lays on the floor having just fallen off a ladder and hurting his leg.

c) *The man is shouting* at you to *STOP* because you had left the building having forgotten to collect your coat.

d) *The man is shouting* in the middle of the road arguing face to face with another man and it looks like they are about to start fighting.

Being presented with each scenario notice how your behaviour would differ in reaction to each context. Would you run towards the man, run away from the man, stop and watch, or not really pay any attention?

You can now understand knowing the context of; where, when and with whom, is important to create an appropriate reaction or behaviour.

LIFE CONTEXT
What aspect of life?

There is yet another element of context that can be considered and that is to do with our aspects of life. These aspects are the different areas of life that we experience. These include (and yet, are not limited to); work, family, romance, health, and finance. These aspects or *contexts of life* provide a framework for varying values and beliefs you hold (see Values and Beliefs). Although there are core values that overlap contexts, there will be values you hold that are exclusive to a single context. As values impact our behaviour, it comes as no surprise that finding what context of life someone is operating in or wanting to create a desired outcome in, is necessary. The following diagram of the *wheel of life* presents an example of contexts that can be present in a whole life.

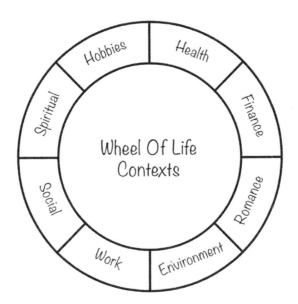

This concludes this section on context, giving you a thorough overview of the importance and understanding of, 'it depends on the context'.

Source Material & Further Learning
(1975) The Structure of Magic, Vol I. Bandler & Grinder: Page 15 (1981) Reframing, Bandler & Grinder, Page 1

PART FOUR:

UNDERSTANDING STATES

STATES OF CHOICE

Before we look at the different types of states a person can experience, let's first define what a *state* is.

WHAT IS A STATE?

The term *State* in NLP represents the sum of conscious and unconscious thoughts or sensory feelings that a person is experiencing at a specific moment in time.

NLP techniques are about positive change - having the objective of putting a person in a desired state of being more resourceful. With this it makes sense to cover off what a *resourceful state* is so you know what you are trying to achieve with NLP techniques. Not all change starts from a perceived negative place, it can be that the desire is to go from a resourceful state to a more resourceful state. That being said we will also cover what an *unresourceful state* is so that you can spot one in yourself or others in order to make those changes towards resourcefulness. Before we break those types of states down let's look at two Presuppositions of NLP;

- *Present behaviour represents the best choice available.*

- *It is useful to make a distinction between behaviour and self.*

These two presuppositions in particular are important to reference when investigating unresourceful states or behaviour. Just communicating and bringing awareness of these statements can enable a person to begin the transformation towards resourcefulness and away from the unhelpful unresourceful state by allowing them to comprehend that rather than being an unresourceful person, they are indeed a person demonstrating an unresourceful state. This acknowledgement alone increases the choices available to them.

Source Material & Further Learning
(1990) Changing Belief Systems with NLP, Dilts: Page 219

RESOURCEFUL STATE

In the simplest of terms, a *resourceful state* is one where a person will feel positive. This positivity will come about due to helpful emotions, choice, and flexibility. This flexibility of behaviour comes as a result of having strategies that either progress them towards a desired outcome or having the option of other strategies available to progress.

Here are some examples of resourceful states that a person can experience or demonstrate;

- Calmness
- Confidence
- Composed
- Happiness
- Enjoyment
- Clear minded
- Clarity of decision
- Being creative
- In flow (or in the zone)
- Sense of effortless

After reading this list it is not hard to realise why resourceful states are those states that we want to elicit and use in a number of NLP techniques. Even though you may or may not have learned about the following techniques yet, for ease of future reference here are some occasions when a resourceful state is useful;

- Ecological Checks (or Congruence) with a Desired Outcome
- Setting a Resourceful Anchor
- Future Pacing Calibration

UNRESOURCEFUL STATE

In simple terms, an *unresourceful state* (or non-resourceful state) is one where a person will feel negative. This negativity will come about due to unhelpful emotions and a lack of choice and flexibility of behaviour. This can be due to a strategy that either hinders progress towards a desired outcome or in some cases, could represent a person freezing due to being stuck (see Stuck State). Here are some examples of unresourceful states that a person can experience or demonstrate;

- Stress
- Anxiety
- Panic
- Unfulfilled
- Fear
- Lack of confidence
- Sense of feeling blocked
- Sense of being stuck
- Sense of unavailable energy to meet the effort required

A *Stuck State* is a result of a person having no choice and an inflexibility of behaviour due to a lack of other strategies or patterns available. Here a person will have negative thoughts and negative feelings creating a scenario where they feel and experience an inability to move. There can be several causes for a person to be in a stuck state such as;

- Confusion due to a *Pattern Interrupt*
- Lack of choice or flexibility due to available strategies,
    - o Lack of life experience.
    - o Inability to create a strategy from a generalised pattern.
- Unconscious mind not recalling an experience.

Source Material & Further Learning
(1990) Introducing Neuro-linguistic Programming, O'Conner & Seymour: Page 49

STATES OF FEELING

Are there times when you think about a memory and you can see the experience through your own eyes as if you were there? Alternatively, are there times when you look back and you can watch yourself as though you are on a TV or on a stage?

It is a common misunderstanding within NLP that these descriptions are describing association and dissociation respectively. This is incorrect, these descriptions are describing 1st person and 3rd person perspectives. Now these two differing perspectives can be methods (of which there are more) to achieve the two states of association and dissociation – but they are accurate descriptions of them.

An *associated* state is where you have a connection to your feelings and emotions (aka with your emotion) and a *dissociated* state is absent from your own feelings and emotions (aka without your emotions), noting that dissociated does not mean emotionless.

ASSOCIATED STATE
With your own emotions

You can encourage an associated state, which is the sense of your feeling of emotion to a situation, by being fully present, internally visualising an experience through the perspective of your own eyes to the extent that it may be possible to experience the senses; visual, auditory and kinesthetic.

You might ask;

- "Be there now."
- "With your own eyes and body, experience it."
- "As you re-live it, what can you see?"
  - o Please note that even after visualising in this way it is still possible for a person to be dissociated from an experience.

Below are some characteristics that will provide you with evidence that a person is associated;

- They are alert.
- They may be leaning forward.

- The colour of their face will match (see Calibration) the experience.
- Their voice may vary in tone (see Calibration).
- Their voice may vary in tempo (see Calibration).
- Movement or kinesthetic change may be triggered by the visualization (see Synaesthesia)

Even though you may or may not have learned about the following techniques yet, for ease of reference here are some occasions when an associated state is useful;

- Anchoring Resourceful States.
- For use within the Perceptual Positions technique.
- Future Pacing and Visualization of a desired outcome.
- Creating Rapport.

There are times when an associated state is unhelpful and the cause of an unresourceful state, which of course is undesirable. This is particularly important to know and understand if you are coaching. Examples are;

- Recalling a phobic response.
- Recalling an unpleasant experience.
- When trying to remove or reduce an emotional response.

DISSOCIATED STATE
Without your own emotions

You can encourage this dissociated state, which is the sense of being disconnected from feelings or emotions to a situation, by visualising an experience through the perspective of an onlooker's or observer's eyes. From this perspective of a situation, it is possible for you to experience the emotions and senses experienced by the observer and therefore you will be unable to experience your own associated emotions or sensory experience.

Considering this, it explains how dissociation is useful in reducing, changing or removing the intensity of a feeling someone may have about a past experience or future experience they are visually constructing or recalling.

You might ask;

- "Look on to the situation yourself."
- "Be the observer now, can you see yourself there?"
- "Can you see the whole of you in what you are seeing?"

Here are some characteristics that provide evidence of dissociation;

- They are talking about the experience in the 3rd person.
- Their physiology demonstrates relaxation.
- Their voice will have less variance and may be monotone
- Have minimal behaviour change when reciting the experience.
- Show minimal emotion when reciting the experience.

For ease of reference here are some NLP techniques and occasions when a dissociated state is useful;

- For recalling unpleasant or unresourceful experiences.
- Achieving 'Going Meta'.

There are times when a dissociated state is unhelpful which is particularly important to know and understand if you are coaching a client. Examples are;

- Anchoring Resourceful States.
- Setting safety (or bail-out) anchors.
- Future Pacing a desired state.

GOING META

The word Meta is a Greek word meaning transcending. It is now more generally used to mean 'about (its own category)' or 'aboutness'.

Within NLP this is used to gain an observer's perspective on a situation or an issue. This can be useful as this dissociated state creates a level of objectivity for a situation by a person being outside of the system being observed – even with that person existing inside the situation.

Going Meta can also be referred to as; sitting in the director's chair, the observer's perspective, view from 10,000 feet, or the helicopter view, all literally meaning to go above and beyond and outside of the situation to create an objective viewpoint.

Source Material & Further Learning
(1985) Using Your Brain for a Change, Bandler: Page 40 (1990) Introducing NLP, O'Conner & Seymour: Page 90 (1988) Change Your Mind & Keep the Change, Andreas/Andreas, Pg 26

STATES OF CONSCIOUSNESS

During the day, while we are awake, there are two states of consciousness that we alternate between. This alternation generally happens at an unconscious level although it is possible for you to be consciously aware of what state you are in at any given moment and intentionally move from one to the other. These two states are called *uptime* and *downtime*.

UPTIME

This is a state of being fully present and having full focused awareness directed outwards to the sensory experience and responding to it directly. You will know you are in *uptime* and present in the moment as;

- You will not have internal visualization.
- There will be no self-talk occurring.
- You will not be experiencing inner feelings.

You can consciously improve your ability to be in and maintain uptime by;

- Focusing on what is currently happening outside of you.
- Focus on being observant.
- Focus on listening carefully to someone.

There are many resourceful uses for an uptime state such as;

- Calibration for rapport.
- Effective communication.
- Playing a competitive sport (boxing, tennis).
- Listening to instructions.
- Listening to a client.
- Making no emotive decisions.

Looking at this list you can see why there is an emphasis on being in an uptime state when coaching a client using NLP. (See Coaching)

DOWNTIME

This is a state of having your focused awareness fully directed inside yourself, paying no attention to the sensory experience that is outside of you. You will become consciously unaware of the moments where you have been in *downtime* when you suddenly become consciously aware of things such as;

- A loss of awareness of time.
- An awareness of just experiencing self-talk.
- Becoming aware of a high degree of Deletion afterwards.
- Having just experienced a flow state of extreme concentration.

You can improve your ability to obtain and maintain downtime by;

- Focusing on Self-talk (reflecting, planning).
- Focusing on Inner Kinesthetics. (sensations/feelings).
- Focusing on Internal Visual (day-dreaming).
- Performing Meditation.

There are many resourceful uses for a downtime state such as;

- Meditation
- Introspection
- Finding meaning
- Hypnosis / Trance
- Relaxation
- Though provoking games (chess)
- Self-healing
- Concentration / Flow State
- Enhanced performance

Source Material & Further Learning
(1975) Frogs into Princes, Bandler & Grinder: Page 163

BREAK STATE

Firstly, let's clear up the fact that a *break state* is not really a state in itself, it is actually a technique named after the desired result of the technique. A *break state* is a rapid change technique that literally means to stop a state or frame of mind that someone is in, resulting in an immediate change away from the one they are currently in.

Break state is frequently used by an NLP Practitioner to shift a client away from an unresourceful state. It can also be utilised to switch a person from being inwardly focused (downtime) to outwardly focused (uptime) which can be useful when wanting to break concentration or switching a person's attention from one thing to another.

The easiest and most effective way to break state is to ask seemingly random questions, as in specifically *not* about the state or the cause of the state the person is currently in. If you were to ask a related question about the state this may encourage the person to go deeper into this state, which would be the complete opposite of what you are attempting to do with a break state.

A breaks state is a crucial step in a number of NLP techniques such as; Anchoring, Swish or Sub-modality Mapping Across where you need to be able to stop a particular state between each stage or it may be to repeat a procedure to reinforce the effectiveness of the technique.

As both a break state and a *Pattern Interrupt* can result in shifting someone to a neutral state there is sometimes confusion between them. A simple way to understand the difference is that a break state is regarding a shift in a single emotional state whereas a Pattern Interrupt is more about recognising an unwanted or unresourceful pattern and disrupting it with an intervention (See Pattern Interrupt)

Source Material & Further Learning
(1990) Introducing NLP, O'Conner & Seymour: Page 80

PART FIVE:
OUTCOMES

SETTING OUTCOMES

Outcomes
What do you want specifically?

Setting specific *outcomes* is extremely important to any change process.

If you do not know, or have what you want defined, how can you take any direction towards the goal? Without any kind of conscious desired outcome defined a person will inevitably wander randomly and aimlessly through life, continually reacting to situations by avoiding what they do not want.

> *'Would you tell me, please, which way I ought to go from here?'*
> *'That depends a good deal on where you want to get to,' said the cat.*
> *'I don't much care where.' replies Alice.*
> *'Then it doesn't matter which way you go,' replies the cat.*
> **Alice in Wonderland, Lewis Carroll**

NLP insists that firstly we must identify a desired outcome so that we can make conscious, purposeful and positive moves towards the specified outcome. Said another way, 'What do you want specifically?'.

Desired Outcome
What do you want that you don't currently have?

A desired outcome suggests by its very existence that it is something you want (or desire) and the components of the defined outcome are things that you currently do not have in your present situation or state. With a desired outcome set, we are able to make a plan, own the plan and take ownership of actions and activities that will move us closer to what we want.

You can see that you need an outcome before you can make a plan or take action, therefore it is important to not *do it* before you have an outcome defined. Sure, *doing* so in the absence of an outcome will provide life experience and yet the value of this experience is questionable as it is undirected and using up one of your finite resources – time! A desired outcome is also different to a goal, target or objective in that all of these are just events or items of achievement. An outcome in comparison must meet some carefully considered criteria or what in NLP we call *conditions*. These conditions combined create well-formed outcomes.

WELL-FORMED OUTCOMES

Neuro-Linguistic Programming lists certain *well-formedness conditions* that outcomes should meet. We will run through each of them looking at the questions you can ask as an NLP Practitioner in order to create a well-formed outcome for either yourself or a client.

Quick Reference:

Summary of the 7 Well-Formedness Conditions of an Outcome

1. Is it Positively Stated?
2. Is there Testable Sensory Evidence to measure progress?
3. Is the Desired State Sensory Specific?
4. Is it Achievable and Maintainable by the Subject?
5. Is it Explicitly Contextualised?
6. Does it Preserve Positive Present Products?
7. Is it Ecologically Congruent with the Subject and System?

The Well-Formedness Conditions.

1) Positively Stated.

The very first condition is that the outcome must be stated positively, using positive language. Said another way, the outcome must be what is *wanted* as opposed to what is *not wanted*. This is based on the logic that a person can only engage in the process of 'doing something' even if that 'doing' is a result of not wanting something else. So, as you cannot *not do something* NLP chooses to focus effort on what we want.

With a reference to meta-programs (see Meta-Programs), you achieve a positively stated outcome by using *towards* language as opposed to *away from* language. Here are some questions you can ask either yourself or a client to obtain information that adheres to this condition;

- Is the goal positively stated?
- What do you want?
- If you don't want that, what do you want?

2) Testable Sensory Evidence.

The outcome must also have a demonstrable evidence procedure, as in there must be a way of measuring not only the achievement of the outcome but also measuring progress against the desired outcome. This allows us to understand whether we are heading towards or away from the desired outcome and can therefore change plans and behaviour accordingly. Here are some questions you can ask either yourself or a client to obtain information that adheres to this condition;

- How will you know when you have completed the outcome?
- What criteria will mean the desired outcome is achieved?
- How would someone else know when you've finished?

3) Sensory Specific Desired State.

You must be able to describe the experience of achieving the outcome with an associated fully sensory-specific description. What will you see, hear, feel, smell, taste and be saying to yourself? Here are some questions you can ask either yourself or a client to obtain data that adheres to this condition;

- What will you see through your eyes when this is achieved?
- What will you hear when you achieve this outcome?
- What feelings will you feel when you finish this outcome?

4) Achievable and Maintainable by the Subject.

Achievement of the outcome itself and progress towards the desired outcome must be able to be initiated and maintained by the person achieving the outcome (the *Subject*). This specifically places ownership and the responsibility for achieving the outcome with the subject themselves. With this taken into account it is not a well-formed outcome if someone else has to achieve it or even change it in some way. Here are some questions you can ask either yourself or a client to obtain information that adheres to this condition;

- Do you have the resources to start?
- What is the first step you will take?
- How will you maintain your plan to achieve this outcome?

5) Explicitly Contextualised.

Achievement of the outcome should be stated within a specific circumstance as opposed to open-ended universal statements such as; *all the time* or *always*. This is also included to ensure that achievement of the outcome provides additional choice to the subject as universals (See Universal Quantifier) can reduce the flexibility of behaviour or response. Here are some questions you can ask either yourself or a client to obtain information that adheres to this condition;

- Who do you want to share the achievement of this outcome with?
- Where will you be when you achieve this outcome?
- When specifically, will you achieve this outcome?
  - Specify an exact date and time.

6) Preserve Positive Present Products

If a desired outcome removes any positive aspect of a present state, then there is a risk of substitution of behaviour which may cause future conflict. This can be identified during an ecology check (See Well-Formedness condition 7: Ecologically Congruent) when a subject demonstrates incongruence by highlighting a *secondary gain*. A secondary gain is a resourceful state or behaviour that occurs as a result of a present state the person wants to change. As this can often be unconscious or initially seemingly unrelated to a present state, it is important for an NLP Practitioner to ensure this condition is adhered to. Here are some questions you can ask either yourself or a client to obtain information that adheres to this condition;

- What do you have now you want to still have?
- When you achieve this outcome what will you have?
  - *Calibrate the response to the positive aspects of the present state.*
- Does this outcome add to your current choices?

7) Ecologically Congruent

Finally, with all the data provided by the other six conditions an ecology check can be run. This is where the Subject should consider the impact and consequences that could occur during the process of achievement and the actual achievement of the desired outcome. The desired outcome should not be pursued if any harm to themselves or other people is identified. Here are some questions you can ask either yourself or a client to obtain information that adheres to this condition;

- When you achieve this what will you gain?
  - *Positive / Positive (+/+)*
- When you achieve this what will you not have?
  - *Positive / Negative (+/-)*
- What will you have if you do not achieve this outcome?
  - *Negative. / Positive (-/+)*
- What will you not have if you do not achieve this outcome?
  - *Negative. / Negative (-/-)*
- Will anyone else be impacted by achieving this outcome?
- Will anyone else lose anything if you achieve this outcome?

The +/+, +/-, -/+, -/- are a line of questions called Cartesian questions. They were formulated and are attributed to René Descartes (1596-1650) a French philosopher and a mathematician who created them for the intention of opening the mind to new alternatives and possibilities.

Source Material & Further Learning
(1990) Introducing NLP, O'Conner & Seymour: Page 10 (1975) Frogs into Princes, Bandler & Grinder: Page 147 (1988) Change Your Mind & Keep the Change, Andreas/Andreas: Page 105

PART SIX:
REPRESENTATIONAL
SYSTEMS

OUR FOUR WORLDS

In 1967 Paul Watzlawick coined the phrase,

"You cannot not communicate."

The introduction of this concept was coupled with his terminology; verbal communication (spoken language) and non-verbal communication (body language).

Later chapters such as rapport will be focused on non-verbal communication (posture, gestures, breathing) but for now let's focus on communicating effectively with verbal language, something that is also extremely useful for techniques such as building rapport, pacing and leading – all things you will shortly learn about.

With reference to the Communication Model, we know that we take in information from the world (territory) through our senses process this data through our filters and then create an internal sensory representation of that data (our map).

For each of the four types of experience, we can sense we have a specific sensory representational system to process the data we receive from those particular worlds in order to provide us with our perception.

Let's take a look at each of them;

- **The world of Space.**
    - The visual world.
    - What we see through our eyes.
    - We see things in a simultaneous way.

- **The world of Time.**
    - The world of sound.
    - The temporal sound through time.
    - We hear things in a linear way.
        - Languages are sounds that have meaning.

- **The world of Sensation.**
    - o   The world of feeling in our body.
    - o   The emotive response patterns we feel.
    - o   What we physically feel or sense with our body.
        - ▪   Including smell and taste.

- **The world of Meaning.**
    - o   The world of attaching meaning to a sense.
    - o   The meaning we attach to a language?
        - ▪   Hearing a language or word being spoken.
        - ▪   Seeing a word written down.
        - ▪   Feeling a texture. (Braille)

Source Material & Further Learning
(1967) In Pragmatics of Human Communication, P. Watzlawick, J. Beavin-Bavelas, D. Jackson

4-TUPLE

V.A.K.D
or
V.A.(K/O/G).D

A *tuple* is a collection of items or things that do not change over time. Think of it as a 'closed list' that cannot and will never change.

In every moment of time, we create a *4-tuple* (closed list of 4 items) representation of that experience from four senses or *modalities* (see Modalities). The way in which we combine these four inputs together creates our perception of the world (map).

These 4 modalities are;

- **V**isual (Seeing)
- **A**uditory (Hearing)
- **K**inesthetic (Feeling)
  - ○ **O**lfactory (Smelling)
  - ○ **G**ustatory (Tasting)
- **D**igital (Meaning via Language)

Before you say anything, I know there are *six* items on this 4-Tuple list of four! In this particular model of the Representational System Olfactory (Smelling) & Gustatory (Tasting); abbreviated as O and G are grouped with Kinesthetic (Feeling) as they are all related to the *world of sensation*. This does not however make this model the 6-Tuple.

Source Material & Further Learning
(1975) Patterns of The Hypnotic Techniques of Milton H. Erickson, M.D. Vol 2, Bandler & Grinder: Page 21

6-TUPLE

V. A. K. O. G. AD

The 6-Tuple is a model that takes into account the fact that we build our models of the world first and then second to that, attach meaning to our experiences. This meaning is processed by a sixth sense, our *language.*

As our self-talk is related to meaning (Digital) and we hear (Auditory) our self-talk (internal language), we refer to this as Auditory Digital (AD). Despite the word Auditory being used, it must be clear that AD is not related to any sensory organ in the body.

Here are the 6 modalities that make up the 6-Tuple;

- **V**isual (Seeing)
- **A**uditory (Hearing)
- **K**inesthetic (Feeling)
- **O**lfactory (Smelling)
- **G**ustatory (Tasting)
- **A**uditory **D**igital (Internal Dialogue)

You will find that when we speak, we will explain our perception of the world or an experience using words that are related to one of the primary senses (Predicates).

A high frequency of use with predicates from a particular sensory representational system will be uncovering which one of the sensory representations we have a primary preference for.

Knowing this information about another person and using the same sensory-specific language can help you be in rapport with that person as you are meeting them at their map of the world. We will cover this further in the section *Predicates* and the section *Preferred Representational Systems.*

INTERNAL & EXTERNAL REPRESENTATION

The last element of Representational Systems to cover is that we can either sense things internally or externally. This variance allows us to build a complete model of our Representational System.

Visual External (V^e)
The images you see with your eyes, outside of you.

Visual Internal (V^i)
Images that you visualise with your mind's eye.

Auditory Tonal External (A^e)
The sounds outside of you that you hear with your ears.

Auditory Tonal Internal (A^i)
Sounds that hear with your mind's inner ear.

Auditory Digital (A^d)
Words that are used to playback or speak with yourself.

Kinesthetic External (K^e)
Tactile feelings as a result of touch, temperature or moisture.

Kinesthetic Internal (K^i)
Internal sensations or visceral feelings like emotion.

Olfactory (O)
Odours that you can smell.
Technically it could be represented as O^i but this can only occur inside of us there is no requirement for Internal to be stated.

Gustatory (G)
Things you can taste.
Technically it could be represented as G^i but this can only occur inside of us there is no requirement for Internal to be stated.

EYE PATTERNS

Have you ever noticed that when people speak, they move their eyes? I'm not just talking about directing you to where they want you to look, but more in the way of moving their eyes around their head. This movement is not a random act and our eye movements have meaning. Depending on whether a person is looking down, up or to the side, their eyes are giving us information about the internal representations a person is using to access information. More often than not, showing what representational system or modality they actually prefer to access information with, something known as their *lead representational system*. As a bit of fun and to witness this for yourself you could ask someone, "Can you please spell out the word 'phenomenal'?" Now watch where their eyes go…

There are six places that a person can be looking to provide you with an idea of what modality they are using to access information from. That being said, be aware of Mind Reading as without thorough calibration, this model can only initially provide a suggestion due to some subtle variance between different people. Around 75-85% of the population are considered to be *normally wired* (see the Eye Accessing Cue Chart) while the other 15-25% are considered to have *reverse eye accessing cues*. This was initially linked to whether a person is right-handed or left-handed person but that link is now considered to not be the case. For ease of teaching, we will use the chart for normally-wired eye accessing patterns as this accounts for the large majority.

NLP PRACTITIONER TIP
In a digital world with video calling, it is possible that you will be looking at a reverse video image of someone. This of course will impact what you are observing. To enable you to build your eye-accessing map for them look for a word in the background or on clothing so you can see if you are actually looking at a mirror image of the person you are speaking with.

The following Eye Accessing Cue Table and Chart allows us to look at each of the six positions. It is important to know that the illustrations depict what you will see by looking at the person you are observing, they are not a representation from an associated perspective. There is one position missed from the table and that is one where someone is looking straight at you; Eyes Straight Ahead, Defocused or Dilated. There is no specific NLP term for this position and yet this gaze-like look is a representation of a person being in a Downtime State (See Downtime) and evidence that they are accessing information from multiple modalities. That being said Visual Internal is most likely to be one of the multiple modalities being accessed.

Eye Accessing Cue Reference Table

Up and to the Right. This would indicate **Visual Recall (Vʳ)** They are remembering seeing the word and picturing it.	
Horizontally to the Right This would indicate **Auditory Recall (Aʳ)** They are remembering hearing the word and hearing it	
Down and to the Right This would indicate **Auditory Digital (Aᵈ)** They are possibly thinking about the last time, the meaning of the word or maybe even the meaning behind the question!	
Up and to the Left This would indicate **Visual Construct (Vᶜ)** They are creating an image in their mind of what it might look like.	
Horizontally to the Left This would indicate **Auditory Construct (Aᶜ)** They are creating a sound of what that word might sound like if someone said it to them.	
Down and to the Left This would indicate **Kinesthetic (K)** It is possible that this word makes them feel a certain way or maybe the question itself makes them feel a certain way.	

Eye Accessing Cue Chart

Putting these together here is a full eye accessing cues chart from the perspective of you looking at another person.

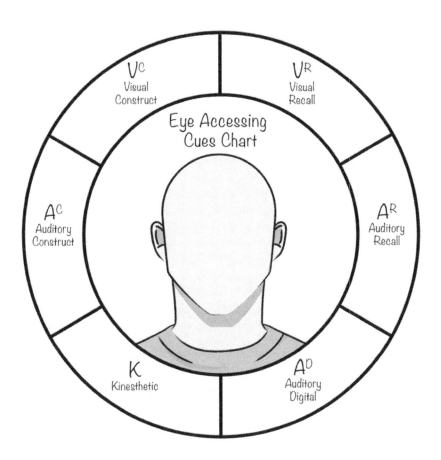

Source Material & Further Learning
(1975) Frogs into Princes, Bandler & Grinder: Page 25

PREDICATES

With reference to the Representational System section, we mentioned that the way a person speaks (words and phrases) can give a good indication of what sensory representational system that person primarily uses to create their model of the world (see Preferred Representational Systems). These sensory-specific words are what we call *Predicates*. To witness this, ask a person about a past experience and you will hear them predominantly respond in one of four ways;

- **Visual.**
  - *What they saw.*
- **Auditory**
  - *What they heard.*
- **Kinesthetic.**
  - *What it felt like.*
- **Digital**
  - *What the logical facts were.*

The next few pages contain lists of words and phrases that you might hear a person say to indicate which particular internal sensory representational system (modality) they are operating from.

If you wish to build rapport and communicate effectively to a person then you should use the language that matches their preferred representational system. In particular, these types of words will have the most impact;

- Verbs – a word that conveys an action an occurrence
- Adverbs - a word used to modify a verb
- Adjectives - a word naming an attribute of a noun

This brings a whole new level of understanding to the phrase 'speaking the same language as someone' doesn't it?

Source Material & Further Learning
(1975) Frogs into Princes, Bandler & Grinder: Page 28

Visual Predicates.

Here are some visual words to listen out for:

• Bright	• Glance
• Clear	• Outlook
• See	• Observe
• Picture	• Clear
• Examine	• Appear
• Vivid	• Show
• Hazy	• Bright
• Focus	• Dim
• Look	• Dark
• View	• Hindsight
• Watch	• Vision

Phrases you might hear a person use with a visually preferred modality:

- It appeared to be
- It looked interesting
- I see what you mean
- Now look here
- Please show me what you mean
- I have tunnel vision
- You've lost perspective
- I can picture that
- That memory is a bit hazy
- Is what I am saying clear?
- Let's look at this a different way
- That is a bright idea
- I like the look of that
- That's my point of view
- It was clear-cut
- You have short-sightedness

Auditory Predicates.

Here are some auditory words to listen out for:

• Heard	• Deaf
• Loud	• Tone
• Talk	• Vocal
• Tell	• Harmony
• Listen	• Beat
• Announce	• Call
• Amplify	• Wavelength
• Mention	• Remark
• Speak	• Stated
• Tune	• Roar
• Ring	• Say

Phrases you might hear a person use with an auditory preferred modality:

- That is unheard of
- Word for word
- Call me when you want
- I'm outspoken
- Don't utter a word
- Describe in detail
- It was as clear as a bell
- We are in-tune
- He gave me an earful
- Lend me your ear
- To tell the truth
- I heard you loud and clear
- Let me voice my opinion
- Sorry I tuned out
- I was tongue-tied at the moment
- We are on the same wavelength

Kinesthetic Predicates.

Here are some kinesthetic words to listen out for:

• Touch	• Sore
• Hold	• Bounce
• Handle	• Flow
• Grasp	• Snap
• Tap	• Push
• Solid	• Break
• Feel	• Weight
• Connect	• Rub
• Catch	• Tied
• Throw	• Stroke
• Draining	• Grounded

Phrases you might hear a person use with a kinesthetic preferred modality:

- Let's get to grips with that
- We are connected
- I'll guide you hand-in-hand
- We need to start from scratch
- We can pull some strings
- I'm all tied up right now
- It all boils down to this
- Hang on there
- That slipped my mind
- I've got a real feel for that now
- That really hit home
- Let's drive this forward
- She was as solid as a rock
- Let's take things one step at a time
- That was a real weight on my mind
- They rubbed me up the wrong way

Digital Predicates (Unspecified Representational System)

Here are some types of Digital (Meaning) words to listen out for:

• Attitude	• Think
• Consider	• Evaluate
• Attentive	• Remember
• Identify	• Wonder
• Conceive	• Aware
• Sequence	• Learn
• Logical	• Information
• Facts	• Data
• Understand	• Remind
• Process	• Emit
• Pattern	• Ignore

Phrases you might hear a person use with an unspecified preferred modality:

- He had a bad attitude
- I'll have to take that into consideration
- We need to identify the problem
- Yes, I'm very logical
- These are the facts
- I'm thinking about it
- I need to understand
- Let me take a moment to process that
- There is a pattern of data
- I need to learn the specific terms for the role
- That reminds me
- I'll evaluate the situation
- Can you wonder what it was like?
- I am aware of it
- Here is the sequence of events
- Here's the information I know

NON-VERBAL ACCESSING CUES

Beyond predicates (verbal) and eye patterns, there are some other non-verbal *accessing cues* that can help us with regards to detecting which sensory representational system someone is accessing information from. The tables below provide some of these indicators for each modality.

Voice Tone

Visual	Auditory	Kinesthetic
Speak in a high voice Speak with a clear tone	Has a melodious tone	Low tone Deep tone Soft tone

Voice Tempo

Visual	Auditory	Kinesthetic
Rapid speed	Medium pace Rhyming & rhythm	Slow Pace Pauses often

Breathing Location & Depth

Visual	Auditory	Kinesthetic
Shallow Short breaths Top of chest	Even breathing Mid Chest	Deep Long breaths Abdomen

Posture & Gesture

Visual	Auditory	Kinesthetic
Tension Extended neck Gesture hands to eyes Often ectomorphic	Rhythmic movement Head tilted Gesture hands to ears Often mesomorphic	Relaxed posture Head down Gesture to abdomen Often Endomorphic

REPRESENTATIONAL SYSTEM PREFERENCES

With knowledge of the 6-Tuple Sensory Representational Systems (V.A.K.O.G.AD), and all the verbal and non-verbal accessing cues to help identify which sensory system someone may be using at a particular moment, we can now look at the different ways and times a person will utilise a preferred representational system.

PREFERRED REPRESENTATIONAL SYSTEM

Before we look at the different types let's get clear on our definition of a *Preferred Sensory Representational System.* Although we use all our senses, one system will provide a person with the most variety, depth and latitude and therefore the most flexibility for processing information for use at different times and for different purposes.

PRIMARY REPRESENTATIONAL SYSTEM

The *primary representational system* is the sensory representational system for which a person prefers to take in and process information from the outside world.

This is due to the fact that the person has the most latitude in sensing and understanding the information they are sensing. You will find a person will use this system as their predominant way of communicating as they have the most variance and flexibility to communicate their meaning.

A person will pay more attention to their primary representational system modality as they are able to make the most efficient comprehensive meaning of as much information as possible. With all this being considered, you can understand that to communicate effectively with a person, if you predominately use their primary representational system this provides information in the sensory modality that they can create the most meaning and understanding of your communication. This is why this particular system is a fundamental element of building and being in rapport with someone.

LEAD REPRESENTATIONAL SYSTEM

The *lead representational system* is the sensory representational system from which a person prefers to access their internal representational information. It is possible for this to be different to the primary representational system.

The lead system can be detected by paying close attention to eye patterns. In particular, look out for the very first eye position following the processing of an external trigger (event in the outside world). Think of the lead representational system as the 'key to the safe', it is the sensory modality that is utilised first to allow access to all the other information and sensory modalities in the person's internal sensory representation (map). As this is the very first sensory modality used it is the modality that will most frequently appear at the beginning of a person's internal T.O.T.E. strategies, in particular the initial sequence of accessing information that eventually will result in behaviour. (See Strategy).

REFERENCE REPRESENTATIONAL SYSTEM

The *reference representational system* is the sensory representational system that is used by a person within a particular strategy to detect whether they know and agree with information they have accessed via the lead representational system.

This process is mostly done in the conscious mind and therefore provides conscious awareness of the reasoning behind whether something is true or false.

If there is a situation where a person cannot connect to any sensory references it may result in a person saying something along the lines of 'I don't know what I want', explaining that they have no frame of reference for the information they have accessed (also see Transderivational Search).

Source Material & Further Learning
(1975) Frogs into Princes, Bandler & Grinder: Page 28

TRANSDERIVATIONAL SEARCH PATTERN

If a person has no *reference representational system* or is finding it hard to make meaning of information this can be detected by witnessing a particular eye pattern consisting of rapid eye movement going from one eye accessing cue to another. This pattern is called a *Transderivational Search (TDS)* and occurs due to the fact the unconscious mind is rapidly accessing and searching across multiple sensory representational systems as well as recalling and constructing the information that is present.

For more information about TDS please see the Milton Model where hypnotic language it is used to create a state of confusion (stuck state) and the calibration for this state is TDS.

SYNAESTHESIA

In most cases, one representational system will happen after another in a linear sequence. For example, a person will access information with the Lead Representational System, then reference meaning with the Reference Representational System and then choose to communicate verbally with Predicates from their Primary Representational System. There are however times when a sequence does not occur and two or more representational systems overlap causing them to exist simultaneously. This is called *Synaesthesia*. An example of *Synaesthesia* might be that when a person sees a colour, they get a taste in their mouth or when they hear a sound, they can see a colour.

Source Material & Further Learning

(1975) Patterns of The Hypnotic Techniques of Milton H. Erickson
Vol 1, Bandler & Grinder: Page 217
(1980) NLP: Vol I. The Study of The Structure of Experience, Dilts, Grinder, Bandler, Bandler, DeLozier: Page 28

PART SEVEN:
RAPPORT

SENSORY ACUITY & CALIBRATION

Sensory Acuity is about having the capability to use your senses to make accurate observations about ourselves and others.

Let us focus on the NLP Presupposition,
'The meaning of the communication is the response that you get.'

With sensory acuity you can read the response you are getting in much greater detail by reading the non-verbal communication you are receiving. Before you can accurately measure any differences in a person's non-verbal communication you need to know from what state you are measuring from, something called a baseline state. This act of observing and measuring against a baseline state is known as *Calibration*. By constantly comparing a person's present state to their baseline state we can begin to accurately read the response and adjust our own behaviour accordingly.

These are nine key non-verbal indicators that allow us to read a person and in-turn calibrate their internal responses in any ongoing interaction;

- Skin colour
- Skin shininess
- Muscle tonus
- Breathing rate
- Breathing pauses

- Lower lip size
- Pupil dilation
- Breathing location
- Breathing depth

In addition to these nine be aware there are many more, such as;

- Head movement
- Eye brow movement
- Lip movement
- Gestures

- Mouth drying
- Tonality of voice
- Tempo of voice
- Volume of voice

Source Material & Further Learning
(1981) Trance-Formations, Bandler & Grinder: Page 201 (1990) Introducing NLP, O'Conner & Seymour: Page 52 (1975) Frogs into Princes, Bandler & Grinder: Page 79

NO MIND READING

A *mind read* is when you claim to know what someone else is thinking or feeling without having any direct communication from that person to base that information on. Calibration is one of the first things that you have learned where you can practice and test your ability to avoid using your own filters and analyse purely the evidence that is being presented. Be aware that you are recognising the sensory-based evidence and *just that*. If you calibrate a change this is highlighting that there has been an internal change in that person, you do not at this stage know what that internal change is or means. To discover what is happening we must ask questions and the answers to these questions will enable us to collect information that leaves absolutely no room for guessing. Guessing is an alternate way of saying 'making an assumption'. As an NLP Practitioner you should not be making any assumptions about anything that the other person is thinking in their mind or said another way, no *Mind Reading* should take place. An NLP Practitioner is interested in gaining information about the other person's map and therefore must leave their own out of the processing of the data being presented.

Here are some examples of mind reading;

- His face told me he was uninterested in what I had to say.
- His look said he was angry.
- She kept her voice down because she was embarrassed.
- You could tell by her breathing that she was calm.

In contrast here are some examples of sensory-based evidence;

- He is blushing.
- She began breathing faster.
- She is speaking more quietly.
- He took in a deep breath with his chest.

Source Material & Further Learning
(1975) The Structure of Magic, Vol I. Bandler & Grinder: Page 105

PACING

Rapport is probably one of the most well-known elements associated with NLP. It is not uncommon for people who have dabbled in learning about emotional intelligence or NLP to know about *mirroring* someone to gain rapport. This section will go into exactly what it is and what is behind it.

Firstly, a definition of the word Rapport,

Rapport is the process of establishing a relationship with another person that illustrates harmony, understanding, mutual trust and mutual confidence.

The first thing to notice is that it is a *process* not a thing. I point this out because it tells us that we can be *in* rapport with someone but we cannot *have* rapport with someone. The process ultimately results in a perceived lack of difference at an unconscious level.

So, why is rapport so important? Well, it turns out that people tend to like and trust people who are *like* them. A high level of trust can influence whether that person is more or less likely to follow someone. The more trust the more likely it is. Interestingly, it is possible to be in rapport with someone who does not *like* you, because the unconscious similarities have resulted in high levels of trust. As an NLP Practitioner if you do find yourself in this scenario it could suggest a line of questioning that could uncover how much (or little!) they like themselves – remember though, no assumptions or mind reading, this is just a prompt to ask some elegant questions.

The other component of rapport that helps build high levels of trust is that you are effectively showing the other person at an unconscious level that you accept them and accept the validity of what is going on in their ongoing experience. You are demonstrating that you can relate to their model of the world. Simply put, people feel good when they feel a person understands and empathises with them.

One last point to cover with regards to rapport is that it does not mean that you just agree with everything that person says. With what you know now I'm sure you can think of people in your life that you trust and yet you can also disagree with. This disagreement does not break your rapport with them. If the disagreement does, you now know there are other things going on with regard to communication verbally and non-verbally that have actually meant you are no longer in rapport with them.

The key to building rapport is something called *pacing*. This is where you take conscious action to meet the other person where they are at. As you progress through this section you will learn about the Representational System and with this knowledge, you can ensure your verbal communication (see Predicates) can meet the other person on their map, for now, though we are focusing on non-verbal communication.

Here are the critical non-verbal things to *pace*;

- Posture
- Gestures
- Voice tone
- Voice volume
- Voice tempo
- Breathing

There are a number of ways for you to consciously build rapport by matching or reflecting these non-verbals. They all have influence and yet the most powerful thing to pace to become in rapport with someone is reflecting or matching breathing. This is due to the fact that the synchronisation of breathing is picked up and noticed by a person's conscious and unconscious mind.

Here are the three techniques you can use to match and reflect to build rapport;

- Matching
- Mirroring
- Crossover Matching

Before you read on you must ensure that you are personally congruent when in the process of building rapport. Any unconscious gestures you present to the other person that are misaligned within you will hinder and possibly destroy any chances of you being in rapport with that other person.

MATCHING

This is where your physiology, words, voice tempo, and voice tonality exactly match what the other person is doing. Think of this like a dance routine where you are repeating the same moves. It is important not to overdo this by repeatedly immediately mimicking to a point at which it is obvious and a focus of the other person as this can negatively impact your ability to be in rapport with them.

MIRRORING

This is the same concept as Matching except your physiology mirrors the person as though they are looking in a mirror. Mirroring has been found to be a slightly more effective method of pacing over Matching resulting in a quicker and deeper level of being in rapport.

CROSS-OVER MIRRORING

This is when you match one part of a person's physiology or behaviour with a different part of your physiology. The easiest example would be to tap your foot or finger on a table to match the tempo of the other person's breathing.

IN RAPPORT INDICATORS

Here are four things you may observe to identify that you are in rapport;

- Nodding of head
- Leaning forward
- Active listening
- Direct eye contact

Source Material & Further Learning
(1975) Frogs into Princes, Bandler & Grinder: Page 79 (1981) Trance-Formations, Bandler & Grinder: Page 33 (1990) Introducing NLP, O'Conner & Seymour: Page 19 (1975) Patterns of The Hypnotic Techniques of Milton H. Erickson, M.D. Vol 1, Bandler & Grinder: Page 12

LEADING

NLP PRACTITIONER CONTEXT
For ease of explanation, the techniques of Pacing and Leading are being utilised within the context of coaching a client.

Until now in this book you have been in observation mode, gaining data and knowledge. As explained Uptime and observation mode is one of, if not the most important state to be in as an NLP Practitioner (see Coaching with States). With an understanding of Calibration, Pacing and Rapport we can now look at how as an NLP Practitioner you are able to begin to facilitate change in a person, moving them towards a more resourceful state or desired state. Having initially detected a *baseline state* and *calibrated* your client, after mirroring, matching or cross-over mirroring the client's physiology as well as using their primary representational system you may then observe you are in Rapport via indicators such as nodding, leaning forward or active listening. You can either continue to hold and be in rapport with the client via *pacing* or you are now in a great position to be able to *lead* the client.

LEADING

Firstly, *leading* cannot take place unless adequate *pacing* is present. This does mean as an NLP Practitioner you can present a *lead* and yet it does not guarantee the client will follow. Let's also get something else very clear, you cannot and therefore should not attempt to try and *lead* a person that is unwilling to be led. From an ecological perspective, this is why as an NLP Practitioner you *must* seek and gain permission from the client before any change work can be done. The purpose of leading is to positively *influence* (See Influence) the possible options and beneficial options available to a client by providing direction to a more resourceful state.

Influence
Introducing options to increase flexibility and choice that may or may not be taken.

With the description above of how you arrive at an opportunity to lead a client, you can understand how this is related to *influence*. As an NLP Practitioner, you are making decisions and taking action (leading) that can influence a direction a client *may* (or may not!) take by introducing the options to the person. You are influencing the options, *not* the client's actual decision. Remember NLP is a Process Model, not a Content Model.

155

Influence vs Persuasive Influence

A high level of trust allowing the options presented for more choices to be considered valid.

You can only have the ability to influence a client if you have first persuaded them that the options you are presenting are valid. The way you can gain *persuasive influence* is by meeting the client in a place where there is a shared presupposed belief of what is true and the options you are presenting (leading) are considered as a beneficial possibility by the client. It is important to acknowledge that you are not telling the client which option to choose, you are merely presenting options that are validated due to them matching their presuppositions. (Also see Beliefs).

Persuasive Influence vs Manipulation

While we are cover the topic of *pacing and leading* let's also cover the word that has the most negatively associated connotation to NLP, that being *manipulation*. As previously explained pacing and leading can be related to persuasion and influence. Complications and misinterpretation are then made by the introduction of the word *manipulation*. Let's look at two definitions of the word firstly to greater understand what that word means but also to get clear how the confusion with NLP techniques occurs;

1. Manipulation: Handling or controlling something in a 'skilful manner'

With reference to a few of the presuppositions of NLP and the NLP Communication Model, you will be aware that the only thing that an NLP Practitioner can 'skillfully control' is their communication to a client. The primary desired outcome of this communication being to present the client with more flexibility of choice, so as to provide the client with a resourceful state to operate from.

What is *not* possible with NLP is to create the actual change in the client, they can only do that themselves. So to this end, you cannot physically (or metaphorically) manipulate a person to behave a particular way and you definitely cannot do anything that a person does not want to do.

2. Manipulation: Handling or controlling someone in a 'clever or unscrupulous way'.

This definition is where I personally feel the negative connotation derives from and it has to do with the inclusion of the word 'unscrupulous',

- *Unscrupulous: showing no moral principles; not honest or fair.*
- *Unscrupulous: done for the benefit or in favour of the manipulator.*

Knowing that all desired outcomes with NLP change techniques are to move a person from an unresourceful present state to a resourceful desired state and that that change process can only be done by presenting possible options for a client to take, and that the client can only choose to take action on themselves, you can see that this word is not relevant, nor is it possible for an NLP Practitioner to unscrupulously manipulate. It goes against all of the core processes, principles and abilities an NLP Practitioner possess.

The only thing as an NLP Practitioner you are in control of and can manipulate is your own communication to another person. Yes, this can *influence* (present options) and yes can be *persuasive* (present an option that a client agrees is possible and valid) but in no way can we *manipulate* (control a person's actions for them) nor are the any intentions to *manipulate* (control actions to reduce choice and flexibility) of another person.

As a person learning NLP, I trust that this provides enough content and commentary for you to be able to communicate a response to an objection or comment of this nature that you may face in the future.

Source Material & Further Learning
(1975) Frogs into Princes, Bandler & Grinder: Page 80

FUTURE PACING

Future Pacing is the method to enable a person to experience a situation in the future as though they are actually there combining their sensory representational systems as well as the additional resources they will have as a result of the desired outcome. Future Pacing is the final step of many NLP techniques as it allows an NLP Practitioner to calibrate a client against the previously identified problem state so as to detect if change has occurred and indeed whether more work needs to be done.

The second beneficial component of Future Pacing is the art of repetitive mental rehearsal. Learning is optimal when a skill is being developed in the real world. This 'real' learning allows for a full range of senses to be experienced in a situation. Repetition benefits learning as it allows for habits (unconscious competent behaviour) to be formed. These habits are a result of experiencing multiple feedback scenarios enabling further improvement via the experience of flexibility being required in a variety of situations. As Future Pacing encourages the use of all senses, it is the next best thing to experience an actual event in real time.

Here are some steps that are required for a successful Future Pace;

- Experience the future event from an associated perspective.
    - o Developing a Visual Internal sense may help
        - o (See Developing a Sense)
- Construct a full sensory experience of the event happening.
    - o As an NLP Practitioner, you can calibrate the moment just after the trigger of the event to see if change has occurred.
- Acknowledging this is a rehearsal.
    - o Notice things within the experience that can be used as feedback to enable further learning and improvement.

Source Material & Further Learning

(1975) Frogs into Princes, Bandler & Grinder: Page 87
(1981) Trance-Formations, Bandler & Grinder: Page 158
(1990) Introducing NLP, O'Conner & Seymour: Page 77

DEVELOPING A SENSE

There are times when it can be useful to focus on or enhance a single specific aspect of sensory awareness. This can be consciously done by considering Miller's Law (7 ± 2) and reducing the information coming from other senses. This reduction allows more conscious awareness of the sense you want to develop. Being able to focus more on Visual Internal, for example, will assist in the ability to Visualise or Future Pace. Other benefits of developing a specific sense could be to;

- Gain more data about a trigger for a coach (See Present State).
- Gaining more detailed data while eliciting a strategy (See Strategy).
- Enhance the awareness of sub-modalities (See Sub-modalities).
- Bringing conscious awareness to a non-preferred system.

Here are some examples of how you can develop each of the particular senses with some practical examples included;

To enhance **Visual Internal (Vⁱ)** be in Downtime and…

Visual (Ve)	Auditory (Ae)	Kinesthetic (Ke)
Close your eyes	Remove noise	Stop moving

To enhance **Visual External (Vᵉ)** be in Uptime and…

Visual (Vi)	Auditory (Ae)	Kinesthetic (Ke)
Open your eyes	Remove noise	Stop moving

To enhance **Auditory Internal (Aⁱ)** be in Downtime and…

Visual (Ve)	Auditory (Ae)	Kinesthetic (Ke)
Close your eyes	Remove noise	Stop moving

To enhance **Auditory External (A^e)** be in Uptime and...

Visual (Ve)	Auditory (Ad)	Kinesthetic (Ki)
Close your eyes	Focus on sounds	Stop moving

To enhance **Auditory Internal Digital (A^{id})** be in Downtime and...

Visual (Ve)	Auditory (Ae)	Kinesthetic (Ki)
Close your eyes	Remove noise	Stop moving

To enhance **Kinesthetic Internal (K^i)** be in Downtime and...

Visual (Ve)	Auditory (Ae)	Auditory (Ad)
Close your eyes	Remove noise	Tell yourself to focus on areas of your body

To enhance **Kinesthetic External (K^e)** be in Uptime and...

Visual (Ve)	Auditory (Ae)	Auditory (Ad)
Focus on the location of the sensation	Remove noise	Tell yourself to focus on location of the sensation

To enhance **Olfactory (O)** be in Uptime and...

Visual Recall (Vi)	Auditory (Ae)	Kinesthetic (Ki)
Visualise images you previously associated with the smell	Remove noise	Stop moving

To enhance **Gustatory (G)** be in Uptime and...

Visual Recall (Vi)	Visual (Ve)	Kinesthetic (Ki)
Visualise images you previously associated with the taste	Close your eyes	Sit Still

OVERLAPPING REPRESENTATIONAL SYSTEMS

Overlapping, also known as 'translating between representational systems', is a form of pacing and leading that helps a person utilise another representational system different from the one they are currently using. Once in rapport and aware of a person's *primary representational system,* an effective flexible communicator can construct language that meets the person in their map and leads them to other resourceful or *preferred representational systems.* The technique is often used by an NLP Practitioner to lead a person towards a Sensory Representational System enabling them to access the modality that will provide them with the most latitude of understanding and therefore flexibility for achieving a resourceful state. It can also be used to direct a person towards a modality that has possibly been deleted, distorted or generalised from their internal representation so they can create a map containing more flexibility. Here are two examples of how overlapping can be utilised;

1. A Salesperson in a sales presentation:
Overlap: Visual > Auditory > Kinesthetic
V > A > K

People generally buy based on how they feel about a product or service. With this considered, for as a salesperson a desired outcome in a presentation or meeting would be for the potential customer to *feel* something about their product or service. Here is how to utilise overlapping in this scenario;

"(i) Here's what our product looks like. Often when you see other people using this product, you will always (ii) hear them say great things and especially mention how (iii) happy and confident it makes them feel. Which is something that you can easily feel too."

i.   **Part 1: Visual (V)**
     Here's what our product *looks* like. Often when you *see* other people with this product, you will always…

ii. **Part 2: Auditory (A)**
     hear them *say* great things and especially *mention* how…

iii. **Part 3: Kinesthetic (K)**
     happy and *confident* it makes them *feel.* Which is something that you can easily *feel* too.

2. NLP Practitioner coaching a client:
Overlap: (Auditory Digital > Kinesthetic) > Auditory > Visual
$(A^d > K) A > V$

During a coaching session, a client may present how they feel (K) about something due to the way they speak to themselves (A^d). This could be an Ad>K cause and effect (see Meta Model) or may even be an Ad/K synaesthesia. If by being in rapport you know that this specific client's *primary representational system,* is Visual (V) it is possible to lead them to use language that enables them to use the modality that provides much more latitude and flexibility to construct a meaningful detailed desired state, enhancing their choices to not only define but also achieving what they want. Here is how to utilise overlapping in this scenario;

"(i) As we sit here knowing how you say to yourself how scared you are of failing when you talk on stage. Take a moment to notice how confident and happy you feel once the moment is over and you begin to (ii) hear clapping and then cheers because despite your concerns once you (iii) look out into the audience you can see people standing and smiling because of what you have said to them all."

i. **Part 1: Auditory Digital > Kinesthetic (A^d>K).**

As we sit here knowing how you *say to yourself* how *scared* you are of failing when you talk on stage. Take a moment to notice how *confident* and *happy* you *feel* once the moment is over and you begin to…

ii. **Part 2: Auditory (A)**

hear clapping and then *cheers* because despite your concerns once you

iii. **Part 3: Visual (V)**

look out into the audience you can *see* people standing and smiling because of what you have said to them all.

Source Material & Further Learning
(1975) Frogs into Princes, Bandler & Grinder: Page 41 (1981) Trance-Formations, Bandler & Grinder: Page 44

NEW BEHAVIOUR GENERATOR

The new behaviour generator is an NLP technique that provides a strategy to enhance the performance of an existing behaviour or capability within yourself or a client via a visually constructed rehearsal. Once you have identified and decided on a situation and a new behaviour follow these step-by-step details to work through the New Behaviour Generator strategy. You will also see the related eye pattern movements with each step that can help to enhance the efficacy of the strategy.

Technique Overview:
New Behaviour Generator.

Action	Representational System	Associated Eye Accessing
1. State your desired behaviour to yourself noting how it is different to your present behaviour.	A^{id}	Down-Left
2. Visualise someone else doing the desired behaviour.	V^{ic}	Up-Right
3. Replace that person's image and sounds with yourself.	V^{ir}	Up-Left
4. Visualise yourself doing the desired behaviour.	V^{ic}	Up-Right
5. Step into the movie and from an associated perspective and access kinesthetic feelings while doing the desired behaviour.	K^{ic}	Down-Right
6. Calibrate the ecological congruency of the desired behaviour and if happy, think of a cue that will trigger the new behaviour & future pace.	K^{ir}	Down-Right
7. If not happy and incongruent identify how to enhance the desired behaviour using words and repeat step 1.	A^{id}	Down Left

Illustration Overview:
New Behaviour Generator

This illustration shows the order of steps and a person's associated eye movements as you work through this NLP technique.

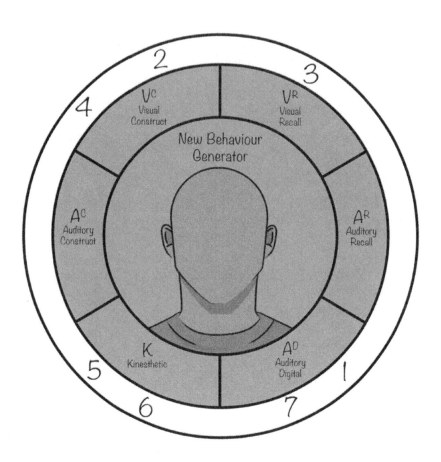

Source Material & Further Learning
(1981) Trance-Formations, Bandler & Grinder: Page 178

PART EIGHT:
COACHING

ROLE & RESPONSIBILITY OF COACHING

As an NLP Practitioner, you will have the ability to consciously acknowledge and manage your own state, something known as 'taking *personal inventory*'. This topic is placed at the end of the Sensory Acuity section as you need the necessary sensory acuity competence to be able to have conscious self-awareness of your own preferences and resourceful states. This is especially important in the context of coaching a client.

Before we look at the state itself let's first look at the role of coaching and the responsibilities of being a coach.

Much like the term NLP, the term *coaching* is often misunderstood, misused and thrown about incorrectly with regard to meaning and how it is performed. Coaching can play an important role in a number of contexts within a person's life. It can fundamentally help a person define and understand their model of the world, in particular;

1.   Where they are at now (Present State) and
2.   Where they want to go (Desired State)

With this future-orientated desired state defined, the secondary role of coaching is to assist the person by making them aware of all the options (flexibility of behaviour) they have available to them to achieve it. This can, in the simplest form mean opening up their awareness of any sensory representations that have been or are being deleted, distorted or generalised in their map, thus providing them with new perceptions and options to achieve their desired outcome.

It is important to note that *coaching* is meeting a person in *their* model of the world (map), where *they* are at now and where *they* want to go using resources and methods *they* choose once the options are made available to them. At no point is any of this about what the Coach wants or advice the Coach thinks the client could take action on to get their outcome!

Let's take this further and look at the characteristics of two terms (and roles) that are frequently incorrectly considered to be the same thing and yet are not; Coaching & Mentoring.

Coach Role	Mentor Role
1. Identify where the client is now	1. Identifies the client's issue
2. Meet the client in their map of the world.	2. The Mentor identifies when they had solved a similar issue.
3. Helps the client define a well-formed outcome desired outcome.	3. The Mentor asks the client if they would like the outcome that they had achieved.
4. Work with the client to discover the options and resources available to the client, helping plot the best route to the client's desired outcome.	4. The Mentor then advises the client based from their own map of the world (i.e. not the clients) and on the strategy to repeat their desired result.
5. Get the client to arrive exactly where they want to be and with many more resources and flexibility available to them for future use.	5. The client follows the instructions to a desired outcome often defined by the Mentor as the 'best' for what the client needs.
6. Ability to check the client is in a more resourceful state once the desired outcome is achieved and be able to offer further support as they understand the client's map.	6. If the client fails it is not their fault as the Mentor's advice did not work for them. The Mentor at this point has no flexibility past their own experience to help.

I'm sure you can recognise now that some Mentors you meet are actually coaching and some Coaches are actually mentoring. Ultimately the role and responsibility of coaching is to provide the client with options, enabling them to have increased flexibility of behaviour and choice, empowering them to be more resourceful, defining and achieving more.

NLP PRACTITIONER & COACH STATE

We have already mentioned at the very beginning of this book that with your NLP knowledge enabling you to impact others, also comes great responsibility. A *coach state* is a reference guide on how to *take inventory* of yourself and best manage your own state to ensure you are serving the other person as best you can. With the role of Coach defined and summarised as offering solutions for the client in *their* map of the world leaving *them* more resourceful, it is clear that a coach must be able to understand and omit their own internal representations from any content they work on with a client.

The technique of *taking personal inventory* enables you as an NLP Practitioner to have increased awareness of your present state, a form of self-calibration if you like. It is not about actually changing your state.

Technique for Taking Personal Inventory.

1. Sit still and quiet, close your eyes and relax
2. Take two slow deep breaths
3. Pay attention and let your awareness focus on your feet
4. Move your awareness up through your body noticing each part.
5. Don't judge what you are feeling just notice the sensation
6. What thoughts do you have now?
7. Are there pictures connected to these thoughts?
8. Is the image still or moving? How far away is the visualisation?
9. Are you hearing any sounds or talking? Are they loud or quiet?
10. Are you talking to yourself right now?
11. Become aware of how you are feeling right now.
12. What emotion are you sensing?
13. Don't try and change anything, just feel what you feel.
14. Now open your eyes and come back to the present.

Once you have taken inventory, you are now able to consciously calibrate yourself into a resourceful coaching state. This section could be considered to be an extension of the Unresourceful and Resourceful State section as we are effectively describing what a resourceful state is in the context of being a Coach. You can use the following list as a guide or a checklist for this Coach state.

A Resourceful Coaching State with Responsibilities.

- Know what a personally resourceful state is for you to;
    - have the flexibility to be an effective communicator
    - have positivity towards the client
    - have positivity towards the client's desired outcome
- Be in Uptime:
    - Externally focused
    - Minimal self-talk (Internal Dialogue / Auditory Digital)
    - Associated
- Be in rapport with the client:
    - Verbal (Primary Sensory Representational Predicates)
    - Non-verbal (Physiology/Auditory Mirror and Matching)
- Be aware to always seek and obtain permission from the client to;
    - ask questions
    - agree the purpose of the relationship
    - be responsible for the process
- Be aware of the role and responsibility to;
    - elicit a client's present and desired state in their map
    - understand and identify a trigger in the client's map
        - to test against in an ecological check
        - to test against in a future pace
    - have the flexibility to ensure the control of the process
    - pace and lead a client to a resourceful state
    - obtain a future-orientated well-formed desired outcome.
    - omit your own experiences, filters and preferences
    - always have a state appropriate for the context

Source Material & Further Learning
(1987) Turtles All the Way Down, Prerequisites to Personal Genius De Lozier & John Grinder: Page 151

PRESENT & DESIRED STATE MODEL

The *Present State* and *Desired States* are a way to describe the start and end points of a change process with regard to a *state*. Simply put;

"What *state* are you in right now and what *state* would you like to be?"

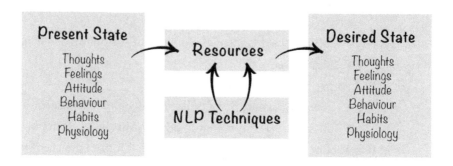

The *Present & Desired State Model* above illustrates where exactly NLP techniques provide ways to assist the change. It also shows that in order for these techniques to be put to work we need to measure two things;

- Where are we right now?
  - Present State
- What outcome do we want to achieve?
  - Desired State

These two elements allow us to understand our progress and ultimately know when we have arrived at our destination. Let's take a look at each of these states in more detail.

PRESENT STATE
Where are you right now?

This state is often referred to as the problem state or symptom within NLP coaching, mainly because if there was no problem or issue then change would not be desired. That being said the present state does not have to contain an issue, in fact by referring to it in this way we can fail to acknowledge any resourceful elements of a so-called 'problem state'. In addition, it may be that the present state is simply the starting point to advance from one resourceful state to another more resourceful desired state.

As an NLP Practitioner, there are a few questions that can be asked that will begin the process of observing and eliciting the present state. We want this to be as rich in data as possible to ensure accurate calibration.

- "What do you want to work through?"
- "What is the current issue you want to overcome?"
- "What is the current problem you want to change?

Once the question has been asked you need to be looking for the following information and aspects of a present state;

- Ensure the *Trigger* (the external event) that kick starts the present *problem state* is;
  - Happening in a single context (See Understanding Context)
  - Is Associated (See States of Perspective)
- Non-Verbal Indicators (See Calibration)
  - Physiology
- Behaviour (See NLP Presuppositions 12.)
  - Sensory Acuity Calibration
    - Predicates & Representation Systems
  - What they are doing
    - Physical movements & gestures
    - Attitude
    - Thoughts
  - What they are feeling
    - Eye Patterns down to the left (if normally wired)

DESIRED STATE
How you want to be.

This state is often referred to as the end state, mainly because it is where the change for the particular issue being worked through ends. That being said the desired state is one that leaves a person in a more resourceful state and therefore could be considered to be a new present state. We must also acknowledge that the desired state should hold the resourceful elements of the initial 'problem state'.

As an NLP Practitioner, there are a few questions that can be asked that will begin the process of observing and eliciting the desired state. We want this to be as rich in data as possible to ensure accurate calibration.

- "If that is how you have been how do you want to be different?"
- "Be there now, what are you seeing, hearing and feeling"
  - Future Pacing
- "What will you feel and have if you achieve this?"
  - Ecological Check
    - +/+
- "What will you not feel if you don't achieve this?"
  - Ecological Check
    - -/-

Once the question has been asked you need to be looking for the following information and aspects of a desired state;

- Sensory specific
  - Including all senses
- Associated
- A resourceful state for the client (or a more resourceful state at least)
  - Calibrating to the problem state
    - Physical movements & gestures
    - Attitude
    - Thoughts
    - Physiology
- Is ecologically sound
  - Does not provide conflict with any secondary gain.

PART NINE:
ANCHORING

STATE MANAGEMENT / ANCHORING

WHAT IS AN ANCHOR?

With NLP we acknowledge that our current state and responses to external events dictate our behaviour and emotions. In order for something to happen or change it has to first start with what we call the *trigger*. So what fires the trigger? The answer to this is an *Anchor*.

An anchor is a naturally occurring sensory stimulus that consistently triggers a particular internal state and emotional response. Said another way, every time you experience the anchor the same state or response will occur within a person. There is no real restriction on what can be an anchor, anything that is possible for you to sense with any of your sensory representational systems can be an anchor. It can be an image, sound, touch, smell or taste.

NLP utilises anchors as a conscious tool and technique for a person to change internal states. This allows a person to access a state in a particular context or situation at will. Anchors can trigger both resourceful and unresourceful states and yet with the NLP techniques available, we can consciously access a resourceful anchor in a given context which therefore reduces, removes or replaces any unresourceful states or negative emotions at a particular moment.

With this considered you can also understand that an anchor can allow us to capture internal states we have experienced, or are experiencing, making the connected internal state available to us in the future. This therefore means an anchor can allow us to move experiences around in time. Anchors can also be used to amend and adjust internal processes that a person runs. This enables that person to change how they can respond to a particular event or experience when it occurs. As an anchor can create an internal state within a person and as you can create your own anchors consciously, it is not that hard to see why this is one of the most important and fundamental NLP techniques and tools for an NLP Practitioner to have knowledge of. To have clear definitions before we continue with techniques;

An Anchor

is a sensory stimulus that is attached to an internal state.

Anchoring

is the process of attaching an association of a sensory stimulus to an internal state to enable the set anchor to be fired in the future.

As we know NLP is the process of modelling behaviour, so before we progress to anchoring and anchoring techniques let's understand a little about how anchors were discovered.

HISTORY OF ANCHORS

There were a few key investigations and lines of research that resulted in the knowledge presented in the NLP syllabus as anchors. The first of these was by the Russian psychologist Ivan Pavlov. He was particularly interested in the 'stimulus and response' aspect of behaviour, something later called 'reflex conditioning' or 'conditional reflex'. His now famous experiment with dogs, hence the name '*Pavlov's Dogs*' saw him ring a bell, present some food to the dogs and then feed dogs. This written with NLP notation would be an $A^e > V^e > K^+$. Breaking that down into more detail he noticed that on the sound of the bell, the dogs would salivate in preparation for the food before the food was even presented. What was discovered was an Auditory Kinesthetic synaesthesia $\{A^cK^iK^+\}$ where there was no decision occurring between the stimulus and the response.

Around the same time a professor of psychology, independent from Pavlov, called Edwin Twitmyer was conducting a study on classical conditioning investigating the patellar tendon reflex. By lightly applying a single tap of a hammer on a person's bent knee he would witness a reflex of the leg extending. He then informed the subjects that he would ring a bell to let the person know when the tap of the knee would occur. By mistake during this testing the bell accidentally rang before a tap and yet the subject extended their leg. By pure coincidence and serendipity, Edwin Twitmyer had discovered the same Auditory Kinesthetic synaesthesia $\{A^cK\}$. Although NLP techniques are known for behavioural change it would be an obvious assumption to make that this is how NLP was first introduced to anchoring, and yet you would be wrong. Bandler and Grinder discovered anchoring via the modelling of Milton Erickson. They witnessed him using auditory anchors, tonality to be specific, to cause a trance state for clients to enable the opportunity for change in the client. It is from here they then developed the variety of anchoring techniques you see as part of the NLP syllabus today.

Noting that anchors are indeed classical conditions it is worth mentioning that even though there are techniques shared over the following pages to create an anchor, the formation of one very rarely happens after one instance of experiencing an anchor. With this in mind, repetition is key. No matter the technique adopted nor whether the anchor is a visual, kinesthetic or auditory repetition will have more of an opportunity to create an effective anchor. In addition to this, techniques you will learn shortly, even after the test of time have gathered no convincing scientific evidence meaning techniques such as chaining anchors can work but they work based on suggestibility or placebo.

CRITICAL FACTORS OF ANCHORING

In the process of anchoring or *setting an anchor*, there are a number of critical factors to do with time, intensity and location, that must be taken into account to make sure the anchoring is successful.

Summary of critical factors of successful anchoring

- **State Purity**
  - *The purity of the state being anchored*
- **State Intensity**
  - *Intensity of the state being anchored.*
- **Intensity Timing**
  - *The timing of the application of the anchor*
- **Anchor Uniqueness and Precision**
  - *The uniqueness of the anchor being set*
- **Replicable Anchor**
  - *The anchor can be easily reproduced*
- **Anchor Strength**
  - *The strength of the anchor being set*

Let's explain the six critical factors in more depth.

State Purity
The purity of the state being anchored

Before we even get to set an anchor, we must identify the desired state that we want the anchor to be associated with and trigger when fired. With this desired state known, we want to experience it in a single context from an associated position to ensure that the desired state we are anchoring is pure. Even if a person can recall multiple instances of a desired state get one single instance as this allows other critical factors such as timing and intensity to be adhered to.

State Intensity
Intensity of the state being anchored.

The intensity of an anchored state is important in that the desired state must have more power than the state at which you want the anchor to change. Much like the pure state we want the person to be associated with a single instance of the experience they are recalling so that the intensity can be maximised.

NLP PRACTITIONER NOTE:
Be aware that there are some memories *(traumas)*, that have such a negatively intense recall of an experience they create synaesthesia, (See Synaesthesia) where the sensory anchor immediately causes an unconscious unavoidable response, known as a *phobic response.* (see Fast Phobia Cure)

Intensity Timing
The timing of the application of the anchor

The timing of the anchor being set is vital. An anchor is to be set at the peak intensity of the pure instance of the state. If you set the anchor too soon or too late you will not be anchoring the pure intense desired state but rather a diluted version or possibly a mixture of multiple states that occur before or after the peak intensity of the desired state. With this considered the best time to begin applying an anchor is as the person is starting to experience the desired state and as the peak of the state is experienced that is the moment of release.

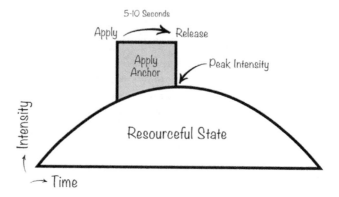

Releasing any later than this will be anchoring the state that follows the desired state. Depending on the desired state and the person the time taken to achieve the peak intensity of a state will vary so if coaching it is important to calibrate the client. Look for non-verbal changes such as breathing, skin tone and muscle tension (see Calibration).

The importance of timing is also why when coaching it is best to have the client experience the desired state at least once so you can observe and calibrate to know the best time to apply and release the anchor on a re-run of the desired state. In general, the time period between applying and releasing an anchor is five to fifteen seconds and yet depending on the client and the experience it could be up to a minute or longer.

Anchor Uniqueness and Precision
The uniqueness of the anchor being set

The uniqueness of an anchor is fundamental to having a conscious ability to trigger a desired state. Without uniqueness, the anchor could be fired by mistake or accidentally at an undesirable moment. For example, a kinesthetic anchor would require a unique location on the body that is not commonly touched (such as a knuckle) and an olfactory anchor could be a strong smell of something not naturally occurring (such as a lip balm).

We must also ensure that this uniqueness is combined with precision. This not only makes it likely to be unique but it also ensures the strength of the anchor. For example, if you were to anchor a knuckle through a glove then there is the opportunity for the position of the anchor to change mid-anchoring, not to mention the strength (as in pressure) of the anchor being diminished.

NLP PRACTITIONER NOTE:

Something to be aware of as an NLP Practitioner coaching a client is that when you set an anchor you are not accidentally setting another anchor with another sensory trigger. By this I mean you are setting an anchor on a person's knuckle and also your other hand is holding their other hand for support. As a coach, you must be conscious that you are only setting a single unique anchor.

Anchor Strength
The strength of the anchor being set

It is important that the anchor is set firmly so there is no mistaking it. In our already shared this would be a firm touch or a strong smell. It is also good practice to gradually increase the pressure or strength of an anchor as a person reaches the peak. Remember that on release this is immediately removed – something to take into account if you are using a smell! Now, even though we say set a strong anchor this obviously does not mean to the point of being uncomfortable or in pain. As an NLP Practitioner, when coaching a client and knowing in advance that a strong anchor will be set it is a good idea to inform the client of the process and gain permission for the process you are about to work through.

Replicable Anchor
The anchor is able to be easily reproduced

This one may seem obvious and yet it must be stated as it is critical for the success of an anchor. What would be the point of setting an anchor that the client could then be unable to fire and repeat? To utilise resourceful anchors a person must be able to fire them themselves, so that must be taken into account when setting an anchor. This is where uniqueness and precision also come into play as a loose anchor on a hand will be hard to replicate and yet a specific point on a knuckle is clearly easier to touch accurately.

Source Material & Further Learning
(1979) Frogs into Princes, Bandler & Grinder: Page 82

KINAESTHETIC ANCHORING

A kinesthetic anchor is an anchor that is set using touch. If you wished to set a visual, auditory or olfactory anchor the same process would be used except you would replace the kinesthetic elements accordingly. It is worth noting at this moment that an olfactory anchor is actually one of the most powerful forms of an anchor due to the fact that our sense of smell is directly connected to our limbic system which is responsible for handling our memories and emotions. This step-by-step is just to explain the process of setting the anchor whereas the NLP techniques that follow will include a thorough walk-through of how you can set an anchor as an NLP Practitioner coaching a client or indeed yourself.

- **Identify a unique location**
- **Gain permission to touch the agreed anchor position**
  - o Add that there will be pressure applied
- **Calibrate Present State and Trigger to enable testing**
  - o Associated
- **Elicit Desired State looking for the peak**
  - o Associated
  - o It is important not to anchor the on the first run-through of eliciting the desired state as you want to observe the peak.
- **Break State**
- **Elicit Desired State Again and Coach apply the Anchor**
  - o Observe and pay attention to the growth of the Desired State.
  - o Just before the peak apply firm pressure to the anchor location
  - o Release the pressure immediately and fully at the peak.
- **Break State**
- **Elicit Desired State Again and Client apply the Anchor**
  - o Recreate the Desire State situation again
  - o Just before the peak apply firm pressure to the anchor location
  - o Release the pressure immediately and fully at the peak.
- **Break State and repeat until the anchor is set.**
- **Test and Future Pace.**
  - o Calibrate

ANCHORING TECHNIQUES

With knowledge of what an anchor is and the success criteria of successfully anchoring, let's look at a few NLP techniques to utilise this powerful state management tool.

A RESOURCE ANCHOR

A resource anchor is an anchor that will enable a person to consciously and intentionally fire a resourceful state at will, such as 'confidence'. This could be particularly useful for a person who wants to be in a resourceful state when doing something they want to excel at such as;

- Just before a presentation
    - o Rather than feeling a nervous state
    - o Resource Anchor will fire a confident state
- Just before (or during) an exam
    - o Rather than feeling a stressed state
    - o Resource Anchor will fire a composed state

The following step-by-step example of this technique is written in the context of you as an NLP Practitioner coaching a client through the process of setting a *kinesthetic resource anchor.*

- **Be in a Coach State**
- **Be in rapport**
- **Explain the process and seek permission for kinesthetic anchor**
    - o *"We are together going to identify a unique location and point on your body that you are able to touch. When you choose to consciously touch this exact point you are going to be able to immediately feel the feeling of a positive state, one of your choosing. This is called setting an anchor."*
    - o *Before we continue can I have permission to apply pressure to the exact location where you decide to place the anchor?*
- **Agree on a unique location**
- **Calibrate Present State**
- **Identify and create a Desired State for the anchor.**
    - o *"Can you remember a time when you were feeling totally (desired state)"*

- o *"Be there now."*
- o *"See what you were seeing, hear what you were hearing and feel what you were feeling."*
- **Break State**
- **Reverse and Elicit Desired State observing the growth and peak**
  - o *"We want to set the anchor at its most powerful peak so go back to the experience you have just created and then go back a little further in time."*
  - o *"Now play out the experience again, see what you were seeing, hear what you were hearing and feel what you were feeling."*
  - o Calibrate the growth and peak moments
- **Break State**
- **Recreate the Desired State and apply pressure just before the peak**
  - o *"Now play out the experience again, see what you were seeing, hear what you were hearing and feel what you were feeling."*
  - o Non-verbal calibration
    - Physiology & Breathing
  - o Apply firm pressure to the agreed location just before the peak.
- **Release the pressure at the peak**
  - o Calibrate and release the pressure at the peak.
- **Break State**
- **Recreate Desired State and client sets the anchor**
  - o *"Now it is time for you to set the anchor as well"*
  - o *"Again, play out the experience again, and just as you feel the peak apply the anchor, letting go at the most intense moment.*
- **Break State and repeat the setting process if required.**
- **Future Pace and Client Fire Anchor** to test the trigger is the last step.
  - o *"Think of a time in the future when you will have this again?"*
  - o *"Be there now"*
  - o *"Fire your anchor, and what is happening?"*
  - o Calibrate

Source Material & Further Learning
(1979) Frogs into Princes, Bandler & Grinder: Page 115

STACKING RESOURCE ANCHORS

If one resourceful state is not enough or a person would like to have an incredibly powerful anchor that combines and piles up a number of complimentary resourceful states to enhance the effectiveness of an anchor, then we can use a process called *stacking anchors.* For example, a single stacked anchor might combine states such as;

Confidence + Calm + Assertive + Strong + Composed

The process of stacking follows the exact same steps as the Resource Anchor, just repeated with a number of different states. If you are stacking multiple resource anchors in one coaching session it is good practice to break state after each state is anchored and test and future pace.

It can also be helpful to mark the exact spot of the anchor to ensure that the location remains consistent as you are stacking. This can be especially useful if time passes between sessions. A good hack is to use a knuckle or a place where the is a freckle on the back of a hand or arm.

- **Coach State**
- **Be in rapport**
- **Explain the process and seek permission for kinesthetic anchor**
- **Agree on a unique location (and possible mark for consistency)**
- **Calibrate Present State**
- **Identify and create a Desired State for the anchor.**
- **Break State**
- **Reverse and Elicit Desired State observing the growth and peak**
- **Break State**
- **Recreate the Desired State and apply pressure just before the peak**
- **Release the pressure at the peak**
- **Break State**
- **Recreate Desired State and client sets the anchor**
- **Break State and repeat the setting process if required.**
- **Future Pace and Client Fire the Anchor**

As anchors can last a lifetime if set correctly (unless removed by collapsing them – see Collapsed Anchors) it does not matter how much time passes between stacking a state to an anchor. This effectively means that over the course of years, you can create an extremely powerful resource anchor for yourself that utilises many experiences from many contexts. All that is required is that the anchor is set to the exact same location when stacking.

Source Material & Further Learning

(1990) Introducing Neuro-linguistic Programming, O'Conner & Seymour: Page 72

COLLAPSING ANCHORS

Not all anchors are positive. Most people have anchors that trigger an unresourceful reaction or state. When we identify one of these unresourceful anchors we can use a technique and pattern called *Collapsing Anchors* to remove them. This can be extremely useful if a person identifies that a particular experience in the past is holding them back from progressing towards something they want. The simple premise of collapsing anchors is to override and remove the 'charge' of an unresourceful anchor with that of a resourceful anchor. The positive resourceful anchor must be powerful enough to neutralise or cancel out the negative unresourceful anchor so if one resourceful state is not enough a person may have to stack resource anchors to create the appropriate power.

The process of setting up the situation to allow the collapsing of an anchor follows the exact same steps as the Resource Anchor, except this time you set two locations; one for the unresourceful state and one for the equal or stronger resourceful state. The two locations must be located in places that allow them both to be fired at the same time in a particular order, which will be covered in the process steps that follow.

- **Be in rapport**
- **Explain the process and seek permission for 2 kinesthetic anchors**
- **Agree a unique locations and possible mark for consistency**
- **Identify the Present State (Problem State) and elicit the trigger.**
  - Depending on the problem state you may want to set a 'safety anchor' prior to associating the client with their problem state.
  - Calibrate
- **Break State**
- **Identify the Desired State**
- **Break State**
- **Stack a number of resource anchors to the resourceful location**
- **Break State**
- **Associate the client with the problem state**
- **Set the kinesthetic anchor once to the unresourceful location**
  - You want the unresourceful anchor to be weak
  - Do not stack negative anchors.

- **Break State**
- **Associate the client to just before the problem state trigger**
- **As the trigger occurs fire both resourceful and unresourceful anchors at exactly the same time with the same pressure.**
  - ○ Observe the physiology of the client as you may witness some bilateral movement. This is called the *Confusion State*.
- **Keep the pressure on the two anchors until the confusion state has passed and the client has stabilized.**
  - ○ Physiology will return to being consistent.
  - ○ This may take up to several minutes
- **Maintaining the pressure on the resourceful anchor for a few more seconds and letting go of the unresourceful anchor.**
- **Break State.**
- **Test unresourceful anchor that has now been dissolved (collapsed)**
  - ○ *"How does that feel, what are you feeling"*
  - ○ There should be no response to this anchor now.
- **Test the problem state trigger**
  - ○ If there is still an undesirable response and yet it is less intense repeat the process until there is no response.
  - ○ If there is no response then future pace.
- **Future Pace and fire the resource anchor on the trigger**
  - ○ This reinforces the process and will fully collapse the anchor even if there are some small calibrations you cannot pick up on as a coach.

If a person has multiple negative unresourceful experiences or problem states be sure to only collapse one anchor at a time. You can repeat the process by reusing the same stacked resource anchor as long as the charge of the resource anchor is positive and powerful enough to neutralise or cancel out the negative charge or the unresourceful problem state.

Source Material & Further Learning
(1979) Frogs into Princes, Bandler & Grinder: Page 106

CHANGING PERSONAL HISTORY

This NLP technique is used when a person's progress is being negatively impacted by something they have experienced in the past and they are somehow held back by a perceived unresourceful kinesthetic limiting belief. If we refer to the NLP Communication Model, paying attention to the universal models of; deletion, distortion and generalisation we witness that a person will behave according to their perception of an event. This technique reconstructs a perception of an event or experience from the past, changing it from being an unresourceful one to becoming a resourceful one. This works by knowing that the person is only behaving according to their current distorted and generalised construction of the event or experience.

To change personal history, we must access multiple representational systems. This allows for the full map of a generated history (memory) to be accessed and positively changed. This also ensures that the changed (newly constructed) experience contains all the critical sub-modalities that we use to create our meaning of an event. This results in the perception of their personal history, from their perspective, has been changed to be enabling. As this process deals with an unresourceful state it is good practice to set a safety anchor for the client before commencing this process.

- **Coach State & be in rapport**
- **Explain the process and seek permission for 2 kinesthetic anchors**
- **Agree on unique locations and possible mark for consistency**
- **Associate the client with an experience from the past of the unresourceful feeling currently holding them back. Label it and elicit this initial trigger.**
  - *"What do you call this feeling?"*
  - Calibrate
- **Set a kinesthetic anchor to the unresourceful anchor location**
- **Break State**
- **Fire the unresourceful anchor setting it as a 'Search anchor'**
  - Holding the anchor in place and having the client go back through time finding other times they felt the (label) feeling is called setting a *'search anchor'*.
  - Encourage the client to find multiple occurrences and go back to the first time they experienced the (label) feeling.

- Note this does not have to be the experience that created this *cause-effect* feeling.
  - Encourage the client to go back as far as they can, preferably when they are younger.
  - *"As you go back through time notice moments of when this feeling occurred"*
  - *"As you experience a time give me a sign"*
- **Calibrate and release the search anchor when moments occur.**
  - *"Fully experience the moment of (unwanted feelings label)"*
  - *"Notice your age as you go back through time experiencing these experiences"*
  - With the search anchor released anchor each instance of the experience to help the client to access these moments.
  - Once the experience's anchor is set release it and reapply the search anchor.
    - *"Now back further through time do you notice any earlier moments when this feeling occurred"*
  - Repeat until the earliest memory has been experienced and anchored.
- **Break State**
- **Ask the client what resources they would have needed to have in all of those experiences for them to have been positive experiences.**
  - These resources must be in the control of the client.
    - This should not be a wish list of how other people could have changed or been different. It is how they could have responded in a more resourceful way.
    - Also, see 'Conditions for well-formed outcomes'
  - Write down the exact words the client is using to describe these resources as they can be used as auditory anchors within this process.
- **Using the auditory anchors elicit a number of resourceful states and stack these to a resource anchor.**
  - The stacked resource anchor must be powerful enough with enough charge and hold enough resources to change the client's history.
  - *"Do you feel that if by having all these resources in the past you would have"*

been able to satisfy your needs in each of your past experiences?"

- Calibrate

- **Break State**
- **With the resource anchor applied invite the client to revisit the past experiences with all the resources they need. You can also use the auditory anchors for an additional charge.**
  - Start with the initial problem state and trigger
- **Still holding the resource anchor, you can assist the client in accessing these unresourceful experiences by firing the anchors that were set for each experience. These anchors hold resourcefulness and can also be collapsed as the client moves back through their experiences.**
  - *"As you pass back through the experience satisfied you now have the resources for that experience, give me a sign as you pass through and are on your way to the next experience."*
  - Calibrate for the sign maintaining pressure on the resource anchor and release the unresourceful anchor
  - Fire the anchor for the next experience
  - Repeat these steps until all the anchored experiences have been satisfied and related anchors have been collapsed.
  - If at any time they are not satisfied ask the client what additional resources they would need and then stack this to the resource anchor and then restart again from this experience.
- **Break State**
- **Test the initial problem state trigger with no anchor**
  - *"What has changed? Have your memory subjectively changed?"*
  - Calibrate
- **Test another problem state trigger with no anchor**
- **Future Pace with no anchor**

Source Material & Further Learning

(1979) Frogs into Princes, Bandler & Grinder: Page 115
(1990) Introducing Neuro-linguistic Programming, O'Conner & Seymour: Page 62

CHAINING ANCHORS

There are times when you may wish to replace an unresourceful state, problem state or stuck state with a single resourceful state and yet there is not enough charge in the resourceful state to collapse the unresourceful anchor. An example of this may be that a person panics when a particular event happens and they would like to remain calm. Panic can be considered a much stronger state than calmness and therefore in isolation calm would not be able to dissolve or collapse the state of panic. This example also illustrates how chaining is about breaking an unhelpful habit, an unconscious strategy with an unresourceful outcome, and creating a new pathway to access a desired resourceful state.

Chaining is a technique that creates intermediary anchors so that smaller consecutive state changes can occur away from the unresourceful state and towards the desired state. This may seem a little complicated at first however the pattern is not too dissimilar from being considered as multiple collapsed anchors.

There is a lot of preparation before the techniques can start as you have to first design the chain before eliciting and anchoring the many states used within the chaining of the anchors.

Success criteria for designing a chain sequence.
To design a successful chain there are conditions that need to be met.

1. A chain must have a minimum of three steps
2. A chain must have a maximum of five steps
3. Each step in the chain must be as small as possible
4. Each step must be doable by the subject
5. Each state is ecological and congruent for the subject
6. Each step must NOT contain a state that is part of the current unconscious strategy being run.
7. The 1st state change (Step 1) must be 'away from' the problem state
8. The 2nd state change (Step 2) must be a neutral or weak state
9. The 3rd state change (Step 3) must be 'towards' the desired state
10. Only begin to install the chain once it has been fully designed

INSTALLING THE CHAIN

- **Coach State**
- **Be in rapport**
- **Explain the process and seek permission for the kinesthetic anchors required for the chain**
  - o   In this example, five anchors are required
- **Agree a unique locations and possible mark for consistency**
- **Identify the Present State (Problem State) and elicit the trigger.**
- **Set a kinesthetic anchor for this state**
  - o   Anchor 1
- **Break State**
- **Identify the Desired State**
- **Set a kinesthetic anchor for this state**
  - o   Anchor 5
    - In this example, we have five states.
- **Break State**
- **Elicit each state used in the chain and set a kinesthetic anchor for each individual state.**
  - o   Break State between each anchor
  - o   When this step is complete you will now have the following five anchors set;
    - Anchor 1: The Problem State
    - Anchor 2: An 'Away From the Problem State' State
    - Anchor 3: A neutral or very weak state
    - Anchor 4: An 'Towards the Desired State' State
    - Anchor 5: Desired State
- **Start the installation by firing Anchor 1 and hold.**
- **As Anchor 1 grows fire Anchor 2.**
- **As Anchor 1 peaks holding Anchor 2, release Anchor 1.**
- **As Anchor 2 grows fire Anchor 3.**
- **As Anchor 2 peaks holding Anchor 3, release Anchor 2**
- **As Anchor 3 grows fire Anchor 4.**
- **As Anchor 3 peaks holding Anchor 4, release Anchor 3**

- **As Anchor 4 grows fire Anchor 5.**
- **As Anchor 4 peaks holding Anchor 5, release Anchor 4**
- **As Anchor 5 peaks break state.**
  - This is an important step at the end due to the fact that the chain is repeated many times and if you do not add this break state or separator state you will create an infinite loop of the last chain (Desired State) circling back to the Problem State. Therefore, undesirably installing another stuck state strategy.
- **Repeat the full installation three times**
- **Break State.**
- **Test the problem state trigger**
  - Calibrate for the entire sequence and that the end state is the desired state.
- **Future Pace and fire Anchor 1 on the trigger**
  - Calibrate to witness the end state being the desired state.

Source Material & Further Learning
(1990) Introducing Neuro-linguistic Programming, O'Conner & Seymour: Page 60

CIRCLE OF EXCELLENCE

The circle of excellence is a stacking technique that allows a person to set a *Spatial Anchor,* the anchor itself being an imaginary circle on the floor that is stepped into. Learning this *self-anchoring* technique can allow a person the capability of creating, building upon (stacking) and consciously triggering an incredibly resourceful desired state throughout their lives. Something that is invaluable for personal development and growth.

Self-Anchoring

Before we cover the Circle of Excellence let's cover the topic of self-anchoring as it is a very important technique to use on yourself. As you will now be aware anchors can be useful in many contexts of life. However, one particular resourceful state you could consider anchoring is in the context of coaching as an NLP Practitioner. You could for example self-anchor a powerful and resourceful internal 'Coach State' that would enable you to have all the positive feelings you want to feel in order to serve your clients as best you can. The very best time to set an anchor is in the present moment of experiencing the resourceful behaviour, feeling and state you wish to anchor. Guess who the best person to know this exact precise moment of a peak state in an experience is, yes - you! The other thing to acknowledge is that *you* are always available to yourself for stacking and reinforcing resourceful states. With knowledge and practice you can be very opportunist in adding resources to an anchor. When self-anchoring you are able to utilise all kinds of sensory anchors as well, whether they are; kinesthetic, auditory, a powerful olfactory one or a kinesthetic spatial one like the one within the Circle of Excellence technique.

Circle of Excellence

There is an alternative version of this technique called the Chi Tool of Excellence which could be considered a Designer Circle of Excellence in that you invite the subject to create their own most powerful alternative to a circle on the floor using their own preferred modalities and critical sub-modalities. For example, instead of a circle on the floor to step into a person may choose to step into a bright light or a large colourful bubble. In the following process, we will cover the traditional technique originally created by John Grinder. There is no kinesthetic interaction between the coach and the client in this technique which makes it an effective technique to use in groups.

- **Be in rapport**

- **Explain the Circle of Excellence outcome before beginning.**
- **Ask the client to associate with a resourceful positive Desired State**
  o Label the Desired State
- **Break State**
- **Ask the client to associate with another Desired State**
  o Repeat this a number of times to get at least 3 Desired States
- **Break State**
- **Ask the client to visualise a circle on the floor**
  o Ensure the circle is big enough to step into.
  o Utilise eye accessing asking them to put the circle in front of their right foot to access the kinesthetic representational system.
  o Add some power to the circle enhancing critical sub-modalities such as colour or brightness to it.
- **Ask the client to be fully associated with the desired state experience.**
  o *"Be there now"*
  o *"What are you seeing through your eyes?"*
  o *"What are you feeling at the moment?"*
  o Use all Representational Systems
- **As intensity of the (label of the desired state) grows ask the client to step inside the circle, allowing the peak to be inside the circle.**
- **Now step back out of the circle.**
- **Repeat this process for each of the desired states.**
- **Repeat the entire process of adding all the desired states 3 times.**
- **Break State.**
- **Future Pace.**
- **Get the client to step into the circle and describe their feeling**
- **Step back out and instruct the client to take this circle with them.**

Source Material & Further Learning
(1990) Introducing Neuro-linguistic Programming, O'Conner & Seymour: Page 60

PART TEN:
LANGUAGE

LINGUISTIC PRESUPPOSITIONS

The *linguistic* element of NLP looks at our structure of language as well as the type of language we choose to use. With reference to Representational Systems, we know that *Meaning* is one of the worlds that we live in. Our *Digital* representation of the world is the one that makes sense of our senses by using language. We know by the Predicates we use we can understand our Primary Representational System and yet language communicates much more to us than our preferred modalities. We have already come across presuppositions within the Presupposition of NLP section understanding that they are *"a thing that is assumed beforehand at the beginning of a course of action."* Even though this is true of Linguistic presupposition also there is another aspect to this collection of items. A linguistic presupposition ultimately highlights language and words that are charged in a way that insinuates something that is actually missing from the actual content of the sentence. Said another way, 'What is not being said?' by what is being said. With knowledge of the linguistic presuppositions, you can not only develop a higher level of linguistic acuity with the use of your own language to improve your communication, but you can also start to highlight these with other people and clients to identify areas for gaining clarity in what they are saying which may provide an opportunity to help that person achieve a more resourceful state. Below is a list of the linguistic presuppositions that we will be covering.

Summary of Linguistic Presuppositions

1. Existence
2. Awareness
3. Adverb and Adjectives
4. Modal Operator of Necessity and Possibility
5. Ordinal
6. Temporal
7. Cause-effect
8. Exclusive or / inclusive or
9. Complex equivalence

Source Material & Further Learning
(1975) The Structure of Magic Vol 1, Bandler & Grinder: Page 211

EXISTENCE

This implies a person, place or thing (or noun) actually exists. It generally suggests that a person has experienced the thing. Acknowledging the existence of a particular thing, also allows there to be an understanding that a situation can occur without that thing present.

- Example within a simple statement
  - *"The ball is there."*
    - The 'ball' exists
  - *"John is angry"*
    - A 'John' exists
- Example of how this may appear with a client.
  - *I'm waiting for the perfect job*
    - This suggests that a 'perfect job' exists

AWARENESS

This is a verb that uses a specified predicate or unspecified predicate to direct attention to a thing.

- Example within a simple statement
  - *"Look at the ball over there*
    - You are seeing the ball with your own eyes
- Example of how this may appear with a client.
  - *"He doesn't realise I'm angry"*
    - There's no question of anger existing, just whether he realises and has an awareness of it.

ADVERBS AND ADJECTIVES

These words add detail to nouns and verbs.

An adjective describes something about a noun or pronoun.

- Example within a simple statement
  - *"It was a great day"*
    - The day is being described as great
- Example of how this may appear with a client.
  - *"I preferred my <u>previous</u> job"*
    - They have a job now, different to the one in the past.

An adverb describes something about the verb or how to do the verb,

- Example within a simple statement
  - *"He is running <u>fast</u>"*
    - He was running at speed.
- Example of how this may appear with a client.
  - *"I just need to work <u>harder</u>"*
    - They are working and yet they are not working as hard as is possible for them.

ORDINAL

These are words that suggest there is an order or sequence to what is being listed, which may or may not be related to time. Words like; First, second, and third are an indication of this and yet any list can be recognised as ordinal.

- Example within a simple statement
  - *"His second time here"*
    - There have been two occasions that he has been here
- Example of how this may appear with a client.
  - *"My first wife liked watching sports"*
    - This presupposes there is another wife now and possibly more past wives.

MODAL OPERATORS OF NECESSITY AND POSSIBILITY

A modal operator refers to the *mode* that a person is *operating* in their map of the world. Modal operators of necessity and possibility are words that modify a verb to either;

Something needs to be done (Necessity).
Words like; need, must, should, have to, and ought to.

- *"I need to eat better"*
  o This *need* presupposes that they are not currently eating well. It also insinuates that there is a desired objective for eating better.

Something that is possible to be done (Possibility).
Words like; can, able, will.

- *"I could leave my job now."*
  o *Could* presupposes that leaving their job is a possible option that exists for them. It also acknowledges that they have a current job.

Also, if something is possible then we must recognise that it can also be impossible (Impossibility). Words like; can and cannot, able and unable.

- *"I cannot leave my job now."*
  o *Cannot* presupposes that leaving their job is a possible option that exists for them even if they are not going to choose that option.

TEMPORAL OR TIME

A word or grammar that related to a sense of time; past, present or future.

As a *verb*, this is shown as the past tense of that verb or the addition of 'ed' or in the present of the verb by adding 'ing'.

- *"I played football"*
  o They are not playing football right now and played in the past. It could also mean that they have chosen not to play football in the future.

As an adverb, this would be words such as; before, now, after, yet.

- *"I must speak with him before we leave."*
  o This presupposes that they have to leave. There will be an order of events that includes; they were not speaking, they were speaking, they leave the house.

CAUSE-EFFECT

This is a situation where something occurs (the *cause*) and then the other thing happens as a result (the *effect*). A person will imply that there is a connection between both the occurrence (X) and the result (Y). (i.e. X leads to Y happening). Good indicators of cause-effect are words such as; because, causes, makes, if... then.

- *"Eating makes me happy."*
  o This presupposes that when they are not eating, they are not as happy. It also suggests there is a past event or an anchor related to the action of eating that triggers happiness. What about eating makes this person happy? Does it always happen? Is the emotion related to specific times, particular foods or potentially the company? All of the above are omitted.

EXCLUSIVE OR / INCLUSIVE OR

This covers both instances of how the word 'or' can be used when creating a dichotomy (two things that are represented as being opposite – also known as a *dilemma*).

Exclusive or suggests that a person can make one choice from their dilemma, either one option or the other. They are unable to have both options. (i.e. X or Y is their only choice). This is often a cause for inner conflict with a person.

- *"I can either stay or go"*
  - o   You cannot physically be in two places at the same time.

Inclusive or suggests that a person has multiple options that enable something to happen. They can choose one or the other or they can have both. (i.e. X, Y or X and Y). In certain circumstances an *inclusive or* actually gives the perception of choice when in fact it is being removed.

- *"You can either pay for it now or pay for it later"*
  - o   Here there is no question that a payment will occur.

COMPLEX EQUIVALENCE

These words imply that there is a meaning synonymous with a person, place or thing. A complex equivalent often makes an appearance describing the identity (X) of a person (Y). (i.e. X is Y)

Good indicators of complex equivalents are words such as; mean, like, is

- *"John being angry means he hates me"*
  - o   An example of a mind read as sensory evidence does not connect these things.

Regarding identity complex equivalents show up with words like; am, be, is,

- *"I am a smoker"*
  - o   The two are not connected. They are a person who smokes

CHUNKS & CHUNKING

Let's jump straight into this section by looking at these two statements;

- Drill *down* into the details of *this idea*
- Let's go *up* and take a helicopter view of *this idea.*

Notice that there is the presence of *an idea* in both and to obtain more information about that idea you can either get into the details or go more generalised and global with your investigation.

Within NLP we utilise a model called the *Hierarchy of Ideas* and this model brings together three concepts of movement;

- Chunking Down,
- Chunking Up,
- Chucking Across (or Sideways).

Before we look at the model itself let's take a look at what a *chunk* is. A chunk basically means a group of bits of information. It is a term that originates from computer programming, one of the many influences within NLP terminology that Richard Bandler brought across from this field.

Chunking refers to how these chunks are interrelated and organised. Considering that nothing has meaning in isolation and there are always chunks interrelated, chunking can be used to find more logical information about the chunk (deductive) or more generalised information about the chunk (inductive). This is done linguistically within NLP by chunking up to find a higher meaning, and by chunking down to find deletions related to specific clarifications.

HIERARCHY OF IDEAS

Chunking is how the Hierarchy of Ideas is ultimately utilised as a linguistic model within NLP techniques. It effectively broadens understanding and creates more choice, flexibility and resourcefulness for the subject.

To better understand the linguistic model, first, let's see how this model works within a physical world example. This diagram of the Hierarchy of Ideas illustrates a simple concept of chunking from a house.

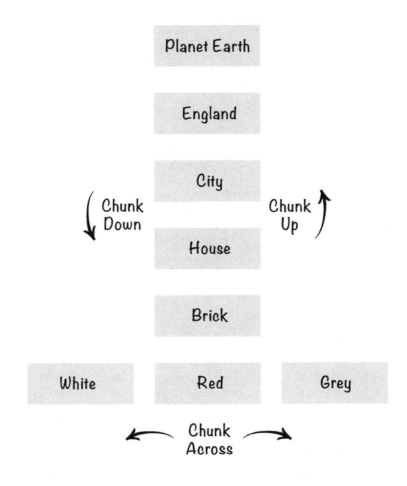

CHUNKING DOWN

When chunking down we are looking to take a chunk (bits of information - which linguistically could be a word, sentence or phrase) and ask questions to find out more specific details about that chunk.

Using the shared illustration of the Hierarchy of Ideas using a house, let's see how this would work. Let's start with finding out where a person lives.

- Coach: *"Where do you live?"*
- Client: *"I live in **England**."*
- Coach Chunk Down: *"Where in England?"*
- Client: *"In the city of **London**"*
- Coach Chunk Down: *"What type of home do you have?"*
- Client: *"It's a **house**"*
- Coach Chunk Down: *"What is your house made of?"*
- Client: *"It's a **brick** house."*

- **Chunking down summary:**
  - England > London > House > Brick

With reference to other sections of this NLP syllabus, chucking down is the discovery of Deep Structure by using Meta Model questions.

CHUNKING UP

When chunking up we are looking to take a chunk and ask questions to discover more general information about that chunk.

This can be beneficial to understand the context of a piece of information or situation as it allows for a broader view or bigger picture of that information being presented.

This can also access abstract information and ideas that provide alternate options and flexibility to a person.

Rather than use the same content from the shared illustration of the Hierarchy of Ideas let's use another example of a chunk, this time a person frustrated by a task they are doing.

- Client: *"I'm frustrated that I have to finish this **poster** today"*
- Coach Chunk Up: *"What are you going to do with the poster?"*
- Client: *"It is going to be used to **advertise our business**"*
- Coach Chunk Up: *"Who does your business serve?"*
- Client: *"We help **people in our community** with gardening"*
- Coach: *"That's great, so the poster will help people in the community?"*
- Client: *"Yes! It makes me happy to see people so happy. I better get it finished!"*

- **Chunking Up Summary:**
  - Poster > Business > People

With reference to other sections of this NLP syllabus, chucking up is the move to Surface Structure by using the Milton Model or Inverse Meta Model questions.

CHUNKING ACROSS / SIDEWAYS

Let's quickly return to the original two statements, we can also add a third;
- (Chunk Down) Drill **down** into the details of this idea
- (Chunk Up) Let's go **up** and take a helicopter view of this idea.
- (Chunk Across) Let's look at this idea **across** from another angle

Returning to the hierarchy of idea illustration of the House, this third aspect of *chunking across* (or chunking sideways) within a level is a process of remaining in the same class (or set) as the idea (or object) and yet changing the item to a related member of that class. For example;

North America	← **Europe** →	Asia
USA	← **England** →	Japan
Village	← **City** →	Town
Flat	← **House** →	Bungalow
Wood	← **Brick** →	Concrete
Grey	← **Red** →	White

Much like chunking up, chunking sideways can provide information that can introduce abstract ideas that bring alternate options and flexibility to a person. Here is a rudimental example of chunking sideways that could be used to bring awareness of options to a person who is stuck.

- Client: *"I'm panicking because our **train** got cancelled to London?"*
- Coach Chunk Across: *"Are there any **other trains?**"*
    o Chunking sideways in the class of Trains
- Client: *"No!"*
- Coach Chunk Across: *"OK, is there any **other transport?**"*
    o Chunking sideways in the class of Transport
        ▪ Bus, Car, Plane, Bike
- Client: *"I will see if there is a **bus** or **taxi**"*

- Chunking Across (one)
    o The Train → Another Train
- Chunking Across (two)
    o Bus ← Train → Taxi

Technically by Chunking Across and changing an element in this way, a person is replacing surface structure detail, unconsciously connecting their mind to the deep structure. It is this that allows for the opportunity of more choice, more flexibility of behaviour and a more resourceful state.

Chunking Across can provide the content for great metaphors, something that we will cover shortly in this book and NLP Syllabus.

Source Material & Further Learning
(1990) Introducing Neuro-linguistic Programming, O'Conner & Seymour: Page 150

SURFACE STRUCTURE & DEEP STRUCTURE

Now let's look at this hierarchy of ideas model from the aspect of linguistics. For this, we need to understand that the sentences we construct and communicate from our map of the world do not present all the information that is possible to obtain from the sentence. What we present verbally is called a *Surface Structure* sentence and by chunking we can obtain the missing information to discover the *Deep Structure* of what we are really saying.

Here is a quick summary of the different types of chunking and what NLP models are used with regard to linguistically chunking;

- **Chunking down**
  - Obtaining more detail or specific information
  - Done linguistically by using the *Meta Model*
    - to obtain *Deep Structure*
      - more specific language
      - uncover subsets
      - increase conscious awareness
      - can create uptime

- **Chunking up**
  - Forcing more general, global or abstract information
  - Done linguistically by using the *Milton Model*
    - to move to the *Surface Structure*
      - more vague and general language
      - discovers or creates sets
      - access unconscious mind
      - can create downtime

- **Chunking across / sideways**
  - Looking at information in terms of something else
  - Can be used linguistically to create *Metaphors*

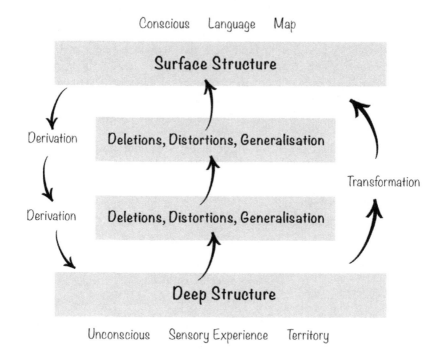

Much like the NLP Communication Model, the Deep Structure and Surface Structure diagram allows us to consider the journey that sensory data from the outside world (territory) takes via deletion, distortion and generalisation to create our internal sensory perception (map) of the world and surface structure language.

TRANSFORMATION

If we were to communicate with the spoken word (verbal language out) purely using an internal sensory map we would be communicating our Deep Structure. However, we do not do that! In our unconscious mind's attempt to be as efficient as possible, multiple automatic conversion processes of deletion, generalization or distortion can take place from the deep structure resulting in a surface structure language being very deprived of deep structure content. This process is called *Transformation*. The process of linguistic challenges and chunking is used to recover the Deep Structure sentence by reverse-engineering these transformations.

DERIVATION

A *Derivation* is a single instance of a deletion, distortion or generalisation that recovers or moves closer to recovering the content of the deep structure. Chunking as previously mentioned is a technique used to discover a derivation.

MODEL OF TRANSFORMATIONAL GRAMMAR

We want to uncover this Deep Structure as it has all the richness of what a person has actually experienced from the perspective of their map of the world. Knowing a Deep Structure may actually assist a person in uncovering information that may allow them to identify triggers that have caused a problem or a *stuck state*. It may also provide information that allows more choice and flexibility by means of additional layers of chunking across. Ultimately knowledge of a Deep Structure will provide a person with more choice and enable change to occur.

Using a simple Surface Structure sentence let's work through a breakdown of *Transformations* to illustrate the missing components presented and what the Deep Structure could look like.

"The boy passed the soccer ball far."

Let's first break apart the components of this sentence. These are what are known as *constituents* and are a way for a native speaker to group together smaller elements of the sentence using their intuition,

"The boy (and) **passed** (and) **the soccer ball far"**

What happens next is that a native speaker will group these constituents together to gain a comprehension or representation of what that sentence means,

"The boy (and) **passed the soccer ball far"**

Let's now look at this tree structure where the words grouped are attached to one node.

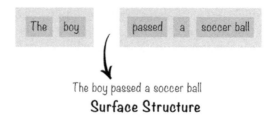

The boy passed a soccer ball
Surface Structure

Now let's look at how this sentence could be fully broken down to a logical semantic level (i.e. the Deep Structure)

Deep Structure

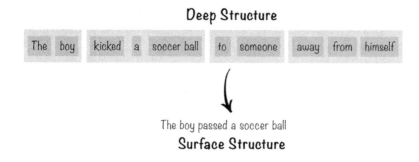

The boy passed a soccer ball
Surface Structure

With this short example, it brings a whole new meaning to the phrase, "He never says that he is thinking!"

The questions required to discover a Deep Structure sentence, giving us a true representation to our unconscious internal sensory experience (map) by uncovering the language removed in a sentence during transformations from Surface Structure sentences is exactly what the Meta Model patterns were created for. So, let's move on and learn about these patterns.

Source Material & Further Learning

(1957) Syntactic Structures, Noam Chomsky
(1975) The Structure of Magic Vol 1, Bandler & Grinder: Page 28
(1995) The Minimalist Program, Noam Chomsky

META MODEL

If you refer back to the section describing the origins of NLP you will know that a fundamental element, the most important element in some people's opinion, during the development of NLP, was the creation of the Meta Model.

One of the first people Richard Bandler, John Grinder and Frank Pucelik modelled was the extraordinarily talented family psychotherapist Virgina Satir. Her exceptional ability was to listen to a client's language and spoken word and chunk down to their Deep Structure using a collection of elegant questions. Once modelled these language patterns became the Meta Model.

Meta Model analyses the sentences (language out) we create and communicate verbally by considering a number of rules that a well-formed sentence should contain. Using these rules as a guide coupled with a list of recognisable repeatable patterns, the Meta Model allows for elegant questioning to recover deleted components of a Surface Structure sentence to discover a Deep Structure sentence.

Said another way, the Meta Model is the linguistic process that enables movement from the Surface Structure to the Deep Structure allowing us to accurately recover deletions and elicit an image from a person's internal sensory representation (map) of the outside world (territory) for the purpose of reconnecting that person to their experience to allow change to be possible.

To put it in a simpler way, the Meta Model is a number of questions available to you to reverse and uncover deletions, distortions and generalisations. There are a variety of reasons that you could use these questions such as;

- collecting data,
- clarifying information,
- clarifying meaning,
- identifying the restrictions causing unresourceful state or behaviour,
- creating new choices for a person to increase resourcefulness
- to use as verbal self-defence if you wish to prove something

There are five types of question (also known as challenges), that will elicit an answer that should gather more specific detailed information;

- What...?
- Which...?
- Who...?
- When...?
- Where...?

The only 'W' question missing from here is the question 'Why?'. The reason for this is that *why* is the only question that actually chunks up rather than down. A *why* question takes a person into their values and beliefs and to overarching reasoning for something or some behaviour. As the Meta Model focuses on chunking down, 'Why?' does not make an appearance.

Please note. Proceed with caution after you learn and put Meta Model patterns into practice as their use can make conversations difficult or awkward for others due to the fact you will be gaining clarification on information that may be being consciously or unconsciously omitted from the communication. Excessive use can break rapport!

WELL-FORMED SENTENCE CONDITIONS

Before we look at the patterns, let's review the guiding rules of a well-formed sentence. As we know, Surface Structure sentences are groups of words that are not well-formed, as in they are reliant on a native speaker's creation of constituents and intuition to enable understanding.

There are seven well-formed characteristics or grammatical conditions for the English language and as therapists themselves, the founders of NLP collated this list of rules which then ultimately provided a desired outcome for what the Meta Model patterns are trying to achieve.

The 7 Conditions of a Well-Formed Sentence.

1. It is well-formed in English.
2. Contain no transformational deletions or unexplored deletions in the portion of the model in which the client experiences no choice.
3. Contain no nominalisations.
4. Contain no words or phrases lacking referential indices.
5. Contain no verbs incompletely specified.
6. Contain no unexplored presuppositions in the portion of the model in which the client experiences no choice.
7. Contain no sentences which violate the semantic conditions of well-formedness.

Let's now look at the Meta Model patterns to recognise when and what strategic questioning is required to achieve a well-formed sentence.

Source Material & Further Learning
(1975) The Structure of Magic Vol 1, Bandler & Grinder: Page 53

META MODEL PATTERNS

In order to *challenge* (to ask questions) the transformations (multiple derivations) that have occurred between the Deep Structure and the Surface Structure sentences, we can listen out for certain patterns to direct our line of questioning and obtain the deleted components of the sentence. These patterns are called Meta Model patterns. The patterns fall under the same categories as the universal modelling processes used to filter information from the territory to create our internal perception of the world (map).

Summary of the Meta Model Patterns:
- **Generalisation** meta program patterns
  - Universal quantifiers
  - Modal operators of necessity
  - Modal operators of possibility & impossibility
  - Generalised Referential index
- **Deletion** meta program patterns
  - Simple deletion
  - Comparative deletion
  - Lack of referential index / Unspecified referential index
  - Judgement
  - Unspecified verb
  - Unspecified noun
  - Nominalisation
- **Distortion** meta program patterns
  - Cause & effect
  - Mind reading
  - Complex equivalence
  - Lost performative
  - Presuppositions

Source Material & Further Learning for Meta Model
(1975) The Structure of Magic Vol 1, Bandler & Grinder: Page 46 to 106

GENERALISATION META PROGRAM PATTERNS

These are the patterns that allow us to identify the elements of a person's map that have become detached from the original experience and now form a representation that represents an entire category of experience in itself.

UNIVERSAL QUANTIFIERS

A phrase or word that takes a result or occurrence of individual events communicates them as one instance at all times with no exceptions. Words such as; *always, never, everyone, no-one, all, constantly, everybody.*

This Meta Model challenge has the aim of recovering information about whether there are any exceptions to the generalisation. This will either highlight exceptions or if there are none confirm the validity of the statement.

Here are some examples of what you might hear to identify this (a) and how you could respond and challenge with a question to recover the generalisation that has occurred (b).

> *a) "He **always** shouts at me"*
> *b) "Always?"*
>
> *a) "**Everyone** is better than me"*
> *b) "Is there anyone who is not?"*
>
> *a) "It would **never** happen"*
> *b) "Really, never?"*

MODAL OPERATORS OF NECESSITY

A phrase or word implying that there is no alternate choice and the action is 100% required. It is an indication that there are beliefs or rules being used to reduce flexibility of behaviour and choice. Words such as; *need, must, mustn't, could, couldn't, have to, should, shouldn't.*

This Meta Model challenge has the aim of recovering a rule or a believed consequence causing a lack of options. Investigating consequences can either open up options for the person or provide an understanding of their model of the world and their perception of ecology. Here are some examples of what you might hear to identify this (a) and how you could respond and challenge with a question to recover the generalisation that has occurred (b).

> *a) "I **should** work tomorrow"*
> *b) "What would happen if you didn't work tomorrow?"*

> *a) "I **have to** do this now"*
> *b) "What would happen if you did it later?"*

MODAL OPERATORS OF POSSIBILITY/IMPOSSIBILITY

A phrase or word that implies choice is or was present and there was an option for a decision. It is an indication that the person can identify the options. Words such as; *can/cannot, will/will not, possible/impossible.*

This Meta Model challenge has the aim of recovering the belief causing the lack of options. Investigating this can either identify an unconscious incompetence providing potential outcomes that could open up options for the person or provide the recovery could provide an understanding of their model of the world and their perception of ecology. Here are some examples of what you might hear to identify this (a) and how you could respond and challenge with a question to recover the generalisation that has occurred (b).

> *a) "I **can't** tell him"*
> *b) "What would happen if you did tell him?"*

> *a) "**That's** impossible"*
> *b) "Has it been possible for anyone before?"*

GENERALISED REFERENTIAL INDEX.

A phrase or word that implies a plural noun with the absence of an occurrence of an individual event (Universal Quantifier). It is an indication that the person can identify the options.

This Meta Model challenge has the aim of recovering specific detailed information that has been generalised to create a plural reference. It may be that there are not any exceptions therefore confirming the validity of the statement.

Here is an example of what you might hear to identify this (a) and how you could respond to recover the deletion that has occurred (b);

> *a) "**People** don't care"*
> *b) "Which people are you referring to?"*

Please observe that recovering this referential index provides much more appropriate detail. Recovering the Universal Quantifier does not get closer to resolving the missing content (e.g. *'All people?'*) nor reframing help (e.g. *'John cares'*) as this just provides an exception rather than retrieving the index content.

DELETION META PROGRAM PATTERNS

These patterns allow us to identify the elements of a person's map that have been deleted from the original experience and now form a representation that focuses on certain elements of an experience by choosing to ignore others.

SIMPLE DELETION

This is where a sentence is left incomplete with an important detail missing. This 'sentence fragment' can be identified due to the fact that a sentence with a simple deletion is often grammatically incorrect. Alternatively, you will hear a word like '*it*' or '*that*' replacing details.

This Meta Model challenge simply has the aim of recovering missing information or recovering more specific information from an incomplete sentence.

Here are some examples of what you might hear to identify this (a) and how you could respond to recover the deletion that has occurred (b);

> *a) "Just do **it**"*
> *b) "Do what?"*

> *a) "**That's** important"*
> *b) "What's important exactly?"*

> *a) "I'm hurt"*
> *b) "Hurt where?" or "Hurt how?"*

COMPARATIVE DELETION

A phrase or word that implies there is a comparison being made and yet details or the basis of what the item is being compared against are missing. Words such as; *better, worse, easier, harder, more, less, good, bad*

This Meta Model challenge has the aim of recovering information about who or what the statement of opinion or comparison is being compared to.

Here are some examples of what you might hear to identify this (a) and how you could respond to recover the deletion that has occurred (b);

> *a) "He is much **better**"*
> *b) "Better than who?"*

> *a) "I'm a **bad** player"*
> *b) "In comparison to whom?"*

LACK OF / UNSPECIFIED REFERENTIAL INDEX

A phrase or word that omits the direct source providing the content of a statement of fact within the sentence. Look out for unidentified plural pronouns such as; *they, people, them,*

This Meta Model challenge has the aim of recovering information about who specifically is being referred to in the statement.

Here are some examples of what you might hear to identify this (a) and how you could respond to recover the deletion that has occurred (b);

> *a) "Just like **they** always say"*
> *b) "Who always says?"*

> *a) "**People** always mess things up"*
> *b) "Who specifically messes things up?"*

JUDGEMENTS

A phrase or word implying the content of a statement is being judged against certain criteria and yet the standards for the judging are missing from the sentence. Not all judgements are wrong, but thoughtless judgment can cause issues. Look out for adverbs such as; *clearly, obviously* or adjectives such as *enough*

This Meta Model challenge has the aim of recovering information about what criteria the statement is being judged against.

Here are some examples of what you might hear to identify this (a) and how you could respond to recover the deletion that has occurred (b);

> *a) "That is an **obvious** improvement"*
> *b) "In what way?"*

> *a) "That is not good **enough**"*
> *b) "What would be good enough?"*

UNSPECIFIED VERB

A phrase or word where the verb and details of the result of doing verb is missing. It leaves you knowing that action was taken or something was done but how it was done is missing.

This Meta Model challenge has the aim of recovering information about what specific action was taken and also missing context or content.

Here are some examples of what you might hear to identify this (a) and how you could respond to recover the deletion that has occurred (b);

> *a) "I failed"*
> *b) "What exactly did you fail at?"*

> *a) "I made this"*
> *b) "What did you do to make it?"*

UNSPECIFIED NOUN

A phrase or word where the person, place or thing is missing or replaced with something else. It leaves you knowing that something was done but you do not know what did it, where or by whom specifically.

This Meta Model challenge has the aim of recovering information about specific people, places or things.

Here are some examples of what you might hear to identify this (a) and how you could respond to recover the deletion that has occurred (b);

> *a) "That's just the way **things** are **here**"*
> *b) "The way what things are and where exactly?"*

> *a) "**It** is for the best"*
> *b) "What is for the best and for whom?"*

NOMINALISATION

A word that has changed a process into a thing. Grammatically this is done by turning a verb into a noun. A frequent indication of this are words ending with '*ion*', '*ure*', '*ity*' at the end such as; *confusion, communication, decision, depression, failure, anxiety,*

This Meta Model challenge has the aim of recovering information about the verb that has created the noun. This can open up options for a person by turning a stationary word into a word that contains motion and therefore has the ability to change.

Here are some examples of what you might hear to identify this (a) and how you could respond to recover the deletion that has occurred (b);

> *a) "There is no **communication** in here"*
> *b) "Who is not communicating?"*

> *a) "We need a **decision**!"*
> *b) "How can we best decide?"*

DISTORTION META PROGRAM PATTERNS

These are the patterns that allow us to identify the elements of a person's map that have become warped from the original experience and now form a representation that experiences an exaggerated category of experience in itself.

CAUSE/EFFECT

A phrase containing two implies that there is a relationship between them in that when one thing (A) happens the next (B) will automatically then happen (A > B). Words such as; *makes, then, because, so, when, automatically.*

This Meta Model challenge has the aim of recovering information about the belief that is causing two things to be connected. This can provide insight into the person's model of the world and also open up options for a person to understand that the two things are unconnected.

Here are some examples of what you might hear to identify this (a) and how you could respond to recover the distortion that has occurred (b);

> a) *"He just **makes** me angry"*
> b) *"What specifically is making you angry?"*
>
> a) *"The whole day is ruined **because** I'm late"*
> b) *"Is there any part of the day not ruined?"*
>
> a) *"I've started **so** I'll carry on"*
> b) *"What would happen if you stopped?"*

MIND READING

A phrase or word that implies that someone knows somebody else's inner thoughts or state with the absence of information from the other person. Think of it as guessing or attributing our own thoughts (or internal sensory representation) to someone else. Words and phrases such as; *I think, he/she thinks, I know, he/she knows, he/she wants*

This Meta Model challenge has the aim of recovering sensory evidence around the statement of potential assumption.

Here are some examples of what you might hear to identify this (a) and how you could respond to recover the distortion that has occurred (b);

> *a) "I don't **think** he cares about me"*
> *b) "Have you ever asked him if he cares about you?"*

> *a) "He **wants** to change"*
> *b) "How do you know? Has he told you that he wants to change?"*

COMPLEX EQUIVALENCE

This is when two unrelated things or concepts are mentioned in a sentence in a way that implies that the two individual things are synonymous. Said another way, they are equal in that if one thing (A) is true then the other thing (B) must also be true. (A = B) Words such as; *means, are, is.*

This Meta Model challenge has the aim of recovering information about the belief that is causing two things to be connected. This can provide insight into the person's model of the world and also open up options for a person to understand that the two things are unconnected.

Here are some examples of what you might hear to identify this (a) and how you could respond to recover the distortion that has occurred (b);

> *a) "If she is quiet, it **means** she is mad"*
> *b) "Can you think of a specific time when she was quiet and not mad?"*

> *a) "Happiness **is** selfish"*
> *b) "How exactly is being happy selfish?"*

LOST PERFORMATIVE

This is a sentence that states a fact, opinion or instruction and yet the direct reference of the original source or person making the statement is missing. Statements such as; *are better/worse, are good/bad.*

This Meta Model challenge has the aim of recovering the source of the statement being made. In some instances, this highlights that a person is making an assumption based on no credibility or fact whatsoever. Alternatively, if you can uncover a direct source it can provide confirmation of the statement or opportunities for further research.

Here are some examples of what you might hear to identify this (a) and how you could respond to recover the distortion that has occurred (b);

> *a) "Mercedes are better cars"*
> *b) "Says who?"*

> *a) "Stability helps growth"*
> *b) "Where did you get that information from?"*

PRESUPPOSITIONS

These are statements that presuppose two or more people believe the rules for which the statement is based, are true and makes sense. An incorrect presumption on the person making the statement is often where this pattern can cause problems. Words such as; *we know, we agree, it is.*

This Meta Model challenge has the aim of recovering the other sources that are believed to share the same truths stated within the statement being made. This can identify potential *mind reads* that may then be worth investigating.

Here are some examples of what you might hear to identify this (a) and how you could respond to recover the distortion that has occurred (b);

> *a) **We all know** this is the best way to do it"*
> *b) "Are we sure everything knows that?"*

> *a) "As **we agreed** this was wrong"*
> *b) "Did we agree?"*

PRECISION MODEL

The Meta Model was created by studying therapists, meaning the primary focus and context of the model was to address personal issues. John Grinder found himself intrigued at how this linguistic model could serve in other scenarios and contexts so with Michael McMaster, Grinder started discovering a model that could be used practically in a business context.

The primary aim was to address the requirement for managers to be effective communicators enabling them to elicit information efficiently and ensure project or business success. This modelling project gave birth to the *Precision Model*, a model that contains a distilled version of the Meta Model with just five patterns, all presented in a way that is relevant to benefit a person in a business or project context.

Much like the Meta Model, the Precision Model provides a manager wishing to extract the Deep Structure information, known as higher quality information within the Precision Model, with a set of responses (labelled (*b*) in the illustration) based on the low-quality information (Surface Structure) being presented (labelled (*a*) in the illustration) enabling the recovery of missing content or the discovery of gaps in knowledge. Here are the five language patterns, known as *pointers* that they found that make up this model;

Summary of the five Precision Model pointers

Pointer	Precision Model Name	Meta Model Equivalent
1st Pointer	Noun blockbuster	Unspecified Noun
2nd Pointer	Action blockbuster	Unspecified Verb
3rd Pointer	Universal blockbuster	Universals
4th Pointer	Comparator	Comparative Deletions
5th Pointer	Boundary crossing	Modal operators

Source Material & Further Learning for Precision Model
(1994) Precision, Grinder and McMaster: Pages *All*

NOUN BLOCKBUSTER: UNSPECIFIED NOUN

The first pointer is a Noun Blockbuster. These result in questions (or challenges) that ensure all parties have a clear understanding of what *things* are being referred to.

This frequently shows up as plurals in statements or sentences, such as words like; *costs, sales, overheads, benefits, numbers, items, resources*

Here are some examples of what you might hear (a) and how you could respond (b) to chunk down and recover the deletion that has occurred;

> a) *"We have run out of some **resources**"*
> b) *"What resources are you referring to?"*

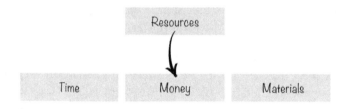

> a) *"We need to reduce some of our **costs**"*
> b) *"What specific costs do we need to review?"*

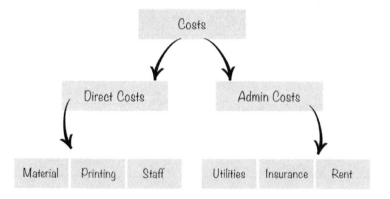

ACTION BLOCKBUSTER: UNSPECIFIED VERB

The second pointer is an Action Blockbuster. These result in questions (or challenges) that ensure all parties have a clear understanding of what *things* need to be done or what specific actions some are referring to. This shows up as words such as; *increase, decrease, enhance, improve, prepare.*

Here are some examples of what you might hear (a) and how you could respond (b) to chunk down and recover the language deletion that has occurred;

> *a) "We have been **improving** our process"*
> *b) "What specific action has improved our process?"*

> *a) "We have to **prepare** for the meeting"*
> *b) "What specific preparation is required?"*

> *a) "We should **enhance** our relationship with the client"*
> *b) "Exactly how can we enhance this relationship?"*

UNIVERSAL BLOCKBUSTER: UNIVERSAL QUANTIFIERS

The third pointer is a Universal Blockbuster. These result in questions (or challenges) that gain higher quality information from generalisations or global descriptions of things, that appear in a statement. Listen out for words such as; *all, every, always, never, nobody.*

Here are some examples of what you might hear (a) and how you could respond (b) to chunk down and recover the language deletion that has occurred;

> *a) "We must **always** do this"*
> *b) "Are there any single occasions when we should not do it?"*

> *a) "**All** the workers agree"*
> *b) "Every single one, with no exception?"*

COMPARATOR: COMPARATIVE DELETION

The fourth pointer is called a Comparator. These result in questions (or challenges) that ensure all parties have clarity on what a particular thing or statement is being judged against. This shows up as words such as; *better, worse, up, down, more, less, best*

Here are some examples of what you might hear (a) and how you could respond (b) to chunk down and recover the language deletion that has occurred;

> *a) "Our profits are **up**"*
> *b) "Up with respect to what metrics and over what time period?"*

> *a) "We've seen productivity go **down** by 20%"*
> *b) "What specific action is down and how did you measure productivity?"*

> *a) "We are the **best!**"*
> *b) "Best at what and compared to whom?"*

BOUNDARY CROSSING: MODAL OPERATORS OF NECESSITY, POSSIBILITY & IMPOSSIBILITY

The fifth pointer is called Boundary Crossing. Where the previous four pointers seek to gain refinement or distinction of a deletion (also see *derivation* or *transformation*) this pointer results in questions (or challenges) that ensure we can understand presuppositions or beliefs that have added bias to the information being presented. This could be a belief about necessity or possibility from the person's experience of the situation (map of the world). The challenges aim to uncover limitations and then cross the boundaries that a person may or may not have done consciously.

Necessity boundaries could show up as words such as; *must / mustn't, should / shouldn't, necessary, have to, need*

Possibility boundaries could show up as words such as; *can / can't, possible / impossible, able / unable*

Here are some examples of what you might hear (a) and how you could respond (b) to chunk down and recover the language deletion that has occurred;

*a) "We **must** finish on time"*
b) "What would happen if we didn't finish on time?"

*a) "We **have to** discount that for them"*
b) "Are there any other ways of creating the same outcome?"

*a) "We all **need to** go to the meeting"*
b) "Is there anyone that doesn't have to be in the meeting?"

*a) "I **can't** stop"*
b) "What would happen if you did stop?"

*a) "That's im**possible**!"*
b) "Has anyone done it or anything similar in the past?"

*a) "We are **unable** to do that"*
b) "What circumstances would allow us to be able to?"

With all of these five pointers, in a business or project situation, you will now be able to obtain high-quality specific information and also ensure your communication is effective by including;

- what specifically?
- where specifically?
- how specifically?
- when specifically?
- compared to what specifically and according to whom?

All this being said, use this model appropriately, timely and for positive outcomes within a business setting. These linguistic challenges could get you into some undesirable situations if you expose a person's ignorance or incompetence in an inappropriate moment in front of the wrong people!

MILTON MODEL

The Milton Model is named after Dr Milton H Erickson. He was the person the co-creators of NLP modelled to create this linguistic model. Where the Meta Model patterns came from therapy and were effective by uncovering missing details in a sentence, Milton Erickson was achieving equally remarkable results with clients as a very successful hypnotherapist and yet his language was vague and ambiguous, looking to remove specific details.

After modelling Milton Erickson, a number of language patterns were discovered that together became known as the Milton Model. These patterns create artfully vague language with the intention of causing the conscious mind to enter a stuck state of confusion. This in turn creates a downtime state for a person something also referred to as a trance.

With reference to the Hierarchy of Ideas, the Milton Model *chunks up*. The Milton Model is sometimes referred to as the Inverse Meta Model as it contains 11 of the same patterns but rather than chunking down the patterns chunk up.

Now although this language originated from a clinical hypnotherapist it turns out that these artfully vague language patterns can be used for other things beyond hypnosis or trance.

Let's quickly refer back to the Meta Model Patterns to explain how we can actually utilise the Milton Model. Meta Model Patterns and questions (challenges) by design chunk down to get more detail and yet by doing so ultimately shares with the other person that you are a little out-of-sync with them with regards to being in rapport – otherwise you would know what they meant right! Milton Model, on the other hand, chunks in the opposite way making statements that cause the other person to search their deep structure to fill in the gaps, this in turn is a great way to build rapport with other people.

In fact, due to the vague language, you can create language that builds rapport with more than one person at the same time having them agree with you and finding common ground as they can all individually relate to what you are saying. This makes Milton language patterns ideal for things such as; political speeches, advertisements, discussions and motivational speeches, where everyone can agree with what is being said or be able to embrace a large group of people to get them all together and feel good

TRANSDERIVATIONAL SEARCH (TDS)

When experiencing Milton Model language, sometimes referred to as hypnotic language, a person has an opportunity to allow their unconscious mind to gather meaning from a surface structure sentence.

In order for the unconscious mind to do this it has to *search* for meaning by running through combinations of possible *transformations* and *derivations* (deletions from the Deep Structure to the Surface Structure), hence the name *Transderivational Search* or TDS as it is commonly referred to. The result of TDS is that a person will get closer to their internal sensory experience creating a wider understanding of possibilities bring greater choice and flexibility for that person. This often results in a new perspective or possible resolution of inner conflict.

With reference to the Eye Patterns section, we know that by witnessing a person's eyes looking in a particular direction, we can identify which sensory modality they are accessing their information, their Lead Representational System. When the unconscious mind performs TDS you will witness the eyes moving rapidly; up, down, side to side as the unconscious searches and makes use of every sensory representation, recalling and constructing to fill in blanks and create meaning.

MILTON MODEL LANGUAGE PATTERNS

This section provides an overview of the Milton Model patterns. Milton believed that a person already had all the resources they need, it was just in some cases they were unable to access them.

The patterns actually utilise the universal filters of deletion, distortion and generalisation to make language deliberately vague allowing a person's unconscious mind to find meaning that is right according to their map of the world.

Summary of the Milton Model Language Patterns

- **Deletion language patterns**
  - Lost performative
  - Lack of referential index
  - Unspecified verb
  - Comparative deletions

  Distortion language patterns
  - Mind reading
  - Cause and effect
  - Presuppositions
  - Complex equivalence
  - Nominalisations

- **Generalisation language patterns**
  - Universal qualifier
  - Modal operators of necessity
  - Modal operators of possibility

- **Pacing current experience**
  - Subordinate clause of time

- **Distracting Conscious Mind with Confusion**
    - Phonological ambiguity
    - Punctuational ambiguity
    - Syntactic ambiguity
    - Scope ambiguity
    - Double binds

- **Accessing Unconscious Resources**
    - Conversational postulate
    - Tag questions
    - Embedded commands
    - Embedded questions
    - Extended quotes
    - Analogue marking
    - Utilisation

Source Material & Further Learning for Milton Model
(1975) Patterns of The Hypnotic Techniques of Milton H. Erickson, M.D. Vol 1, Bandler & Grinder: Page 219 (1981) Trance-Formations, Bandler & Grinder: page 100

LOST PERFORMATIVE

The aim of this pattern is to acknowledge judgment is taking place and yet make no mention or suggestion of the source of the judgment.

- *"That's right."*
- *"That's better."*
- *"It's easy…"*

LOST REFERENTIAL INDEX

The aim of this pattern is to use expressions without specific reference to who or what the speaker is referring to.

- *"This is what love is about"*
- *"I agree with that"*
- *"It's better to move in that direction"*

UNSPECIFIED VERB

The aim of this pattern is to omit exactly how the person will take an action to produce an outcome of a digital predicate (unspecified representational predicates). A simple way to do this is by adding the *"As you"* or *"You are"* to the beginning of your statement.

- *"As you make sense of this…"*
- *"As you discover them…"*
- *"You are achieving awareness…"*

COMPARATIVE DELETIONS

The aim of this pattern is to state a comparison for a thing and yet omit what the thing is being compared to allowing the person to construct their own comparison. These statements can be used to pace someone in their present state.

- *"As you feel happier."*
- *"You will end up more resilient."*
- *"You will learn to understand more."*

MIND READING

The aim of this pattern is to claim to know the internal processes or thoughts of another person. Your statement should be made with the use of digital predicates (unspecified representational predicates).

- *"I know you think that is right."*
- *"You are wondering."*
- *"You will love it."*

CAUSE AND EFFECT

The aim of this pattern is to casually suggest there is a connection between two things or events where one thing happens or exists as a result of the other thing. (A > B).

- *"When you listen carefully, you will learn…"*
- *"Once you walk through the door, you'll be ready to act…"*
- *"If you concentrate you will be happy…"*

COMPLEX EQUIVALENCE

The aim of this pattern is to attach two beliefs or things together to insinuate they are synonymous. It is best to connect one that is known to be true and one that can become accepted as true.

- *"As you are hearing me you are learning…"*
- *"As you see the word focus you will focus…"*
- *"Being happy is freeing…"*

PRESUPPOSITIONS

The aim of this pattern is to make a statement that presupposes something happens as a result of something else being true.

- *"How amazed will you be, when you win a chess game."*
- *"Considered how easy it is to learn to play guitar."*
- *"Listening now you are already in a trance."*

NOMINALISATIONS

The aim of this pattern is to convert an action or movement and distort it into a noun (a thing) therefore removing the movement of the word – stopping it in time.

- *"As you make a decision."*
- *"With your visualization."*
- *"Your relaxation is increasing."*

UNIVERSAL QUALIFIER

The aim of this pattern is to make an absolute generalisation that can be applied to a set or class of people that includes the subject. The statement should also be absent of any reference.

- *"Everyone can be calm."*
- *"We all know this to be true."*
- *"There are opportunities for us everywhere."*

MODAL OPERATOR OF NECESSITY

The aim of the model operator of necessity is to modify a verb to construct a statement that opens up an action or an outcome that must happen or be fulfilled by saying so.

- *"You should think hard."*
- *"You need to be open."*
- *"You must now think."*

MODAL OPERATOR OF POSSIBILITY

The aim of the model operator of possibility is to modify a verb to construct a statement that opens up an action or an outcome to be possible by just saying it is so.

- *"You can be open."*
- *"You are able to take the action."*
- *"You may stop yourself."*

SUBORDINATE CLAUSE OF TIME / PACE & LEAD

This is an essential element of the Milton Model as it can be used to pace and lead, which is often why this language pattern is used to open up a hypnosis session. The aim of this pattern is to use sensory-based language to describe what they are experiencing in the now and leading them, through time, closer to a resourceful state.

- *"(1)As you sit now… (2)when you are hearing my voice…(3) already discovering ideas… (4) then you visualise… (5) during which you relax more… (6) and you begin to wonder… (7) and then breathe deeply*

  - (1) Sit & now
    - Sensory = Kinesthetic
    - Time = Now
  - (2) When & hear
    - Sensory = Auditory
    - Time = Happening & simultaneously
  - (3) Already & discovering
    - Sensory = Digital
    - Time = Happened and simultaneously
  - (4) Then & Visualise
    - Sensory = Visual
    - Time = Next
  - (5) During & Relax
    - Sensory = Kinesthetic
    - Time = Happening & simultaneously
  - (6) Begin & Wonder
    - Sensory = Digital
    - Time = Next
  - (7) Then & Breathe
    - Sensory = Kinesthetic
    - Time = Next

PHONOLOGICAL AMBIGUITY

The second phase of a Milton Model session is to confuse the conscious mind and to encourage TDS (Transderivational Search). The aim of this particular ambiguity is to use *homophones*. These are words that sound the same and yet have a variety of spelling and therefore meanings. Here are some examples of homophones and how they can be used in the context of the Milton Model;

- *"As you put the sea shell to your ear, can you see the sea*
  - o See/Sea
- *"Sat here, hear the trees*
  - o Hear/Here
- *"He knows to follow his nose"*
  - o Nose/Knows
- *"When you write 'right' you know when it is right, right?"*
  - o Write/Right

PUNCTUATION AMBIGUITY

The aim of this particular ambiguity is to merge two statements or sentences using words or phrases to overlap the end of one and the beginning of another. Often this ambiguity can utilise homophones and yet it is not a necessity. Here are some examples of how homophones can be used in this way for the Milton Model;

- *"There are some things **I don't know** if you can consider this today"*
  - o There are some things **I don't know**
  - o **I don't know** if you can consider this today

- *"Consider that you are **right** me a letter today"*
  - o *Consider that you are **right***
  - o ***write** me a letter today"*

- *"That's great, when you get **here** me say come in"*
  - o That's great, when you get **here**
  - o **hear** me say come in

SYNTACTIC AMBIGUITY

The aim of this particular ambiguity is to use a verb or an adjective that leaves the context of the action undefined or unattached to the subject doing the action. This pattern can be constructed in two ways. One is using '*Verb+ing Noun*' and the other is '*Nominalisation+of the+Noun*'. Both allow the verb and the adjective to exist. Here are some examples of how this can be used in the Milton Model;

- *"**Flying planes** can be dangerous"*
  - o Verb: 'Flying planes' as in flying a plane
  - o Adjective: 'Flying planes' as in planes that are flying
- *"Look they are **working horses**"*
  - o Verb: 'working horses' they are putting horses to work
  - o Adjective: 'working horses' as in horses that do work
- *"**Challenging people** can be hard"*
  - o Verb: 'Challenging people' as in to challenge a person
  - o Adjective: 'Challenging people' as in describing a group of people as challenging.

SCOPE AMBIGUITY

The aim of this particular ambiguity is to use a word that could be an adverb or adjective and through a lack of context it blurs what aspect the word is being used for in the sentence. It can also be constructed with the word *and* where the adjective is missing from the second item. Here are some examples of how this can be used for the Milton Model;

- *"**Old** men and women"*
  - o Does this mean *old men* and *old women*?
  - o Does this mean *old men* and *women of any*?
- *"I'm discussing this with you as a **knowledgeable** person"*
  - o Does this mean *you* are knowledgeable?
  - o Does this mean *they* are knowledgeable?
- *"That team has **amazing** players and fans"*
  - o Are just the players amazing?
  - o Are the fans and players both amazing?

DOUBLE BINDS

The aim of this particular language pattern is to provide choice and yet whatever is chosen will include a predetermined outcome. The result of this is a person will normally focus on the choice disregarding that the outcome for something predetermined has already been accepted purely by the fact they are making a choice from the options presented. Here are some examples of how this can be used for the Milton Model;

- *"Will you **turn up** early, on time or late?"*
  - Every choice presupposes that they are turning up
- *"Do you want to **take the next step** with help or by yourself"*
  - Each choice presupposes you will take the next step
- *"Take a red **pen**, a blue **pen** or a black **pen?"***
  - Each choice presupposes you will take a pen
- *"Are you **buying this car** now or later?"*
  - Each choice presupposes you will be buying the car

CONVERSATIONAL POSTULATE

The third phase of the Milton Model is to use language that will allow the unconscious mind to access resources in order to provide the person with more choices. The unconscious mind will not interpret these patterns as commands, rather it will choose to use them to provide suggestions for accessing unconscious resources. The aim of this particular pattern is to provide a question that on the surface could be answered with a binary (or digital) yes/no answer and yet on a deeper level it can be interpreted as a command and therefore an unconscious suggestion to access more information. Here are some examples of how they can be used in the context of the Milton Model;

- *"Can you imagine…"*
  - Surface: Yes/No
  - Deep: The person begins to imagine
- *"Would you be able to consider that to be true…"*
  - Surface: Yes/No
  - Deep: The person begins to consider

TAG QUESTIONS

The aim of this particular pattern is to provide a question at the very end of a statement or sentence to cause the verification of agreement from the person for what has just preceded it. Although this is a question, it should be spoken as a statement to encourage the unconscious mind to access resources by considering the statement to be true at least in some context or capacity. Here are some examples of how they can be used in the context of the Milton Model;

- *"You are changing now,* **aren't you...**"
- *"It is working well for you,* **isn't it...**"

A tag question can also be used to create confusion by presenting incongruent time periods between the statement and the tag question;

- *"You are changing now,* **haven't you...**"
- *"It is working well for you,* **didn't it...**"

EMBEDDED COMMANDS

The aim of this particular pattern is to provide a command encased or covertly placed within the structure of a sentence. This sends one surface message to the conscious mind and another suggestion to access resources to the unconscious mind. Here are some examples of how they can be used in the context of the Milton Model;

- *"I don't know if you will, share this information after you read this."*
  - o Embedded Command: share this information.
- *"Maybe it's possible for you to, go into a trance, after reading this.*
  - o Embedded Command: go into a trance

Embedded commands can also be fragmented within a longer sentence;

- *"Let yourself relax. People can easily, consider how to, begin to, be better."*
  - o Command: Let yourself, consider how to, be better.

EMBEDDED QUESTIONS

The aim of this particular pattern is to provide an indirect question encased or covertly placed within the structure of a sentence. Even though not asked directly the person will answer the question internally as though it was asked directly to them. Here are some examples of how they can be used in the context of the Milton Model;

- *"Are you intrigued to know if you know what is concerning you?"*
  - Embedded Question: what is concerning you
- *"I don't know if you will tell me when did you go there last…"*
  - Embedded Question: when did you go there last

Embedded questions can also be fragmented within a longer sentence;

- *"Can you, relax as people, think of, many things and end on a solution"*
  - Question: Can you, think of, a solution?

EXTENDED QUOTES

The aim of this particular pattern is to provide a quote within a statement that allows you to attribute what was said to someone else who is not the speaker. This can remove responsibility for the phrase and also allow the person to use their sensory representational systems to either recall or construct a person saying the quote. It is also useful to enhance validity as a quote provides an opportunity for a narrative and context to be added to the sentence. Here is an example of how a quote can change the impact of a phrase by switching the ownership from the speaker to a third person.

- *"Anyone learning Milton Model must learn quotes to fully understand it"*
  - Said only by the speaker
- *"John was so excited once he had learned all the Milton Model patterns from me, I remember him saying 'Anyone learning Milton Model must learn quotes to fully understand it' and at that point, I knew he had fully understood the power of quotes.*
  - Said by a 3rd person adding to the validity of the quote

ANALOGUE MARKING

This is actually a non-linguistic mode of communication that can split a sentence up into segments or units. It can be performed by using visual or auditory cues such as;

- Tonality of voice
- Volume of voice
- Gestures
- Movements

For the examples below, say them out loud or use your self-talk and when you see a **bold** word either raise the volume or change the tonality to emphasise it. You will notice how by doing so it provides an embedded statement.

- *"I know you will **feel clever as you hear this**"*
- *"I have no doubt you will **remember this sentence** later"*

UTILISATION

The aim of this pattern is to take what has been said by a person and reuse the content in your communication, presenting it back as though you were in agreement (a shared presupposition) with their statement before it was made. This can be used to pace and lead someone from an unresourceful state to a resourceful state and should utilise all the language (sensory predicates) that has been used by the other person so you can fully align with their map of the world and internal sensory representation.

- *"I can't see how to do it."*
  - Utilisation + Visual
  - ***"That's right, you can't see how to do it**, yet...*
- *"I don't feel I know if I understand this yet."*
  - Utilisation + Kinesthetic
  - *"As we **sit, knowing you feel you don't know if you understand this yet,** consider that **holding** awareness of this is a **step** towards **connecting** to how you can understand..."*

METAPHORS

Metaphors were extensively used by Dr Milton H Erikson which is why this is a great place in the syllabus to cover this topic. With the knowledge that each person has their own preferred sensory systems and associated meaning of experiences, metaphors provide an excellent way to communicate meaning and understanding to a person in their own map of the world. Metaphors are a linguistic technique used to refer to the content of one subject by referring to the content of another concept or experience.

Within NLP we can refer to a metaphor in a number of ways;

- Chunking Across
- An alternate sensory comparison with a similar meaning
- An alternate contextual comparison with a similar meaning
- A story or parable
- A restrictional violation (giving things and beings human qualities they can't by definition possess)

What all these definitions have in common, along with the Greek definition of being 'to carry beyond', is the desired outcome. A metaphor is not about chunking up or down for more information, rather it is used as the best way to access the unconscious mind and resources by presenting a narrative parallel to the issue or experience so that a person can adapt it for very their own experience and meaning.

Source Material & Further Learning for Metaphors

(1978) Therapeutic Metaphors: Helping Others Through the Looking Glass, David Gordon: Page 8

SHALLOW METAPHORS

There are different types of metaphor, the first being a *shallow metaphor*. This type provides a simile or simple comparison in order to provide an alternate understanding.

- She's as cold as ice.
- That school was like a zoo.
- My computer is as old as a dinosaur.
- She is as sly as a fox.
- The open tin was as sharp as a razor.
- It's as tough as an old boot.

DEEP METAPHORS

Deep metaphors, take the form of stories. Storytelling is one of the most powerful communication techniques available to us and stories can provide many levels of meaning.

A deep metaphor (story) can pace and lead a listener through multiple states which, depending on the reason for the story, mirror a present state to a desired state including potential resources embedded within the story. To do a deep metaphor in this way, the content of this story and the content of the issue the client is experiencing will be different in that it is chunked sideways.

Milton Erickson used these types of metaphors with his clients and found they work best when the client is in a trance, allowing the unconscious mind to search for meaning and resources as a result of hearing the deep metaphor.

PART ELEVEN:
STRATEGIES

STRATEGIES AND MODELLING

If we refer back to the term Neuro Linguistic Programming, we now know that the Programming component refers to the strategies and processes a person runs within their conscious or unconscious mind.

- **Programming**
  The code behind our actions that achieve an outcome.

These *strategies* are a series (or sequence) of conscious and unconscious behaviours that we run in order to achieve an outcome. These strategies and also outcomes may or may not be conscious. Considering that our unconscious mind will always work towards a positive intent we can understand that when we see the result of a strategy it is a result of that strategy working perfectly and with excellence.

This now brings an understanding of NLP being the;

- *"Study of human excellence"*

We can gain an understanding of the term *Modelling* by looking closely at the definition Richard Bandler presents for NLP;

*"An **attitude** and a **methodology**, which leaves behind a **trail of techniques**."*

With *methodology* being.
- Modelling a behaviour to discover excellence

And *Trail of Techniques* being
- The structure and repeatable processes to produce excellence

These two components give us a rounded explanation of what *modelling* is and it also brings awareness to the fact that modelling is fundamental and core to NLP. All of the *NLP techniques* you will discover in this syllabus are actually a result of modelling repeatable strategies, coding them and transferring the excellent behaviour and outcome to you.

This is hopefully the section of the syllabus where as an NLP Practitioner you understand that NLP is modelling and that the techniques you learn are actually strategies that have been modelled by the founders and other early contributors to NLP which is why they are presented as part of the syllabus. The techniques in themselves are not NLP they are models.

Therefore, we can define Modelling as;

- Identifying an excellent behaviour for an outcome
- Capturing the structure and repeatable process that produces excellence
- Coding the sensory representational system structure and sequence of the identified process (the strategy)
- Having the ability to consistently replicate the strategy to achieve the particular excellent behaviour for the outcome
- Having the ability to repeatedly transfer the strategy to produce excellent behaviour to others.

STRATEGY VS META-PROGRAM

Before we get further into the topic of strategies let's clarify the difference between a Strategy and a Meta-program. With reference to the Meta-program section, you will know that a Meta-program is a filter and a way in which a person processes data from their senses to form an internal representation (map) which in turn influences our behaviour. A strategy is about how we go about behaving, therefore Meta-programs determine how and what strategies we perform in-order to achieve a desired state.

STATE VS STRATEGY

There are moments when learning NLP certain terms can be confusing with regard to others terms especially if they appear to be doing something similar. *State* and *Strategy* are two of these terms. Both of these terms represent a collection of other things and therefore it is easy to be confused. So, let's look at them together so it can be clear what the differences are. A *State* is the sum of conscious and unconscious thoughts or sensory feelings that a person is experiencing at a specific moment in time. This makes a state an outcome.

A *Strategy* is a series (or sequence) of conscious and unconscious behaviours that we run in order to achieve an outcome. This makes a strategy a process to achieve an outcome (which could be a state!).

MERCEDES MODEL.

With State and Strategy explained, let's add some more complexity in that an internal state can actually impact your behaviour and the strategies you run.

Think of a scenario where the calmer you are (internal state) the better you are at making a logical decision (strategy) and the more flustered you are the harder it is to be logical and rational. This illustrates that there is a relationship between them. This relationship can be explained with a model known as the *Mercedes Model.*

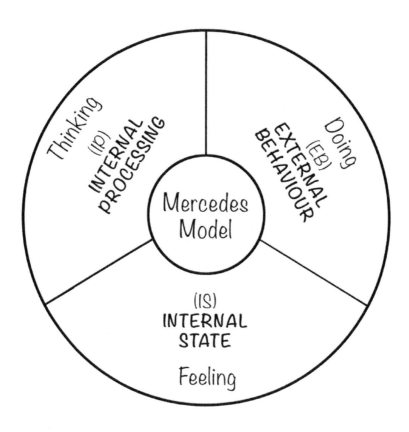

The Mercedes model is one of the oldest psychological models that illustrates the three-way relationship and connection between our emotions, thinking and behaviours so that we can understand a human.

- **Internal Processing**
  - ○ Thinking
  - ○ Internal Sensory Representations
    - Visual (Images)
    - Auditory (Sounds)
    - Auditory Digital (Self-Talk / Inner Dialogue)

- **Internal State**
  - ○ Feelings
  - ○ Emotions
  - ○ Values
  - ○ Beliefs

- **External Behaviour**
  - ○ Posture
  - ○ Gestures
  - ○ Breathing
  - ○ Movement

What this effectively shows is that each of these components can have an impact on the other.

This knowledge can be useful when modelling behaviour as it can provide insight into lines of inquiry if you are not able to replicate the excellent behaviour.

TYPES OF STRATEGY

Strategies can be conscious and unconscious and it is not a prerequisite for a strategy to take a long time or have lots of steps within a sequence especially with our unconscious mind having prime directives such as (See Prime Directives of the Unconscious Mind);

- *To seek optimum functioning with minimal parts*
- *To follow the principle of least effort*

Before creating strategies, we must understand how they are named as this is fundamental to being able to consciously choose a relevant strategy in the future. It is actually quite simple; a strategy is named in accordance with the outcome it produces. For efficiency, we hold a number of strategies within us that we use. These fall under five common categories;

- **Decision Strategy**
  - o How do we decide to act when presented with options
- **Motivational Strategy**
  - o How we motivate ourselves to take action
- **Reality Strategy**
  - o How we know to believe something exists
- **Learning Strategy**
  - o How we learn new material
- **Memory Strategy**
  - o How we create and store memories

With the generic nature of the terms; Decision, Motivational, Reality, Learning, and Memory, it is easy to see that a strategy can help in many contexts, not just one specific task. Knowing this we can understand that strategies lead to generative change and in fact all NLP techniques are generative by design.

Source Material & Further Learning
(1980) NLP: Vol I. The Study of The Structure of Experience, by Dilts, Grinder, Bandler, Bandler, DeLozier: Page 39

THE MODEL OF STRATEGY / T.O.T.E.

NLP uses a basic 4-part model when creating strategies and models. This model is called T.O.T.E. - which stands for; Test, Operate, Test, Exit.

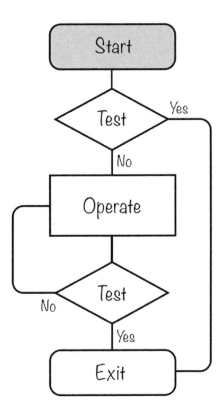

This psychological model was originally developed by George A. Miller, Eugene Galanter and Karl H Pribram in the late 1950s and published in a book called The Plans and Structure of Behaviour in 1960. Up until this point the understanding of a stimulus and then response (See State Management and Ivan Pavlov) remained in a so-called 'black box', they knew outcomes were predictable and reliably worked and yet the mechanics of this were unknown. The work undertaken by Miller, Galanter and Pribram aimed to combine known learning theory (how a person learns) with a cognitive model of learned behaviour (what a person has learned and can remember to do). The result of this was the T.O.T.E model.

Working with this model Grinder and Bandler along with Judith DeLozier and Robert Dilts evolved it further by adding elements from the NLP body of knowledge such as the Communication Model and Anchoring. The addition of this allowed them to pursue their mission of replicating excellence. Let's take a look at each stage and component of the TOTE model.

1. First Test (Comparison)

In this step, the present state is immediately compared to the desired state. This means you cannot start a TOTE unless you have outcome criteria defined. Once a comparison has been made, if there is a difference between the present state and the desired state we move to the next step, operate

2. Operate (Action)

This step is about taking action. This action has the objective of gathering data and then either achieving the desired state or moving the subject closer to the desired state.

3. Test (Comparison)

This second test is again to compare the present state to the desired state. This time though it is assessing whether the action completed in the operation step has resulted in a new present state having with less of a difference from the desired state than the previous present state.

- **If differences exist: (Feedback Loop)**
  If there are still differences detected then the next Operation in a strategy is triggered, in order to get the subject closer to the desired state. This operation is followed by the next Test. This looping process of Test-Operate-Test-Operate... is called a feedback loop and continues until the present state matches the desired state.

- **If there are no differences:**
  Move to the Exit step.

4. Exit (Decision)

This is a digital decision point in that it is a decision that consists of and requires a binary 'yes' or 'no' answer to whether the present state is equal to the desired state.

- **Yes - Same** (also see acceptable errors below)
    o Exit the strategy
- **No – Still a difference**
    o Back to an appropriate operation step

There is an addition to this in that it could be possible for a present state to still contain differences and yet they are acceptable differences (or acceptable errors). An example of this could be when using a 'Searching for a house strategy'. You would have defined a perfect criteria list, some of which are non-negotiables such as '3 bedrooms' and yet the list also contains non-essential criteria such as 'painted white'. In this example if the house you were looking at had 2 bedrooms you would keep searching and if it had 3 bedrooms and is painted light grey this might be an acceptable difference and your search could be over allowing you to exit the 'Searching for a house strategy' and move on to buying it.

STREAMLINE (STREAMLINING)

It must be noted that strategies always work and they always create an outcome. If a strategy produces an undesirable outcome, then a review of the strategy must take place knowing that it ran perfectly. After investigating and understanding which operation step caused a variance that resulted in moving away (creating a greater difference) from your desired outcome, you are able to make changes to that specific operation. It is also possible that a particular step is not required and to make a strategy more efficient you can remove it with no detrimental impact on the excellent outcome. This process of identifying unnecessary or redundant steps and either editing or removing them from a strategy is called *streamlining*.

Source Material & Further Learning

(1980) NLP: Vol I. The Study of The Structure of Experience, by Dilts, Grinder, Bandler, Bandler, DeLozier: Page 194

WELL FORMED CONDITIONS FOR STRATEGIES

Strategies also have a list of conditions that allow us to accept them as being well-formed. These can fall into two categories;

Structural Conditions

- The outcome is well-defined
- The desired outcome is ecologically sound
- All three major representational systems are used in the strategy
  - Visual, Auditory, Kinesthetic (VAK)
- The strategy follows the T.O.T.E model
- Each loop has an exit point (also known as a decision point)
- It contains an external check
  - The complete strategy is not completely constructed from a subject's subjective experience.
- The strategy sequence has the minimum amount of step to achieve the outcome
- The sequence is logical and easily replicable.

Functional Conditions

- The trigger starts the strategy and carries with it the final criteria.
- Decision points alter the present state towards the desired state
- At a test point, there are clear criteria in place to compare the present state against the desired state.
- Decision points that determine progress are based on a congruence or incongruence of the test comparison.

Source Material & Further Learning

(1980) NLP: Vol I. The Study of The Structure of Experience, by Dilts, Grinder, Bandler, Bandler, DeLozier: Page 204

WORKING WITH STRATEGIES

There are two reasons (or desired outcomes for the NLP Practitioner) for wanting to elicit the strategy the person is running causing them to make a particular decision or produce a particular behaviour. These are;

- To discover and replicate an enabling strategy so that you are able to transfer that excellence to others.
- Discover and gain an understanding of how a person is operating that results in an undesirable outcome for them, thus enabling the opportunity for change.

No matter what the desired outcome for the NLP Practitioner, an elicitation process requires an NLP Practitioner to be in a Coach State (See Coaching State section) as you want to be sure that you are catching everything that the client is providing you such as;

- Eye Accessing Cues
- Non-Verbal Communication
    - Gestures
    - Breathing
    - Voice Tonality
- Predicates

Before we get into the actual elicitation process, let's cover how you document the steps of the T.O.T.E. strategy that you are witnessing.

STRATEGY NOTATION

You are going to want to document a strategy in a way that allows others to replicate it. For this, you are going to need to use a language that others understand, common symbols, notations and language. This section provides you with a guide for documenting the necessary information;

- Sensory Representational Systems
- Focus of Perspective.
- Construct or Recall
- Sound or Language
- Positive or negative feelings
- Symbols for additional information

Sensory Representational Systems.

Code	Sensory Representational Systems.
V	Visual
A	Auditory
K	Kinesthetic
O	Olfactory
G	Gustatory

Please note with reference to the 6-Tuple and 4-Tuple the absence of AD (Auditory Digital) or D (Digital) respectively in this list. This is not a mistake it is just that these are noted in another way. (See the following codes)

Focus of Perspective.

Code	Focus of Perspective
i	Internal
e	External

Construct or Recall.

Code	Construct or Recall.
c	Construct
r	Recall

Sound or Language (Meaning).

Code	Language (Meaning)
d	Words and meaning (Digital)

Please note that when referring to Internal Digital (Self-Talk) this is referred to as *id (Internal & Digital)* there is no requirement for a *'e' (External)* to be used when hearing or seeing words externally *(External & Digital)*. This is just noted as *'d'*.

In addition, if it is an external sound being witnessed in a strategy this is noted by just the absence of *'d'*.

Positive or Negative Feelings.

Code	Construct or Recall.
+	Positive Feeling
-	Negative Feeling

As this is only connected to feelings you will on see this after a Kinesthetic (K) notation.

Symbols

Code	Symbolic Meaning
□	Step Container (Test or Operation)
◇	Decision Point Container (Exit)
→	Next Step (These connect containers)
/	Comparison
{}	Synaesthesia

There are other symbols but for now and for the purpose of an elicitation of a strategy for an NLP Practitioner these are sufficient.

With these elements broken down and explained next let's see how they are combined to document a strategy. The following provides an easy reference list of common combinations that are used when documenting a strategy.

COMMON STRATEGY NOTATION LISTS

Visual Notation Codes

Code	Meaning and Description
V^e	**Visual External** An event outside of you that you see with your eyes
V^{ir}	**Visual Internal Recall** Visualising an image from the past
V^{ic}	**Visual Internal Construct** Visualising an image that has not happened
V^d	**Visual Digital** (this can appear after a V^e or V^i) Bringing meaning to a word or symbol you have seen

Auditory Notation Codes

Code	Meaning and Description
A^e	**Auditory External** An event outside of you that you hear with your ears
A^{ir}	**Auditory Internal Recall** Imagining a sound from the past
A^{ic}	**Auditory Internal Construct** Imagining a sound that you have never experienced
A^d	**Auditory Digital** (this can appear after an A^e or A^i) Bringing meaning to a sound you have heard
A^{id}	**Auditory Internal Dialogue** Words that you are saying to yourself (inner self-talk)

Kinesthetic Notation Codes

Code	Meaning and Description
K^e	**Kinesthetic External** An event outside of you that you a feeling
K^i	**Kinesthetic Internal** A sensation you feeling inside of you
K^{ir}	**Kinesthetic Internal Recall** Remembering a feeling that you have experienced in the past
K^{ic}	**Kinesthetic Internal Recall** Imagining a feeling that you could have
K^+	**Kinesthetic Positive** Depicting a positive feeling
K^-	**Kinesthetic Negative** Depicting a negative feeling

Olfactory Notation Codes

Code	Meaning and Description
O^e	**Olfactory External** Experiencing a smell
O^{ir}	**Olfactory Internal Recall** Imagining a smell from the past
O^{ic}	**Olfactory Internal Construct** Imagining a smell that you have never experienced
O^d	**Olfactory Digital** Bringing meaning to a smell

Gustatory Notation Codes

Code	Meaning and Description
G^e	**Gustatory External** Experiencing a taste
G^{ir}	**Gustatory Internal Recall** Imagining a taste from the past
G^{ic}	**Gustatory Internal Construct** Imagining a taste that you have never experienced
G^d	**Gustatory Digital** Bringing meaning to a taste

Examples of Notations using Symbols

Code	Meaning and Description
$V^e \rightarrow A^{id}$	**Visual External** leads to **Auditory Internal Dialogue** *When I see something, I ask myself a question*
$\{V^e K^i K^-\}$	**Visual External** immediately causes (synaesthesia) a **Negative Kinesthetic Internal** *When I see something, I immediately feel bad*
A^e / A^{ir}	**Auditory External** being compared to **Auditory Internal Recall** *Comparing what you are hearing to what you remember hearing*

ELICITING A STRATEGY

The following process is how you can elicit a strategy from another person. This is written out as a full session for an NLP Practitioner to follow.

- **Identify your own outcome.**
  As the NLP Practitioner identify the outcome for the strategy elicitation.
  - o Discover behavioural excellence to replicate
  - o Discover a strategy to assist positive change in a client
- **Be in rapport**
  - o Calibrate
- **Identify and agree on the outcome of the strategy**.
  - o Agree on the final decision point.
- **Client Association**
  - o Act out the strategy in real-time if it is possible in the current environment and context or,
  - o Recall a time when they used the strategy.
    - Tell the client to;
      - o *"Be there now"*
      - o *"Can you remember the last specific time…"*
      - o *"What is causing you to know you needed this?"*
    - Elicitation can only start when a client is associated as that is the only time you can accurately document a strategy as it is happening as opposed to a client just remembering the strategy.
- **Communicating in present tense asking the client to walk through a step-by-step description of what is happening.**
  - o *"As you experience this what is the first thing you are doing?"*
  - o *"Is this the first step?"*
  - o *"What are you doing/ seeing/ hearing/ feeling now?"*
  - o *"What's happening now?"*
  - o Calibrate and observe eye accessing to ensure association.
- **Document your observations using NLP notation methodology**
- **Document TOTE steps Next Steps, Actions and Test Criteria**
  - o *"What's next?"*
  - o *"What is the very next thing you are doing?"*

- o Use a *Contrast Frame* to test and compare outcomes and discover the difference that makes the difference for achieving a desired outcome (See Framing)
  - *"How do you know it is right/wrong?"*
  - *"What do you consider before moving on?"*
- **Re-run steps to gather more data.**
  Gather more information and also confirm previous documentation.
  - o Use a *Backtrack Frame* and use Meta Model to chunk down (See sections Framing, Meta Model, Chunks and Chunking)
    - *"Can we go back a run through what you did at this step?"*
    - *"Remind me again how we came to be here at this decision."*
- **Check Well Formed Condition.**
  Re-run the entire strategy again confirming the conditions are met;
  - o Uses all major Representational Systems
  - o The strategy is logical
  - o Each Feedback loop has an exit decision point
  - o The strategy contains an external check.
- **Break State**
- **Re-run the entire strategy.**
  Taking the client through the strategy ensures that it makes sense to them.
  - o Calibrate throughout for editing and streamlining opportunities.
- **Break State**
- **Take the next appropriate action depending on your outcome.**
  - o If appropriate test the strategy for yourself to see if it works.
    - See Installing a Strategy
  - o If appropriate investigate the strategy to identify opportunities for change if the strategy is causing an unresourceful state.
    - Be sure to check ecology before any change work.

Source Material & Further Learning
(1980) NLP: Vol I. The Study of The Structure of Experience, by Dilts, Grinder, Bandler, Bandler, DeLozier: Page 60

INSTALLING A STRATEGY

Once you have elicited a strategy that reliably provides an excellent outcome the next thing to do is to learn or *install* that strategy. The following steps run through how to install any strategy that you wish to learn.

- **Associate yourself with a Coaching State.** (See NLP Coach State)
- **Be in rapport and calibrate.**
- **Identify and agree on the outcome of the strategy being installed.**
- **Future Pace a Mental Rehearsal.**
  From an associated perspective, run through the sequence of operational sensory representational steps and decision points within the strategy to ensure that it provides the desired outcome.
  - o It is important not to edit or streamline the strategy in any way.
  - o Utilise conscious eye movement (see Eye Accessing Patterns) to assist the repetition of the representational systems within a step.
    - V^c: *"Look up and to the right as you take this step"*
    - A^{id}: *"Look down and to the left as you take this step"*
  - o To achieve unconscious competence, repeat the strategy a number of times (minimum of 3). Ensure that you Break State between each run-through.
- **Chaining Anchors.** (See Chaining Anchors)
  - o Set increasingly resourceful anchors to each step in a strategy
    - Ideally, no more than 5 anchors should be chained.
- **Associated Future Pace**
  - o Using a time when the client knows they want to use this strategy
  - o Alternatively, you can use a Metaphor
- **Dissociated Future Pace**
  - o Using a time when the client knows they want to use this strategy
  - o Alternatively, you can use a Metaphor

Source Material & Further Learning
(1980) NLP: Vol I. The Study of The Structure of Experience, by Dilts, Grinder, Bandler, Bandler, DeLozier: Page 220

PART TWELVE:
SUB-MODALITIES

SUB-MODALITIES?

Let's start by explaining what a sub-modality is. Technically speaking, they are subjective subdivisions or subclassifications of our sensory modalities and they allow us to describe our external experiences in much greater detail. However, sub-modalities have a much more powerful use other than just providing more detail for the purpose of description. They are actually responsible for the coding, arranging, ordering and in turn creating our meaning connected to experiences. The power comes from the awareness that not only can sub-modalities provide us with meaning but we can consciously amend a sub-modality and that in turn changes the meaning.

For example, Richard Bandler found during his discovery of sub-modalities that the sub-modality most likely to change the meaning of something in a person is their location and distance from what they are visualising. This is why a common way to commence sub-modality NLP techniques is to start with visual representations and then notice the kinaesthetic and auditory information that comes with that visualisation.

Source Material & Further Learning
(1985) Using Your Brain for a Change, Bandler: Page 22
(1988) Change Your Mind & Keep the Change, Andreas & Andreas: Page 11
(1989) Insider's Guide to Sub-modalities, Bandler & MacDonald: Pages All
(1990) Introducing Neuro-linguistic Programming, O'Conner & Seymour: Page 58

SUB-MODALITY LISTS

Below you will find a comprehensive list of sub-modalities that can be components of how we structure our internal sensory representation.

Visual
What can you see?
- Colour: Colour or Black & White
- Distance: Near or Far
- Position: Location
- Brightness: Bright or Dim
- Scale: Size of the image
- Perspective: Associated or Dissociated
- Focus: Focused or Unfocused
- Movement: Changing or Steady
- Framing: Framed or Panoramic
- Animation: Movie or Picture
- Depth: 3D or 2D

Auditory
What can you hear? Are there any sounds accompanying the visual?
- Position: Location
- Direction: Movement of the sound
- Volume: Loud or Quiet
- Speed: Fast or Slow
- Pitch: High or Low
- Tonality: In tune and harmony or out of tune and harmony
- Timbre: Scale of quality and clarity of the sound
- Tempo: Consistent or pauses
- Duration: Scale of how long the sound exists
- Language: Words or Sounds

Kinesthetic

What can you feel? Are there any feelings or sensations accompanying the visual?

- Position: Location on or in the body
- Size: Large or Small
- Perspective: Internal or External
- Shape: Make-up of the feeling
- Intensity: High or Low
- Direction: Movement of the feeling
- Pressure: Scale of high to low
- Heat: Hot or cold
- Weight: Light and Heavy
- Movement: Growing or Shrinking

Olfactory

What can you smell? Are there any smells accompanying the visual?

- Intensity: Strong or Subtle
- Duration: Scale of how long the smell exists
- Quality: Pleasant or Putrid

Gustatory

What can you taste? Are there any tastes accompanying the visual?

- Intensity: Strong or Subtle
- Duration: Scale of how long the smell exists
- Quality: Sweet, Sour, Salty, Bitter or Umami

Although this is an extensive list, it is not definitive and if you are able to identify more sub-modality categories within a modality then these can be added too. When using sub-modalities within NLP techniques this list is converted into a checklist (See Sub-Modality Checklist). Some of the NLP techniques in this book will use the full sub-modality list in practice and yet for ease of reading and learning a condensed version mentioning just a few sub-modalities as examples will be included. Know that when you come to run the techniques in live coaching situations use as many sub-modalities as is appropriate to get the full benefit of the techniques.

TYPES OF SUB-MODALITY

As you review the sub-modality list you may notice that the criteria for a response is varied depending on the category. Some responses can be binary and yet others can be on a sliding scale. These two types are called *analogue* sub-modalities and *digital* sub-modalities.

ANALOGUE SUB-MODALITIES

These types of sub-modalities are modalities that are always present, continuous and infinite. Think of them as always being *on*. That being said they can vary in form and this variance is somewhere between two limiting qualities. Here are some examples from the list of analogue sub-modalities;

- Visual: Brightness: **Bright <> Dim**
  - *"Notice how bright or dim the image is"*
- Auditory: Speed: **Fast <> Slow**
  - *"Notice how fast or slow the sound is"*
- Kinesthetic: Pressure: **High <> Low**
  - *"Notice how high or low the pressure is"*

DIGITAL SUB-MODALITIES

These types of sub-modalities are modalities that present no scale, they exist as an either/or with instantaneous change. Think of them as being like a binary *on/off* switch. This also means that both variations cannot co-exist. Here are some examples from the list of digital sub-modalities;

- Visual: Perspective: **Associated or Dissociated**
  - *"Are you looking through your own eyes or looking at yourself?"*
- Auditory: Language: **Words or Sounds**
  - *"Do you hear words or is it sounds?"*
- Kinesthetic: Perspective: **Internal or External**
  - *"Is the sensation inside you or something touching your skin?"*

You now have an understanding that there are variations of qualities and criteria for sub-modalities and these variations are the details that go into creating our internal sensory representation that in turn provides us with meaning to an experience. This allows us to understand that our sub-modalities *code* our experience and meaning of reality.

As mentioned, if you consciously change your internal sensory representation by changing the quality of a sub-modality that will in turn change your comprehension and meaning of that experience. We will cover how you can do this in the following NLP techniques.

Before we look at those though it must be understood that not all sub-modalities are equal with regard to their influence on the meaning you put to an experience. You have what is known as *critical* sub-modalities and within those critical sub-modalities, you will have a *driver* sub-modality.

CRITICAL SUB-MODALITIES

Consciously changing a *Critical Sub-Modality* will result in a change of meaning. Whereas non-critical sub-modalities will have little or no impact on your meaning. As our behaviour and state depend on our meaning of a situation, Critical sub-modalities will vary depending on a person's state.

- Visual: Perspective: **Associated or Dissociated**
  - *"No zoom out of your body and look at yourself?"*
- Visual: Brightness: **Bright <> Dim**
  - *"Turn the brightness of the image up"*
- Sound: Volume: **Loud or Quiet**
  - *"Turn down the volume of the noise"*

DRIVER SUB-MODALITIES

A *Driver Sub-Modality* is the one critical sub-modality that has the most impact on the meaning. If the Driver Sub-modality is consciously changed then all the other Critical Sub-modalities will also change. Think of the Driver Sub-Modality as the first domino or a vital linchpin to a system.

SUB-MODALITY TECHNIQUES

With an understanding of what Sub-Modalities and knowing the power they have in creating meaning which in turn impacts how we behave towards an event, let's look at the NLP techniques you can use as an NLP Practitioner and work through how to utilise them for powerful interventions either for yourself or a client you are coaching.

ELICITING SUB-MODALITIES

Before any change technique can be run, we need to find out what we are working with – a baseline so to speak. To do this we need to collect the sub-modality data (or code) of a particular state. This is done by *eliciting sub-modalities*. Below is the step-by-step process of eliciting the sub-modalities (or the code) of a client's state:

Eliciting Sub-Modalities

- **Coach State.**
- **Be in Rapport and Calibrate.**
- **Select the state you wish to elicit sub-modalities of.**
- **Pace and lead the client into an appropriate resourceful state.**
- **Ask the client to experience that state.**
- **Start with asking about the Visual modality.**
  - *"What pictures do you have?"*
  - If this is hard for them to visualize you can;
    - Ask *"If you could see a picture what would it be like?"* (See 'as if' frames)
    - State *"I know you are not aware of an image but pretending there is one, what image have you made up?"*
    - If these do not work then you could continue with another modality assuming an experience of darkness.
- **Gain more detail using the sub-modality checklist.**
  - Once the person acknowledges they have a representation of the experience you can begin to ask

questions about what they are experiencing. The questions you ask will be relevant to gaining detail for each sub-modality on a sub-modality checklist made up from the list you have in the previous section.

o   Be sure to be direct and keep the pace up when asking your questions as it is possible for a person's experience to change as they are describing it.

o   Remember to look for non-verbal cues also such as; eye-accessing patterns, gestures and movements.

o   With awareness of a Coach State, be sure not to suggest or install sub-modalities into the person's experience with your line of questioning. For example

- Don't ask *"As you see this image through your eyes"* assuming Association. Instead, ask *"Are you seeing this through your own eyes or are you in the picture?"*

- Don't ask *"What colour is the image"* assuming Colour. Instead, ask *"Are you seeing images in colour or black & white?"*

- **On completion, Break State**

o   Once you have run down the full checklist and filled it in you now have the detailed code for how that person experiences that state. Once you are complete be sure to break the state (see *Pattern Interrupt and Break State*) bring the person back into uptime and present conscious awareness. An example question for this as a coach could be;

o   *"Nice shoes, where did you buy those from?"*

o   *"Now open your eyes, what colour socks you are wearing today?"*

With the fully completed sub-modality checklist and elicitation complete you are now able to elicit another state. The other state will depend on the desired outcome of the change and also what NLP technique you are using.

CONTRAST ANALYSIS

Contrast analysis is a method for identifying critical sub-modalities, the sub-modalities that have the most contribution to the meaning of the experience. Once you have elicited two states and have full sub-modality checklists complete, compare them and highlight the differences between the two experience structures. These highlighted differences can be pulled out for use in the change techniques as they are the critical sub-modalities that contribute to the difference in meaning across the two states. One of these critical sub-modalities will be the driver sub-modality, however, all the critical sub-modalities are used in the following techniques so it is not essential nor a requirement to know exactly which one is the driver sub-modality.

MAPPING ACROSS

Having completed the elicitation of multiple states and performed a contrast analysis on them to identify the critical sub-modalities you now have all the data you require to proceed with some NLP techniques that utilise this data for change. The concept of *mapping across* is required for you to work through the techniques as it is the essential component for creating change. With the knowledge that consciously changing our sub-modalities will impact our meaning of an experience, mapping across is the process of doing just that. With the critical sub-modalities identified you can have a person create a visualisation of a state and then lead them to change the property of that critical sub-modalities to be that of the desired state within the process, hence the term mapping a sub-modality across from one state to another. Before we move to actual use cases for mapping across it is worth highlighting that in some instances and techniques, it is required to create more than 2 states and a so-called neutral state must be elicited. The reason for this is the concept that if you map over a critical sub-modality over another then it is possible you could create a stuck state as the unconscious mind cannot perform the change. Think of this third state as an eraser, therefore you have a critical sub-modality from the problem (or present state), you then erase this critical sub-modality using the neutral code, and you then write the desired state critical sub-modality to the experience.

Source Material & Further Learning

(1985) Using Your Brain for a Change, Bandler: Page 103
(1989) Insider's Guide to Sub-modalities, Bandler & MacDonald: Pg 73

SUB-MODALITY CHECKLIST

Below is a checklist that you can use for sub-modality elicitation.

	State 1	State 2	State 3	State 4
State Names				
Visual. What can you see?				
Colour / B&W				
Near / Far				
Bright / Dim				
What is the Size				
Where is the Location				
Associated / Dissociated				
Focused / Unfocused				
3D or 2D				
Framed / Panoramic				
Movie / Still				
Changing / Steady				
Auditory. What can you hear?				
Where is the Location				
Direction of Movement				
Loud/Quiet Volume				
Tempo Fast /Slow				
High Pitch / Low Pitch				
Harmonious / Out of tune				

Clarity of the sound				
Consistent / Pauses				
Duration of sound existing				
Words / Sounds				
Kinesthetic. What can you feel?				
What is the Size				
Where is the Location				
Inside you / Outside you				
Any Shape to the feeling?				
Intensity High / Low				
Direction of Movement				
Pressure High / Low				
Hot / Cold				
Heavy / Light				
Growing / Shrinking				
Duration of feeling existing				
Olfactory. What can you smell?				
Strong or subtle				
Duration of smell existing				
Pleasant / Putrid				
Gustatory. What can you taste?				
Strong or subtle				
Duration of taste existing				
Sweet/Sour/Salty/Bitter/Umami				

CHANGING LIKES & DISLIKES

This NLP Technique is used to help people give up a habit they dislike or is unresourceful for them. This could be a food, drink or a habit such as smoking. The process below follows a full coaching session so that you can follow it in the context of being an NLP Practitioner.

- **Coach State**
- **Be in Rapport and Calibrate.**
- **Identify the issue**, habit or thing they would like to dislike.
    - *"What do you like now and would prefer to dislike?"*
        - Example: Stop drinking cola
        - Example: Stop eating chocolate
- **Present State & test the trigger**.
    - Get the client to visualise a moment when they last had this.
    - *"Think back to a moment when you last had this"*
    - Calibrate the response.
- **Ecology Check.** Check for any secondary gain so as to not make a change that creates a conflict elsewhere for the client.
    - *"If you dislike this, what would you have?*
    - *"If you dislike this, what would you not have?*
    - *"If you didn't dislike this, what would you have?*
    - *"If you didn't dislike this, what would you not have?*
- **Desired State** Assuming you did not pick up an imbalance or incongruence you are now able to find a desired state. In this instance, the desired state is something they do not like as this is the code you will want to elicit the sub-modalities for.
    - *"Can you think of something with a similar consistency or texture to what you like and yet you currently really dislike or would not want to consume?"*
    - NOTE: An assumption in this example is made that the *thing* the client wants to dislike is a food or drink.
- **Elicit State 1.** Now with the present state, desired state and congruence we can elicit the states. Get the client to visualise the present state and using the sub-modality checklist, ask the relevant questions to allow you to build up how they code this experience.
    - *"Go back to a moment where you were having the thing you like."*

- o   *"What image can you see?"*
- o   Continue eliciting the sub-modalities with the checklist
- **Break State**
  - o   *"Can you hear that rain outside?"*
- **Elicit State 2.**
  - o   *"Now, think of the thing with a similar in consistency or texture and yet you currently dislike"*
  - o   *"What image can you see?"*
  - o   Continue eliciting the sub-modalities with the checklist
- **Break State**
- **Perform Contrast Analysis**
  - o   Find the differences, the Critical Sub-Modalities
- **Recreate Present State.** Get the client to visualise the thing they like and prepare them for the process.
  - o   *"Now, go back to a moment where you were having the thing you like, with experiencing all the experiences you described earlier"*
  - o   *"What I'm now going to do now is ask you to make some changes to what you are seeing, hearing and feeling."*
- **Map Across** the critical sub-modalities by asking the client to make these changes. These are examples of what this might look like, but please use the critical modalities specific to the client.
  - o   *"Change the picture from colour to black & white"*
  - o   *"Move the sensation from your chest to your gut"*
  - o   *"Change the temperature from hot to cold"*
- **Anchor** this in place
  - o   *"Now, noticing all of this, lock all of this in place"*
- **Test** with a re-run of the Present State
  - o   *"Go back again to that moment of having that thing and what are you noticing now? What is happening?"*
- **Future Pace** and testing the trigger is the last step.
  - o   *"Think of a time in the future when you will have this again. Be there now and what is happening?"*
  - o   Calibrate

VISUAL SWISH PATTERN

This technique is similar to 'Changing a like to a dislike' with the addition being it can be used to change unwanted behaviour and responses. A *visual* swish is the most commonly used Swish Pattern and yet the process can work with any representational system (See Designer Swish). The process below follows a full coaching session so that you can follow it in the context of being an NLP Practitioner.

- **Coach State**
- **Be in Rapport and Calibrate.**
- **Identify the Problem State (Present State) and trigger.**
    - o   Create an associated image of this state.
- **Break State.**
- **Identify the Desired State.**
    - o   Create an associated image of this state.
- **Change two visual analogue critical modalities of the Desired State**
    - o   *"Turn up the brightness of this image"*
    - o   *"Make the colour of the image more vibrant"*
    - o   *"Notice how you are feeling even more positive."*
- **Break State**
- **With eyes closed put both pictures in the same frame.**
    - o   *"Close your eyes and relax, take two deep breaths"*
    - o   *"Create a visual with both of these two images side-by-side"*
- **Shrink the size of the frame of the desired until it is a dot.**
    - o   *"Reduce the size of the desired state image until it is a dot."*
- **Move this dot to the bottom right of the problem state.**
    - o   *"Move the dot to the bottom right of the present state image."*
    - o   Looking down and to the right will create an eye-accessing cue for Kinesthetic encouraging the client to witness feeling.
- **Bring the dot back with ever-increasing velocity.**
    - o   *"Now notice the dot getting larger as it is coming back towards you."*
    - o   *"As it gets closer it is picking up more and more speed"*
- **The image returning is a bright vibrant desired state.**
    - o   *"As the dot gets close enough for you to see the image you can only see the desired state image, even brighter and more vibrant than before"*

- **Build intensity with volume and tempo of voice and as the image passes through them, say the word '*Swish*'.**
  - o *"The image is moving so fast you realise it is not going to stop!"*
  - o *"It is getting closer and closer, faster and faster!"*
  - o *"As the image hits you and you it passes straight through the image, bright vibrant desired image with a flash – SWISSHHHHHH!"*
- **Now in that brightness, clear the screen of what you are seeing.**
  - o *"As you are now deep inside the vibrant clear and colourful image of the desired state, notice how positive and resourceful you are feeling."*
  - o *"Now clear the screen."*
- **Break State** (See Pattern Interrupt)
  - o *"Open your eyes, shake your hands"*
  - o *"What way did you come in this today?"*
- **Repeat the Swish three to five times.**
  - o *"Close your eyes and relax, take two deep breaths"*
  - o *"Bring back the original image with the dot to the bottom right"*
    - Include evolutions of change with each version
      - o *"This old picture is duller than before"*
      - o *"Notice that it is harder to get this old picture back up"*
- **Test the original trigger**
  - o *"Go back to just before the (trigger), be there now."*
  - o *"As you experience the (trigger) what are you feeling?"*
  - o Notice Recall Eye Accessing Cues
  - o Calibrate
- **Future Pace the trigger in the future**
  - o *"Think of a time when you might experience the (trigger) again."*
  - o *"As you experience the (trigger) what are you feeling?"*
  - o Notice Construct Eye Accessing Cues
  - o Calibrate

Source Material & Further Learning
(1985) Using Your Brain for a Change, Bandler: Page 131 (1989) Insider's Guide to Sub-modalities, Bandler & MacDonald: Pg 64

DESIGNER SWISH

This process follows the same steps as the Swish with slightly different content, tailoring the pattern and technique to an individual's critical sub-modalities. This is more likely to be effective in creating change as the technique is using critical sub-modalities that already have meaning attached to them for the person working through the technique. The process below is the Swish again with the steps Designer Swish variances in bold for ease of reference.

- Coach State, Rapport and Calibrate.
- Identify the Problem State (Present State) and trigger.
  - Create an associated image of this state.
- **Elicit sub-modalities of this state.**
- Break State
- Identify the Desired State
  - Create an associated image of this state.
- **Elicit sub-modalities of this state.**
- **Contrast Analysis and identify two analogue critical modalities**
- **Change two analogue critical modalities of the Desired State**
  - ***"Turn up ..."***
  - ***"Make more ..."***
- Break State
- With eyes closed put both pictures in the same frame.
  - *"Close your eyes and relax, take two deep breaths"*
  - *"Create a visual with both of these two images side-by-side"*
- Shrink the size of the frame of the desired until it is a dot.
  - *"Reduce the size of the desired state image until it is a dot."*
- Move this dot to the bottom right of the problem state.
  - *"Move the dot to the bottom right of the present state image."*
  - Looking down and to the right will create an eye-accessing cue for Kinesthetic encouraging the client to witness feeling.
- Bring the dot back with ever-increasing velocity.
  - *"Now notice the dot getting larger as it is coming back towards you."*
  - *"As it gets closer it is picking up more and more speed"*
- **Critical modalities of desired state image are even more enhanced**

- o *"As the dot gets close enough to see the image you can only see the desired state image, more (critical modalities) than before"*
- Build intensity with volume and tempo of voice and as the image passes through them, say the word *'Swish'*.
  - o *"The image is moving so fast you realise it is not going to stop!"*
  - o *"It is getting closer and closer, faster and faster!"*
  - o *"As the image hits you and you it passes straight through the image, bright vibrant desired image with a flash – SWISSHHHHHH!"*
- Now in that brightness, clear the screen of what you are seeing.
  - o *"As you are now deep inside the vibrant clear and colourful image of the desired state, notice how positive and resourceful you are feeling."*
  - o *"Now clear the screen."*
- Break State (See Pattern Interrupt)
  - o *"Open your eyes, shake your hands"*
- Repeat the Swish three to five times.
  - o *"Close your eyes and relax, take two deep breaths"*
  - o *"Bring back the original image with the dot to the bottom right"*
    - Include evolutions of change with each version
      - o *"Notice that it is harder to get this old picture back up"*
- Test the original trigger
  - o *"Go back to just before the (trigger), be there now."*
  - o *"As you experience the (trigger) what are you feeling?"*
  - o Notice Recall Eye Accessing Cues
  - o Calibrate
- Future Pace the trigger in the future
  - o *"Think of a time when you might experience the (trigger) again."*
  - o *"As you experience the (trigger) what are you feeling?"*
  - o Notice Construct Eye Accessing Cues
  - o Calibrate

Source Material & Further Learning
(1989) Insider's Guide to Sub-modalities, Bandler & MacDonald: Pg 81 (1988) Change Your Mind and Keep the Change, Andreas and Andreas: Page 50

CHANGING LIMITED BELIEFS

With reference to the Values section, we can understand that a *Belief* is something that operates mostly at an unconscious level and is something that we know to be true in relation to a *Value* we have.

With the information shared in the Meta Model, we also know how to identify beliefs by understanding how they will appear linguistically as either a Cause-Effect or Complex Equivalent statement

- **Cause-effect**. A person implies a connection between when something occurs (the cause) and another thing then happens as a result (the effect).
  - *"Eating makes me happy"*

- **Complex equivalence.** A person describes an identity that implies there is a meaning synonymous with a person.
  - *"I am not confident"*

So, what is a *limiting belief?* This is a type of belief that operates at an unconscious level, holding us back from achieving what we want to achieve by stopping a particular personal strategy from beginning or playing an alternative strategy. Let's take a closer look at the four different types of limiting beliefs that exist.

FOUR TYPES OF LIMITING BELIEFS

Belief about Cause

This type is if a person has a belief that there is a specific *cause* that is limiting options. The word *because* is generally a key word to highlight these.

- *"Life is a struggle because I never get what I want."*

Belief about Meaning

This type is if a person has a belief that impacts behaviour due to it impacting the meaning you place on your internal sensory representation of the world.

- *"Marriage prevents freedom."*

Beliefs about Impossibility

This type is if a person has a belief that something is impossible therefore creating a scenario where there is no point in even trying.

- *"I just don't know how I can be a good friend to him."*

Beliefs about Identity

This is where a person has placed limitations on the type of person they identify themselves to be.

- *I'm not good enough to be successful*

TWO-STAGE CONTRAST ANALYSIS & MAP ACROSS

We have covered all the techniques used within this technique and pattern of belief change and yet there is a slight variance to complete this process correctly and make it as effective as possible.

As we know now our sub-modalities create and change *meaning* and their impact on a *belief* is no different. For every belief, we will have a sub-modality code for it. With this considered the Belief Change technique is one where we want to take a belief with a resourceful positive code and install that to replace the code associated with the unresourceful, disabling, limiting belief.

IMPORTANT NLP PRACTIONER NOTE:

It is important to acknowledge the two stages of this process as we are dealing with a person's beliefs with this technique. The two-stage element is fundamental in ensuring that we do not leave a client with beliefs coding that is mixed up or in conflict after the work is complete.

The aim of this technique is not just to overwrite the limiting belief with an empowering belief, it is actually to remove the limiting belief and then add an empowering belief.

The process below follows a full coaching session so that you can follow it in the context of being an NLP Practitioner.

- **Coach State, Rapport and Calibrate.**
- **Identify the issue**, or belief they would like to change.
  - *"What issue do you want to work through?"*
  - *"What belief is holding you back?"*
- **Present State & test the trigger.** Get the client to visualise a moment when they experienced the limiting belief.
  - *"Think back to a moment when you last had this"*
  - Calibrate the response.
- **Desired State** Get the client to define their desired outcome.
  - *"If that is how you are, how do you want to be different?"*
- **Ecology Check.** Check for any secondary gain so as to not make a change that creates a conflict elsewhere for the client.
  - (+/+) *"If you have this, what would you have?*
  - (+/-) *"If you have this, what would you not have?*
  - (-/+) *"If you didn't have this, what would you have?*
  - (-/-) *"If you didn't have this, what would you not have?*
- **Break State**

- **STEP 1: MAP 'NO LONGER TRUE' TO 'CURRENT BELIEF'**
- **Elicit State 1: Present state 'Limiting Belief' (Current Belief).** Having the present state, desired state and congruence we can elicit the sub-modalities of these states. Get the client to visualise the present state and using the sub-modality checklist, ask the relevant questions to allow you to build up how they code this experience.
  - *"Go back to a moment where you were experiencing this."*
  - *"What image can you see?"*
  - Continue eliciting the sub-modalities with the checklist
- **Break State**
- **Elicit State 2: A belief that is 'No Longer True'.**
  - *"Now, think of something that you used to believe and you no longer do."*
    - Childhood memories and beliefs are good for this.

  o *"What image can you see?"*
  o Continue eliciting the sub-modalities with the checklist
- **Break State**
- **Perform Contrast Analysis** to obtain Critical Sub-Modalities
- **Recreate Present State.** Get the client to visualise the 'Limiting Belief'.
  o *"Now, go back to a moment where you were you were aware of this limiting belief, picture all the experiences you described earlier. Be there now."*
      - Associated
  o *"What I'm now going to do now is ask you to make some changes to what you are seeing, hearing and feeling right now."*
- **First Map Across the 'No longer True' to the 'Current Belief'.** Using the identified critical sub-modalities ask the client to make changes to the sub-modalities so that they match the 'No longer True'. Here are examples, but use the client's specific critical modalities;
  o *"Change the picture from colour to black & white"*
  o *"Move the sensation from your chest to your gut"*
  o *"Change the temperature from hot to cold"*
- **Anchor** this in place
  o *"Now, noticing all of this, and lock all of this in place."*
- **Test** with a re-run of the Present State
  o *"Go back again to that moment of experiencing the belief?"*
  o *"What is happening now?"*

- **STEP 2: MAP 'ABSOLUTELY TRUE' TO 'DESIRED BELIEF'**
- **Elicit State 3: Desired state.** Get the client to visualise the desired empowering state and using the sub-modality checklist, ask the relevant questions to allow you to build up how they code this experience.
  o *"Think of a moment where you were experiencing how you want to be."*
  o *"What image can you see?"*
  o Continue eliciting the sub-modalities with the checklist
- **Break State**
- **Elicit State 4: A belief that is 'Absolutely True'.**
  o *"Now, think of something that you know to be 100% true, absolutely true."*
      - A common example is a sunrise.
  o *"What image can you see?"*

- o Continue eliciting the sub-modalities with the checklist
- **Break State**
- **Perform Contrast Analysis** to obtain the Critical Sub-Modalities
- **Recreate Desired State.** Get the client to visualise the 'Desired State'
  - o *"Now, go back to a moment where you are how you want to be, picture all the experiences you described earlier. Be there now."*
    - *Associated*
  - o *"What I'm now going to do now is ask you to make some changes to what you are seeing, hearing and feeling right now."*
- **Second Map Across the 'Absolutely True' to the 'Desired State'** Using the identified critical sub-modalities, ask the client to make changes to the sub-modalities so that they match the 'Absolutely True' sub-modalities.
- **Anchor** this in place
  - o *"Now, noticing all of this, and lock all of this in place."*
- **Test** with a re-run of the Desired State
  - o *"Go back again to that moment of how you want to be."*
  - o *"What is happening now?"*
- **Break State**
- **Future Pace and testing the trigger** is the last step.
  - o *"Think of a time in the future when you will have do the (trigger) again?"*
  - o *"Go to a moment just before it is happening"*
  - o *"Be there now and what is happening?"*
  - o Calibrate

Source Material & Further Learning

(1985) Using Your Brain for a Change, Bandler: Page 103
(1988) Change Your Mind and Keep the Change, Andreas and Andreas: Page 179

COMPELLING FUTURE

The technique of creating a *compelling future* utilises some of the prime directives of our unconscious mind, our Direction Filter meta-program, as well as some neuroscience. Let's pick out these specific prime directives of the unconscious mind;

- To control and maintain all perceptions
- To generate and maintain instinct and habit in order to respond
- To build habits after experiencing repetition
- To follow the principle of least effort

With reference to these, if we construct a thorough compelling future event using all of our sensory representational systems our unconscious mind will look out for opportunities to achieve this with the least amount of effort.

So, what actually makes something compelling? If something is compelling it will make use of our Direction Filter meta-program (Towards or Away) and in the case of a compelling future, towards pleasant or away from unpleasant.

Neuroscience also comes into this NLP technique as with a clear compelling future our Reticular Activating System (RAS) is activated. This is responsible for many things but in the context of this technique, it controls what we pay attention to, or said another way, what we do not delete from our experiences. This clearly impacts our map of the world and has a big impact on our perceptions. This is why RAS is connected to concepts like the law of attraction. With a mention of the Law of Attraction, I must draw attention to the fact that in NLP we believe in *action* as well as manifestation, a common omission from using this technique! (See 3 Legs of NLP)

With the background of this technique in place let's look at the process of actually creating a compelling future with sub-modalities so as an NLP Practitioner you can either create one for yourself or help clients create the kind of world and future they want.

The process that follows is how a full coaching session could be performed so you can see it working in the context of being an NLP Practitioner.

- **Coach State, Rapport and Calibrate.**
- **Identify a compelling future state.** Ask the client to visualise a consequence that compels them to take action. If the client wishes to keep the compelling consequence private, they can also do this. All you will need to know is whether they are motivated towards a pleasant consequence or away from an unpleasant one.
    - *"Can you think of something that would compel you to take action?"*
    - *"Be there now."*
    - *"Tell me if you moved away from something or towards something?"*
        - Example Action: Cooking your favourite dinner
        - (Towards) Eating great food you like.
        - (Away): Not being hungry.
- **Elicit 'Compelling' State.** Elicit the sub-modalities with the checklist
    - *"What image can you see?"*
    - *"What sounds can you hear?"*
    - *"What feelings can you feel?"*
    - *"What thoughts can you think?"*
- **Break State.**
- **Identify an uncompelling future state.** Ask the client to visualise a consequence that is unpleasant and does not compel them to take action. Be sure to get the client to use the same Direction Filter (Towards or Away) as they create this consequence.
    - *"Can you think of something that would not compel you to take action?"*
    - *"Be there now."*
    - (Away) *"Losing weight and yet I still do not exercise enough"*
    - (Towards) *"Getting fitter and yet I still do not exercise enough"*
- **Elicit Sub-Modalities of 'Uncompelling' State.**
- **Break State.**
- **Ecology Check.** Check for any unconscious conflict that would occur if you made the current example of uncompelling compelling.
    - *"Imagine taking action on the thing that is currently uncompelling?"*
    - *"Does any part of you have any objections?"*

- If the answer is *'yes'* then deal with these objections accordingly before moving on.
- If the answer is *'no'* move to contract analysis
- **Perform Contrast Analysis** to obtain the Critical Sub-Modalities
- **Map Across the 'Compelling' to the 'Uncompelling'** Using the identified critical sub-modalities ask the client to make changes to the uncompelling sub-modalities to be like the compelling sub-modalities.
- **Anchor** this in place by saying
  - *"Now, noticing all of this, and lock all of this in place."*
- **Test** with a re-run of the uncompelling future state
  - *"Go back again to that moment of experiencing the uncompelling (trigger)?"*
  - *"What is happening now?"*
- **Break State**
- **Future Pace a compelling future for a well-formed outcome**
  - All Well-Formed Outcome Conditions were adhered to with specific attention placed on ecology.
  - *"Thinking of all that you want to achieve in the future. Think of a moment after you have achieved it all."*
  - *"Be there now. Notice what you are noticing."*
    - *"What are you seeing and hearing having achieved this?"*
    - *"What can you smell in the moment?"*
    - *"What are you feeling having achieved this"*
- **Enhance 'Compelling' sub-modalities.**
  - An optional additional step can be placed here to increase the intensity of the critical sub-modalities.
- **Break State**
- **Calibrate**

Source Material & Further Learning
(1988) Change Your Mind and Keep the Change, Andreas and Andreas: Page 34

SUB-MODALITIES OF TIME

Sub-modalities are the distinctions and details a person has to distinguish between experience and therefore meaning. If we refer to one of the prime directives of the unconscious mind;

- **Organise Memories**
    - To store our memories our unconscious mind organises them using indexes. One such index is the perception of time:
        - Temporal: Past, present and future.
        - Atemporal: Independent of and unaffected by time.

With this, we can understand that one of the most important distinctions a person can have with regard to memories is that of time. Specifically, how we put experiences into a sequence and what we measure to understand events that have happened before and after other events.

ELICIT A TIMELINE

As with all the other aspects of a map, each person uses their own filter for processing time. As an NLP Practitioner, we can learn to understand how a person measures time by initially eliciting their timeline. The basis for this technique is simple, you find two points in time (*the past* and *the future*) and then connect them with a straight line. This being the person's *timeline*. The process that follows how as an NLP Practitioner you can facilitate a client eliciting their timeline.

- **Associate the client.**
    - *"Relax and take two deep breaths"*
- **Identify the past.**
    - *"If you were to point to your past. Where would that be?"*
    - If a client finds it hard then calibrate for a gesture.
- **Identify the future.**
    - *"Now, point to your future. Where would that be?"*
- **Identify the 'now'.**
    - *"Now, point to where 'now' is. Where would that be?"*

In most cases the results will be one of the following;

- Past is behind the person and the future is in Front
- Past to one side (often their left) & future on the other side
- The now is inside the person
- The now is slight in front of the person

Whichever the result given, if you would have them create an imaginary line drawn from the *past* point to the *future* point, through the *now* point that is what we call a person's timeline.

SORTING IN-TIME OR THROUGH TIME

The next aspect of how a person can organise time is that they are either what we call; *Through Time* or *In-Time*. These are important distinctions as they provide much more information about a person's preferences and behaviour than you might think.

Through Time

A *Through Time* person generally has their timeline outside of themselves often seeing memories being recalled from a dissociated perspective. Their future and past can be from side to side slightly in front of them with the 'now' being a spot just in front of where they physically are. They have a good awareness of time, whether that is the duration of an event or being on time for an event to start, feeling negative if they are late. They prefer to plan, stick to schedules and work to deadlines. If we make reference to meta-programs their *Adjustment Response* preference is usually '*Judging*', giving them a good sense of value and appreciation for time.

In-Time

An *In-Time* person generally has their timeline run through their body with their future normally in front of them and past behind, with the 'now' being associated inside of themselves. They live being associated in the present and also recalling memories from an associated perspective. They have a poor awareness of time passing, preferring not to plan and being free-spirited reacting to events and seeing how things go, both qualities that align with the meta-program of *Adjustment Response* preference for being a '*perceiver*'.

TIME LANGUAGE PREDICATES

With all of these aspects of time considered you can now understand that, much like the sensory modalities and sub-modalities have their predicates, when people communicate using words related to time, they are actually communicating how they perceive and measure time. Below are some examples of words and phrases that can help you identify a person's time preferences.

• After	• Past
• Before	• Periodically
• Beginning	• Restart
• Consecutive	• Since
• Elapse	• Stop
• End	• Succession
• Finally	• Then
• Finish	• Until
• Last	• Waiting
• Next	• While
• Now	• Yet

Phrases you might hear a person use with a visually preferred modality:

- *"Time is always on my side"*
  - o Through-Time
- *"Let's plan ahead of time"*
  - o Front / Back
  - o Through Time
- *"I like to be in the now"*
  - o In Time
- *"When I look back at the past"*
  - o Front / Back
  - o In Time

PART THIRTEEN: FRAMING

FRAMING

To explain framing let's first look at two pieces of information;

1. One of the ways we represent the world; is the World of Meaning.
   - *The world of attaching meaning to a sense*
   - *The meaning we attach to a language?*

2. The 4-Tuple of sensory representation;
   - *Visual (Seeing)*
   - *Auditory (Hearing)*
   - *Kinesthetic (Feeling)*
     - *Olfactory (Smelling)*
     - *Gustatory (Tasting)*
   - *Digital (Meaning via Language)*

With reference to these let's consider that an event in itself has no meaning. The meaning only comes from what we sense and then attach a meaning to. With this meaning also comes context and depending on the context our meaning and understanding of information can be impacted.

The meaning we derive from context is what we call *Framing*. There are a number of *frames* identified and used within NLP, each impacting the line of questioning required to obtain more information and understanding about an actual event.

Source Material & Further Learning
(1979) Frogs into Princes, Bandler & Grinder: Page 175 (1981) Reframing, Bandler & Grinder: Page 162 (1994) Precision, Grinder & McMaster (1994) The Enneagram and NLP, Linden & Spalding

BACKTRACK FRAME

This frame is simply a verbal recap and repeat of the information presented in the immediately preceding portion of a conversation.

This could be used to;

- Bring a conscious refresh of important information
- To update or bring up to speed, a new person to a discussion

OUTCOME FRAME

This frame is simply a statement that presents and in turn, directs a discussion towards a desired outcome. The frame should have specific information defined enabling the agreement of what is relevant to a discussion in order to take the next steps.

This is appropriate to use;

- At the start of a conversation or discussion that has the intention of achieving a desired outcome
- In combination with a Relevancy Challenge Frame to decide if the direction of the discussion is on track and relevant to achieve the outcome.

RELEVANCY CHALLENGE FRAME

This frame's purpose is to challenge a point (content) being made by connecting the point to the desired outcome and seeking the belief that it is a relevant contribution for the purpose of progressing towards the outcome. A relevancy frame removes any interpersonal issues in a discussion due to its focus on the Outcome Frame.

This could be used to;

- Keep a discussion on track
- To provoke a deeper explanation of the content presented

AS IF FRAME

This frame is one that pretends something is true or has already happened in order to see what is possible and what would be the consequences of an action that was the result of a decision to be made. Here are four ways you can 'play out' an event to either check congruence with a proposed decision to enable full agreement or to discover current deletions in reasoning;

- Context of Time.
    o A future moment when an event has happened.
- Context of People
    o A moment when a particular person is present
- Context of Information
    o A moment when all the required data is available
- Context of Function
    o A moment where all the actions required to achieve the outcome have been fulfilled

This frame is about possibility so another way of understanding the options you have for an *As If Frame* could be to consider what the very opposite of this frame is where it is pointless even proceeding or imagining the outcome is possible, which could be called the 'Impossible Frame' or 'Helpless Frame'.

OPEN FRAME

This frame is one that enables a discussion to have no predetermined options for the contributor to choose or answer from. This allows for a broader spectrum of information to be obtained. This is done by being asked open questions where a contributor can provide information based on their interpretation of how they wish to answer.

- How would you describe it?
- What do you think is possible?

The opposite would be closed questions with a binary set of answers;

- Would you like option A or option B?

DISCOVERY FRAME

This frame has the purpose of freeing up imposed restrictions and expectations in order to discover new information and options or allow the opportunity to learn by ignoring limiting beliefs.

Example questions to elicit this frame could be;

- "Imagine if you knew you couldn't fail"
- "Just for a moment forget about the outcome and think about what action you could take"

CONTRAST FRAME

This frame simply compares and evaluates the difference between two or more things. Most NLP techniques and successful strategies contain contrast frames as it is the function of which to test results to consider whether progress towards a desired outcome has happened or is happening. In particular, the frame is responsible for understanding what the difference that makes the difference is (a very well-known NLP phrase).

This could be used to;

- Test a result against a desired outcome
- Test a result to see if action within a strategy is progressing towards a desired outcome
- Compare information to discover differences
- Compare outcomes to discover the difference that makes the difference in achieving a desired outcome

ECOLOGY FRAME

This frame is a future-orientated frame. It focuses on evaluating the impact of an outcome on a wider context of meaning and over a period of time that extends past the achievement of the outcome.

It also takes into account the impact and consequences of the outcome on the wider system of life contexts such as family, friends or professional pursuits, in accordance with your values and beliefs.

To collate information for this frame it can be beneficial to look at the outcome (or consequences of) dissociated and through their eyes – associated with them.

This could be used to consider the;

- Long-term impact of your actions & outcome
- Impact of the outcome on other aspects of your life
- Impact of the outcome on other people and stakeholders
- Gain a dissociated opinion free from your own emotions

AGREEMENT

This frame takes into account that we all operate from our own maps of the world which include; beliefs, and attitudes and therefore make decisions and judgements based upon them. The frame provides us with a way to effectively communicate acknowledging this and therefore reducing resistance in a discussion. To summarise the frame is stating something that can be agreed on.

There are a number of linguistic rules for this frame that allow a response to build upon a contribution in a discussion as opposed to shutting it down or dismissing it. Here are some opening phrases to use;

- "**I agree** with what you are saying **and…**"
- "**I respect** the point you have made **and…**"
- "**I appreciate** that **and…**"

Although it may seem similar, do not use the word '*understand*' as a variation of these phrases as that word is a predicate from the digital representational system used for meaning and its use ignores the fact that we are all operating from our own unique maps and that we cannot possibly fully understand another person's point from their map.

You will also notice the word *'and'* being used at the end of each example shown. It is important to use *'and'* and not use the word *'but'* in an agreement frame as the word *'but'* communicates that you have negated, dismissed and deleted the contribution the other person has previously stated. For example,

- "**I agree** with what you are saying **but**…"
  - *'but'* = dismissive, deletion and exclusion
- "**I agree** with what you are saying **and**…"
  - *'and'* = acknowledges, addition and inclusion

An agreement frame can work well to;

- Find a resolution when there is conflict within a discussion
- Open a negotiation
- Reduce resistance in adding alternative opinion

ABSURDITY

This frame can create a change of thinking by exaggerating certain aspects of a statement. By making a situation ridiculous it can challenge thought patterns and create new options. Although this frame at first may trigger negative states or stuck states in people, ultimately it can induce creativity for new ideas and solutions.

This could be used to;

- A change or thinking on an opinion, strategy or outcome
- Break out of a stuck state where there is an apparent lack of options.

PART FOURTEEN:
REFRAMING

REFRAMING

With the information shared in the *Framing* section, we can understand that an event in itself has no meaning. The meaning only comes from what we sense and then attach a meaning to. With this meaning also comes context and depending on the context our meaning and understanding of information can be impacted. Where *Framing* is about obtaining more data and information via particular frames to derive what meaning we have attached to an event in a context, *Reframing* is a way to change a perception of an event therefore changing the meaning. We know that we behave in a particular way based on an external event (trigger) and our understanding of that event. With this considered, *reframing* can be used to change a person's meaning of an event and in turn, create a change in response and behaviour. There are two basic types of reframing that we can use to change our meaning of an external event;

CONTEXT REFRAME

Context Reframing is where we focus on making a behaviour constant and comparing contexts. It is a form of generalisation that works well for issues such as limiting beliefs. With a Context Reframe you can recall a time when you were behaving in a desired way in another context, then acknowledging the behaviour is possible, you change the context to the one where you believe that behaviour is not possible and yet you want it to be. Here is an example for someone who wants confidence in public speaking at work;

Initial Frame
- *I'm too passionate in management meetings.*
    - o **Behaviour**: too passionate
    - o **Situation Context**: management meetings
    - o **Life Context**: work

Reframe
- The behaviour is constant and context changes
    - o Where would this behaviour be useful?
        - *Being that passionate is exactly why you are a great salesperson.*
    - o In what situation would this behaviour serve you well?
        - *Being that passionate makes you such a great football manager.*

CONTENT REFRAME

Content Reframing is where we focus on keeping the content of a trigger consistent and yet change the meaning or intent of an external trigger (event) enabling our response and therefore our behaviour to change. This works well when a person finds themselves in an unresourceful state as a result of an event and wants to be able to change their response. With a Content Reframe, you can think of a situation when you witnessed the same sensory evidence (content) of the trigger and yet it had an alternate meaning. Here is an example of someone upset with comments from their boss at work;

Initial Frame
- *Before I go home my boss keeps upsetting me by always commenting and criticising my work leaving me no time to react.*
    - o **Content:** Boss comments on work before going home
    - o **Meaning:** To criticize my work with no time to react
    - o **Response:** Upset

Reframe
- The content is constant and the meaning changes
    - o What is the positive intention of this behaviour?
        - *It must feel good that your boss wants you to do the best work you can.*
    - o What else could this behaviour mean?
        - *Is he commenting on improvements so you can get a promotion?*

Whether you are coaching a client or self-coaching, whichever reframe you choose Context or Content the outcome should be moving towards a more resourceful state.

Source Material & Further Learning
(1981) Reframing, Bandler & Grinder: Page 162

SIX-STEP REFRAME

To help explain the six-step reframe let's first look at two pieces of information;

1. NLP Presupposition
   - Present behaviour represents the best choice available
     - *The reasoning behind every behaviour is a positive intent*
     - *The behaviour is the best choice available*

2. Prime Directives of the Unconscious Mind.
   - To run the system
   - To preserve the system
   - To take direction and follow orders
   - To have the inability to process a negative
   - To build habits after experiencing repetition

This information builds a consideration that some of our behaviour is out of our conscious control and it is controlled by our unconscious mind to adhere to one or more of its prime directives. The one we wish to focus on with the six-step reframe is that all behaviour has a positive intent. It is either positive by nature or it is the best option available to us.

Now the issue with the behaviour being unconscious is that you are unable to consciously stop or change the behaviour. This results in either you responding in a way you consciously do not wish to or it can result in a lack of action in something you wish to do but your unconscious habits are stopping you.

The six-step reframe is an NLP technique that acknowledges that you cannot consciously change an unconscious habit or response with just your conscious mind. The evidence for this is that if you just wanted to stop behaving in a certain way then you just would by thinking about stopping it!

When you are struggling to stop a habit, it is a good indication that there is an unconscious secondary gain that is important to you that benefits from the undesirable behaviour.

The aim of this NLP technique is to find the intention, discover another way to congruently satisfy the intention and ensure that way is more ecologically sound for you.

The six-step reframe works by creating what is called a second-order change. It is accessing the positive intent of the behaviour and using the principle of systemic thinking, in that the functions and intent of our behaviour can be replaced to create a better equilibrium of the whole system.

This may be a technique that, on the path to becoming an NLP Practitioner, can offer some challenging concepts as it can actually be fully effective purely at an unconscious level. Something that possibly before the Unconscious and Conscious Mind section you would not have been able to comprehend. By working purely at an unconscious level, we mean that consciously you may have absolutely no conscious answers as you follow the steps and yet the process will be operating perfectly well.

Another aspect of the six-step reframe is that the technique uses something called *parts*. Let's look at these in more detail and explain what they are.

PARTS

Parts is simply a metaphor for a part of you wanting one thing and another part of you wanting either the same thing or something different. Either way, each Part must be acknowledged, respected and framed as existing.

Here are a few examples of when finding the positive intent of the unconscious mind with the *Six-Step Reframe* is useful;

- Unwanted habits
- Psychological blocks
- Undesirable Physical Symptoms
- Feeling of Sequential Incongruence
- Reframing the secondary gain

Let's move on to the technique with importance placed on the first step in defining the behaviour you want to change. Make sure it is the right one!

The Six-Step Reframe Pattern.

Step 1: Present State

First, you need to identify the behaviour. You can do this by asking

- *"What behaviour would you like to change?"*
- *"What issue do you want to work through?"*

As an NLP Practitioner, as previously mentioned it is not important for you as the coach to know the behaviour, as long as the client knows that is fine.

Look out for language such as;

- *"I want to do this, but something stops me"*
- *"I want to stop doing it but I can't"*
- *"I don't want to do this, but I seem to keep doing it just the same"*
- *"I want to break this habit"*

Step 2: Establish communication with the responsible part.

Next, you need to go into your unconscious mind to communicate with the specific part of you that is responsible for generating the unconscious behaviour.

You want that part to communicate with your conscious mind by sending a signal of some kind. Start by asking,

- *"Will the part of me that makes me do this be willing to communicate with consciously?"*

Now pay attention, this communication may be a sensation or involuntary movement (K), it may be a picture (V), a sound (A) or an inner voice (Ad). It may not be a signal in the format or form you might expect.

When you get the communication or signal the next thing to do is thank the part for communicating and to then establish that response as an affirmative

BECOME AN NLP PRACTITIONER WITH NLP PRINCIPLES

response from the part. You do this by simply asking.

- *"Thank you for communicating"*
- *"Will it be possible to use this signal as a sign of being in agreement? As though you are saying 'yes'?"*

At this point, you should be able to witness the signal again and calibrate it as a 'yes' response. If for whatever reason the signal does not reoccur then you can ask for a 'yes' response and pay attention for a response. You can at this stage also request a 'no' answer which may appear as a variance in sub-modality such as; brightness, volume or intensity depending on the modality.

Step 3: Establish and separate positive intent.

In order to separate the behaviour from the positive intention we first must identify what the positive intent is. You can do this by asking,

- *"I am aware that the behaviour has good intentions and it has served me well in the past and we intend to hold onto this positive intention."*
- *"Would the part responsible for the behaviour be willing to let me know consciously what you are trying to achieve that has value for me?"*

If you get a 'no' response you can ask

- *"Can you recognise a circumstance where this would be possible"*

If you get a 'no' response still then you can try reframing or possibly start to use chunking up (see Milton Model) questions until you get a 'yes'. With a 'yes' signal the next stage of this step is to get conscious confirmation,

- *"With awareness of this does your conscious mind accept this intention of the behaviour?"*
- *"Do you have the right part that generates this behaviour?"*

With conscious acceptance of the positive intent of the behaviour, which can be the moment where secondary gain comes to conscious awareness for the first time, it is time to ask the Part if it can be open to separating the behaviour from the positive intent.

- *"If there were ways to accomplish your positive function that would work as well as, or better than this behaviour, would you be interested in trying them out?"*

Look for a 'yes' signal and acknowledge this with a thank you.

- *"Thank you"*

Step 4: Create the alternative behaviours

The next step is one that does not actually require any conscious awareness of the work being undertaken.

First, we need to acknowledge there is a *creative part* of you that is able to create a number of alternate creative solutions (new behaviours) to achieve the desired positive intent. We can then communicate to it.

- *"Is the part responsible for this behaviour aware of the creative part of you? The creative part that has access to everything the unconscious mind holds."*
- *"Can you communicate with the creative part and ask it to search through all memories and experiences to generate more choices to accomplish the same positive intent that are at least as good if not better than the original option"*
- *"Thank you to the Creative Part for helping and generating and providing us with these options"*
- *"Can the part responsible for the original behaviour signal a 'yes' when it selects and accepts a new choice and keep going until three have been selected."*

Look for multiple 'yes' signals before moving to the next step.

Step 5: Get acceptance of responsibility

The next step is to future pace your unconscious mind and the part responsible for the behaviour to obtain acceptance of responsibility for using these alternative behaviours. Do this by asking

- *"Is the part responsible for the behaviour willing to take responsibility for using the three new alternatives in the appropriate context?"*

If you get a 'no' response at this stage, go back to the creative part and ask for more alternatives that are better than the original behaviour.

Step 6: Check ecology and integrate fully
Ensure congruence

The last step checks the new behaviours for any conflict that may occur. Ask the question,

• *"Is there any part of me that objects to any of the three new alternatives?"*

Depending on the response it may be that you have to loop back to Step 4 and create new alternatives. If there is a persistence of a negative response at this stage then it may mean you have to repeat the technique from Step 1, but this time with a more awareness consciously and unconsciously of the behaviours.

Source Material & Further Learning

(1979) Frogs into Princes, Bandler & Grinder: Page 137
(1981) Reframing, Bandler & Grinder: Page 114
(1994) Trance-Formations, Bandler & Grinder: Page 147

PARTS INTEGRATION / VISUAL SQUASH

The NLP technique called *Parts Integration* can help resolve an issue related to incongruent values that are in conflict. Let's consider the Presuppositions, *'Present behaviour represents the best choice available'*. As every behaviour has a positive intent, we can understand that the *part* of the person making a decision based on a particular value is choosing the best choice of behaviour available to it at any moment in time based on what it is aware of. The aim of Parts Integration is to make two conflicting parts aware of a higher-level positive intent and possibly an overarching Value that both of the parts share. Having this perspective will then bring more choice and flexibility of behaviour and resolve the conflict. The process shared below is known as a *Visual Squash* which is a method of integrating parts that utilises visual anchors. The process is documented in the context of a full session and assumes that you already have elicited the hierarchy of values for the client.

- **Be in Coach State**
- **Be in rapport and calibrate**
- **Identify the Problem State (Present State) and trigger.**
  - o The client will most probably present this as a dilemma.
    - *'On one hand [x] and on the other hand [x]'*
- **Break State**
- **Identify the two conflicting values**
  - o Referred in this procedure as Value A and Value B
- **Apply the Part for Value A to the palm of a hand**
  - o *"Hold both your hands out in front of you in the air palms faced up."*
  - o *"On one hand hold a representation of the value being held by a part."*
  - o *"Make it a clear representation of what you see, feel and hear."*
    - Associated and VAK sensory representations
- **Apply the part for Value B to the palm of the other hand**
- **Starting with the most unresourceful part find the positive intent**
  - o *"Starting with the most unresourceful part I like you to consider what the intent behind that value is"*
  - o *"Can you think of an example and give me a sign when you have it."*
    - Calibrate for a sign and confirm with the client
  - o Using the Meta Model find the highest-level positive intent for

that Part. On each question tap under the hand to suggest with a kinesthetic touch to the person to go higher.

- Seek permission to touch the hand first then
- Tap and ask *"What is the purpose of…"*
- Tap and ask *"What is important about…"*

o Indications of highest intent are;

- Repetition
- You hear *'that is it'* or *'because it is'*
- A Nominalisation
- An End Value from their elicited Hierarchy of Values

- **Repeat the process for the second hand.**
  o It's possible the client may reach the same intent for each part.

- **Consciously identify the resources associated to each Part**
  o *"With the awareness of each part, acknowledge that they both hold useful resources that can help you."*

- **Open communication and cooperation of the Parts**
  o *"Each part can now recognise the resources the other part brings to you."*
  o *"Knowing this information and understanding the conflict is preventing the achievement of their intention, each part can now consider the good in the other part and use these resources to be more efficient and effective."*
  o *"Each part is now aware they have a lot in common and agree to integrate"*

- **Integrate the Parts together**
  o *"Holding the parts, turn your hands inwards, palms are facing."*
  o *"As quickly or as slowly as your unconscious mind wishes bring your hands together and bring each part together to form a whole part.*

- **Integrate the whole part inside**
  o *"With this single whole part in your hands, pull your hands towards your body and recognise all the resources within it that are now available to you.*
  o *"Hold them inside of you and seal them in"*

- **Test the original trigger, and future pace the trigger.**

Source Material & Further Learning
(1979) Frogs into Princes, Bandler & Grinder: Page 129

PERCEPTUAL POSITIONS

An important piece of knowledge you have as an NLP Practitioner is that everyone has their own map of the world (territory). With this comes a variance of meaning and perception. The Perceptual Position technique is used to provide insight into another person's perspective and understanding of a shared experience or situation. To use a metaphor imagine you are in a field with three friends all facing each other. In the middle of you all is a big 6ft high and wide, three-sided column on the floor, each side big enough for you not to be able to see around the corners. Each side of this box is a different colour. As you look at the colour it creates a feeling inside of you. Although you are all looking at the same object it is not possible for you to see the colour that your friends are seeing. Later you are describing to another friend what you have seen. You all agree that the box existed and yet each of you describes a completely different feeling and colour of the experience. With this example we can understand that no one is wrong in their description of the box and experience, all of the descriptions are 'partially' true. Each one is a limited experience depending on each person's perspective. Based on the work of Gregory Bateson, John Grinder and Judith DeLozier we are provided with a model of three perspectives;

First Position
This is a perspective of a person's own reality out of their eyes. This is the '*I*' position. A person in this position is said to be in an associated state to the experience, connected to their emotions.

Second Position
This is from an associated perspective through the other person's eyes. It is how that person sees the world with you in it. This is the '*You*' position. This is the basis for empathy if the person is in an associated state and the basis of understanding if the person is in a dissociated state. To achieve this position, you will hear things like;
- Step into their shoes
- See it through their eyes into this situation
- Hear it from their perspective
- Think how they would think

Third Position
This is also an associated perspective and yet it is generally a dissociated state from the perspective of the third person. It is how that person sees the world

with both you (First Position Person) and the other person (Second Position Person) in it. This is the 'They', 'Meta' or 'Observer' position. This is the basis for seeing an unbiased relationship between two people due to the dissociation from the situation. This position is used for independent reasoning.

The Perceptual Position techniques we will cover are with regard to the context of relationships.

PERCEPTUAL POSITION TECHNIQUE

This technique explores the relationship two people have together. By using perspectives, the technique aims to bring awareness and resolve issues such as conflict that are causing an unresourceful state in a person.

- **Coach State**
- **Be in rapport**
- **Present State (Problem State) Identify what to work through.**
  - o Understanding an interaction
  - o Understanding an unresourceful state triggered by a person
  - o Explore a resourceful relationship
- **Problem State & find the trigger.**
  - o Get the client to visualise a moment when they experienced the limiting belief.
  - o *"Think back to a moment when you last had this"*
- **Desired State** Get the client to define their desired outcome.
  - o *"If that is how you are, how do you want to be different?"*
  - o *Understand the relationship*
- **Ecology Check.** As an NLP Practitioner, you would now check for any secondary gain so as to not make a change that creates a conflict elsewhere for the client. This is done via an ecology check.
  - o (+/+) *"If you have this, what would you have?*
  - o (+/-) *"If you have this, what would you not have?*
  - o (-/+) *"If you didn't have this, what would you have?*
  - o (-/-) *"If you didn't have this, what would you not have?*
- **Break State**
- **Set the three positions**

o *"Please choose three locations in this environment to represent each of the three positions. The first location will be your associated position. The second will be the associated position from the other person's perspective. The third position will be an associated position for an unrelated neutral onlooker to the relationship and situation of you and the other person."*

o It is good to encourage the client to choose a location for the third position at a distance that allows them to visualise the entire situation.

- **Elicit First Position**

  o *"Please be in location one, position one, be there now (describe the present state situation if necessary), seeing what you see, hearing what you hear, feeling what you feel."*

  o *"As you consider the relationship what is happening from your perspective?"*

  o Check for associated language 'I'

  o Calibrate

- **Break State to neutral current time**

- **Elicit Second Position**

  o *"Please be in location two, position two, and let's look at this relationship from another perspective, the perspective of the other person. Become that person, see what they see, hear what they can hear, feel what they can feel."*

  o *"As you become this person describe in their words the relationship what is happening?"*

  o Check and ensure the client becomes associated (perspective) as them using the language 'I'

  o Calibrate

- **Break State to neutral current time**

- **Elicit Third Position**

  o *"Please be in location three, position three, and let's look at this relationship from another perspective, the perspective of an unrelated neutral person detached from this situation with no preconceptions. Become that person, see what they see, hear what they can hear, feel what they can feel as they look at you both."*

  o *"As you become this person describe in their words the relationship and what is happening?"*

  o Check and ensure the client becomes associated (perspective) as them using the language 'I'

- o Calibrate
- **Gain advice and insight from the third position.**
  - o *"I'm curious to know the opinion of this person as you are experiencing the relationship. What advice would you give these two people about their relationship at this time?*
  - o Check and ensure the client becomes associated as them using the language 'I'
  - o Calibrate
- **Break State to neutral current time**
- **Return to First Position**
  - o *"Please be in location one, position one, be there now (describe the present state situation if necessary), seeing what you see, hearing what you hear, feeling what you feel."*
  - o *"Now, as you acknowledge the other two positions, consider and take inside all that has been said."*
  - o *"As you consider the relationship now what is happening from your perspective? What do you now know?"*
  - o Check for associated perspective language 'I'
  - o Calibrate
- **Break State to neutral current time**
- **Future Pace**
  - o Calibrate

Source Material & Further Learning
(1985) Using Your Brain for a Change, Bandler: Page 37 (1981) Turtles All The Way Down, De Lozier & Grinder: Page 197

META MIRROR

Robert Dilt's evolved this technique to include a fourth position, calling it a Meta Mirror. With this fourth position or *meta-meta* position, a person is able to dissociate further from the advice provided by the third position. As the pattern and process is similar to the Perceptual Position the process is condensed below only expanding on the variances.

- **Present State (Problem State). Identify what to work through.**
- **Problem State & find the trigger.**
- **Desired State**
- **Ecology Check.**
- **Break State**
- **Set the four positions**
  - o *"Please choose four locations in this environment to represent each of the four positions. The first location will be your associated position. The second will be the associated position from the other person's perspective. The third position will be an associated position for an unrelated neutral onlooker to the relationship and situation of you and the other person. The fourth location will be an associated position of someone observing the person in the third position."*
- **Elicit First Position**
- **Break State to neutral current time**
- **Elicit Second Position**
- **Break State to neutral current time**
- **Third Position**
- **Gain advice and insight from the third position.**
- **Break State to neutral current time**
- **Fourth Position (Meta-Meta or Meta Observer Position)**
  - o *"Please be in location four, position four, and consider the advice, reaction and feeling the third person has provided."*
  - o *"How is the third person specifically relating to you in the first position? What are their feelings towards you in the first position?"*
  - o *"How would you in the fourth position describe the attitude, emotions and feeling of the person in the third position?*

- o   Elicit this Third Position information
- **Break State to neutral current time**
- **First Position with Third Position opinion**
  - o   *"Please be in location one, position one, be there now (describe the present state situation if necessary)."*
  - o   *"Now seeing what you see, hearing what you hear, associate yourself and feel all that the third Position feels. Feel, (List third position information)"*
    - • *For example, "Now feel as angry as the third position feels"*
  - o   Calibrate
- **Break State to neutral current time**
- **Return to Second Position**
  - o   *"Please be in location two, position two, be there now."*
  - o   *"Consider how the relationship is different to before with all that is now known and seeing the (first position) with all these new resources."*
  - o   *"What do you now know?"*
  - o   Check for associated language 'I'
  - o   Calibrate
- **Break State to neutral current time**
- **Return to First Position**
  - o   *"Please be in location one, position one, be there now (describe the present state situation if necessary), seeing what you see, hearing what you hear, feeling what you feel."*
  - o   *"Now, as you acknowledge the other positions, consider and take inside all that has been said."*
  - o   *"As you consider the relationship now what is happening from your perspective? What do you now know?"*
  - o   Check for associated language 'I'
  - o   Calibrate
- **Break State to neutral current time**
- **Future Pace**

Source Material & Further Learning
(1990) Changing Belief Systems with NLP, Dilts: Page 190

PART FIFTEEN:
LEARNING

CIRCLE OF LEARNING

As we come to the end of the NLP Practitioner syllabus this seems to be a perfect place to introduce the *Circle of Learning*. This model can be referred to by several titles; Maslow's Learning Circle, the Awareness Model, the 4 stages of Learning, the Learning Ladder or the Hierarchy of Competence.

I'm sure by now you have realised that the NLP Practitioner syllabus contains a lot of learning for you, some of which you still need to review and practice. You will also have awareness that this content is just the start of the knowledge to be gained within the discipline of NLP.

This model reveals the journey that you have been taking through competence and awareness on your path to mastering this new capability. Although we refer to it as the Circle of Learning if we are to return to the origin of this model it would be called the *Hierarchy of Competence*, first published by Martin M. Broadwell in 1969. The model follows 4 stages;

1. Unconscious incompetence
2. Conscious incompetence
3. Conscious competence
4. Unconscious competence

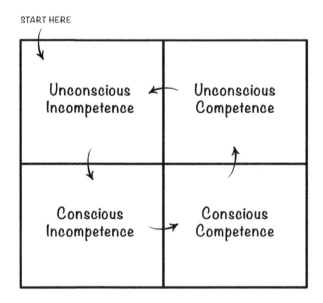

332

Let's take a look at what is happening at each stage.

Stage one: Unconscious Incompetence
You are not aware of what you do not know.
This is where a person does not consciously know what they don't know. This is a place of ignorance resulting in no associated negative emotion or feeling and can result in a person being overconfident in a situation when they are unaware of a deficit in knowledge or capability.

Stage two: Conscious Incompetence
You are aware of what you do not know.
This stage is where a person becomes consciously aware that they can't do something or the amount of knowledge they are lacking in a subject or capability. This is the stage where negative emotions can occur as a person considers the gap between their abilities and what is required. If there is no perceived value in the competence being achieved this is where a person can exit. At this stage via practice, mistakes happen and these should be considered a valuable path to learning competence.

Stage three: Conscious Competence
To perform what you know requires focus.
Here a person becomes aware that the capability is possible for them and they are able to do the thing that they are learning. At this stage focus and attention are still a requirement and yet with it the person can be fully capable. This is the stage where confidence is built.

Stage four: Unconscious competence
To perform what you know does not require focus.
At this stage, you have a learned skill. The capability has become habitual to the extent that you can perform with ease at an unconscious level, requiring no conscious attention or focus. This is the stage that can lead to mastery.

Stage five (or one again!): Unconscious Incompetence
You are not aware of what you do not know.
You will notice that there is an arrow in the unconscious competence box that loops back to unconscious incompetence. This is not a mistake! When things become an automatic skill or second nature, being overconfident in a situation and unaware of a deficit in knowledge or capability can once again occur resulting in a new instance of Unconscious Competence can occur.

I wonder, 'What stage are you at with your NLP learning?'.

FEEDBACK 'SANDWICH' MODEL

We already know that feedback lets you know if you are getting or getting closer to what you want. Although Feedback has made an appearance in the Presuppositions of NLP and also Well-Formed Outcomes in that; 'There is no such thing as failure only feedback' that however is not the specific aspect of feedback we are covering here. Feedback is information that flows between people that has to do with their interactions in the here and now. When the information which proceeds backwards from the performance is able to change the general method and pattern of performance, we have a process called learning. This section looks at how you can provide and indeed receive feedback in the most effective, resourceful and ecological way. Let's look at giving feedback first. The model we will use is one often referred to as the hamburger model or sandwich model. As common as it is known, it is equally misunderstood and misused.

GIVING GOOD FEEDBACK
Most importantly before giving any feedback whether you are in a coaching role or not you must be in rapport with the person receiving the feedback.

With that let's look at the model and steps.

THE MODEL
This way of casing the criticism reduces the impact of triggering a negative response from the receiver as well as making the whole experience much more positive. There is also the additional benefit of our unconscious mind taking in the comments and digesting them to influence future behaviour appropriately.

1) Start with something positive.
"What did they do well?"
State something positive about what you are giving feedback on.
2) Explain what could be improved.
"What would have been even better if?"
Give a recommendation to improve something from your perspective. The aim being to provide corrective feedback resulting in a change a behaviour.
3) End with something positive.
"What you also did well is?"
End your feedback with something more positive.

RECEIVING FEEDBACK EFFECTIVELY

When requesting and receiving feedback it is important to get yourself in the correct state and mindset to enable yourself to maximise the benefits. Within NLP, feedback is seen as an essential component to progressing and achieving outcomes. As you now can see feedback can only ever be useful and once in possession of it, you can choose from your perspective whether it is useful and helpful or not. As Wyatt Woodsmall frequently comments during his training 'Feedback is the breakfast of champions'!

A State for Feedback

Here are a few other things to consider when on the receiving end of feedback. Firstly, ensure that the person giving feedback has the sandwich model. With that in place, you can focus on you and the feedback.

1. Be in a resourceful state
2. Be in Uptime
3. Maintain Rapport
4. Don't take it personally!

With learning being the ultimate outcome here is a guide on how you should receive and embrace feedback positively.

Positive - Do	Negative - Do Not
• Listen Carefully • Acknowledge • Clarify • Check • Evaluate • Incorporate • Observe further • Gratitude	• Argue • Deny • Justify • Surrender • Defend • Distort • Forget • Sulk

EXTENDED EDITION: MASTER PRACTITIONER CONTENT

BONUS PART ONE:
META-PROGRAMS

INTRODUCTION META-PROGRAMS

If we refer to the Communication Model let's pay attention to the filters that impact our internal representation (map) along with the universal models of; deletion, distortion and generalisation. This section focuses on one of these filters, the filter called Meta-programs. The filter named meta-programs is actually more of a category that contains a number of filters (or programs) that we run on the data we receive. We use these individual meta-programs to process our internal representation of the world and they therefore impact our thoughts and behaviour. These meta-programs operate mostly at an unconscious level although we are able to bring awareness to them, which is the intention of this section. As a result of the research and work completed initially by Richard Bandler, Leslie Cameron-Bandler and later by David Gordon, Robert Dilts, Maribeth Meyers-Anderson and Wyatt Woodsmall, a list of meta-program patterns that are common amongst us all were discovered. These patterns (meta-program filters) provide preference structures which impact our preferred behaviour based on the data our sensory representational systems were processing. They therefore considerably impact our decisions and course of action to achieve outcomes and in some instances could actually change the desired outcomes. Meta-programs are frequently confused and misunderstood as putting an identity on a person based on their meta-programs or preferences. With a focus on the word 'choice' and with flexibility in mind, if we were to consider that these meta-programs mean this is the ONLY way a person can process information then we would be removing choice and flexibility of behaviour. What meta-program patterns present are decision points for which a person unconsciously makes a choice. This unconscious choice will be made to move towards resourcefulness and away from unresourcefulness and yet we must acknowledge that the *choice* is there and the option to take either path is possible. This in turn allows us to know there is no right or wrong path to take there is only a preferred one that left unchallenged the unconscious mind will always take. With all this in mind, a meta-program preference can be affected by the context in which it is being run.

Source Material & Further Learning for Meta-programs

(1988) Time Line Therapy & Basis of Personality, James & Woodsmall: Page 91
(1990) Metaprograms, Wyatt Woodsmall (Self-published)

META-PROGRAM PATTERNS

The following pages share the meta-programs along with questions that you can ask to gain an understanding of a person's preferences that lead to behaviour. As an NLP Practitioner, these will give you a clearer understanding of another person's map of the world.

Meta-program	Meta-program preference types
External Behaviour	Introvert /Extrovert
Internal Processing	Sensing /Intuition
Internal State	Feeling / Thinking
Adjustment Response	Perceiving / Judging
Direction Filter	Towards / Away
Action Filter	Proactive / Inactive / Reactive
Frame of Reference	Internal / External
Reason Filter	Options (Possibility) / Procedure (Necessity)
Relationship Filter	Difference / Sameness / Same with Exception
Scope Filter	Global / Detail
Convincer Channel	See / Hear / Read / Do
Convincer Mode	Automatic/ Times / Chronological / Consistent
Primary Interest Filter	People / Place / Thing / Activity / Information
Work Preference Filter	People / Place / Thing / Activity / Information
Management Filter	Self / Self & Others / Others

EXTERNAL BEHAVIOUR
Introvert / Extrovert

This meta-program reveals the preference for gaining energy. In particular, it will uncover whether the source of energy is inside or outside of a person. If someone gains energy from other people or outside influences this is *extroversion* and a person who prefers to gain energy from within by spending time with their own thoughts shows a preference for *introversion*. Here is an example question with answers to enable insight into this preference;

- *"When you are low on energy and need to recharge your batteries, do you prefer to be with others or alone?"*
  - *"With others."*
    - Extroversion
  - *"Alone."*
    - Introversion

INTERNAL PROCESSING
Sensing / Intuition

This meta-program reveals the preference for our source of information. In particular, it will uncover how a person likes to gain and process data. If someone prefers to use their senses (Visual, Auditory, Kinesthetic) to obtain information and fact is considered as *Sensing* and a person that prefers to use their unconscious Digital sense of meaning to process data is considered as *Intuition*. Here is an example question with answers to enable insight into this preference;

- *"When you make decisions, is observing evidence important to you or do you generally work off of your hunches?*
  - *"Evidence is important and the more the better."*
    - Sensing
  - *"Even if evidence is there I tend to just know."*
    - Intuition

INTERNAL STATE
Feeling / Thinking

This meta-program reveals what we prefer our internal state to be when making decisions. In particular, it will uncover the elements of a decision strategy that are important to them to make the best decision. If someone prefers to be guided by an emotional connection to the decision even if it appears illogical, this would suggest *feeling* and a person who prefers to use logic, criteria and a dissociated view of the decision and outcome shows a preference for *thinking*. Here is an example question with answers to enable insight into this preference;

- *"Do you consider how a client will feel after a successful project or do you just want specifications so you can start?"*
  - o *"I just want the client's definition of success criteria to start"*
    - o Thinking
  - o *"The client feeling happy is the most important thing."*
    - o Feeling

ADJUSTMENT RESPONSE
Perceiving / Judging

This meta-program reveals how a person prefers to deal with the outside world. In particular, it will uncover the elements of a decision strategy that are important to them to make the best decision. If someone prefers to live with structure and purpose valuing things such as systems, plans and schedules this would suggest *judging* and if a person prefers to be more spontaneous, the kind that goes with the flow this could show a preference for *perceiving*. Here is an example question with answers to enable insight into this preference;

- *"When you are organizing a party do you have a clear plan or do you just invite people and see how it goes, looking forward to embracing any surprises that brings?"*
  - o *"Oh no, I need a plan!"*
    - o Judging
  - o *"What's the point in planning, it will be what it will be!"*
    - o Perceiving

DIRECTION FILTER
Towards / Away

This meta-program reveals a motivational preference. In particular, it will uncover whether a person moves *towards* what they want or whether they prefer to move *away* from what they don't want. Note that this is an important meta-program with regards to 'well-formed outcome conditions' as no matter the personal preference an outcome must always be stated with towards language. Here is an example question with answers to enable insight into this preference;

- *"What would you like the outcome of the game to be?"*
  - *"Well, I don't want to lose!"*
    - Away
  - *"I want to win of course!"*
    - Towards

ACTION FILTER
Proactive / Inactive / Reactive

This meta-program reveals the preference you have for combining taking action and being reflective. Your preference here is about how and when you start to take action. Someone proactive will reflect on the go not analysing before they start whereas a reactive preference will see a person reflect before taking action. A Reflective preference is just that and no action is taken. Lastly inactive is absent of reflection and action. Here is an example question with answers to enable insight into this preference;

- *"When you something needs to be done what do you do?"*
- *"I start! The quicker you start the better! Assess as you go."*
  - Proactive
- *"I assess the situation and then take appropriate action."*
  - Reactive
- *"I like to gather as much information as possible before I start"*
  - Reflective
- *"I have a habit of putting things off that need to be done"*
  - Inactive

FRAME OF REFERENCE
Internal / External

This meta-program reveals where someone will prefer to judge information and results from. In particular, do they seek *external* sources of information to compare against or do they base the comparison on their own *internal* inner standards? In addition, a good sign of a person being *internal* is that they interpret an external instruction as information to process and consider rather than it being a decision made for them to take immediate action. Here is an example question with answers to enable insight into this preference;

- **"What do you judge your standards against when someone says you have done a good job?"**
  - *"The fact they have told me it's a good job."*
    - External Referenced
  - *"They might say 'good job', but I know I could've done better."*
    - Internal Referenced

REASON FILTER
Options (Possibility) / Procedure (Necessity)

This meta-program reveals why someone is motivated to choose a particular option. In particular, it will uncover whether they do things due to necessity or because they want to open up opportunities. People with a preference for *necessity* tend to ask how to do something as opposed to why and like to follow *procedure*. A person with a preference towards *possibility* and *options* will like to investigate options and feel the need to expand on any lists provided with their own contribution. Here is an example question with answers to enable insight into this preference;

- **"Why did you do it that way?"**
  - *"That is how it must be done."*
    - Procedure (Necessity)
  - *"We looked at all the ways to do it and decided that was right."*
    - Options (Possibility)

RELATIONSHIP FILTER
Difference / Difference with Exception / Sameness with Exception / Sameness

This meta-program reveals the primary preference for how a comparison is made between a group of items, behaviours or ideas.

This meta-program can be linked to how a person is generalising data. A person noticing the similarities is considered to have a *sameness* preference. Someone who immediately notices the difference across things is considered to have a preference of *difference*.

The blurred lines within this meta-program are that of a person who notices both the same and difference. Even though both are being utilised it can be seen that there is a slight variance in the way a person that sees the similarities first and then sorts the group by what they then see is different, known as *sameness with exception*. In much the same way a person can have a preference for spotting differences and then goes seeking for similarities, *difference with exception*.

Here is an example question with answers to enable insight into this preference;

- *"If you were to look at your current job and your last job, how do they compare?"*
    - *"It's in the same industry, same role, same hours"*
        - Sameness
    - *"It's in a new town with new people and better opportunities"*
        - Difference
    - *"It's the same job but with a different company"*
        - Sameness with exception
    - *"It's a new company but the same job"*
        - Difference with exception
        -

SCOPE FILTER
Global / Detail / Global then Detail / Detail then Global

This meta-program reveals the preference for receiving information with regard to the chunk size.

In particular, it will uncover whether the person prefers to only get the *details* so they can take action. People with a *detail* first preference are focused on the sequence of events, the step-by-step details trusting the process to get the outcome, or not having any investment or connection to the outcome.

People with a *global* preference will like to see and feel connected to the overall picture and overview of the main outcome with little to no requirement on how to actually obtain the outcome.

There is obviously a place between these two extremes for people who have a preference for the big picture and then require the details, *global then detail*, and people that want to know what to do next and yet feel the need to be connected to the overall direction, *detail then global.*

Here is an example question with answers to enable insight into this preference;

- **"If we are to start working on this today, what do you need to know from me?"**
    - o *"Why are we doing this and what is the end goal?"*
        - o Global
    - o *"I just need to know what the first thing you need done is."*
        - o Detail
    - o *"What is the end goal and what do you need me to do."*
        - o Global then Detail
    - o *"What needs doing first and provide me with the plans so I can review the overall spec later.*
        - o Details then Global

CONVINCER CHANNEL
See / hear / read / do

This meta-program reveals the preference for which sensory representational system is used to convince someone to believe something is true. The preference reveals a person's preferred modality to trigger a belief; visual (see something), auditory (hear something), kinesthetic (feel or experience something) or digital (connect meaning). Here is a question to gain insight;

- *"How do you sense and know someone is good at what they do?*
- *"I will see them do it with my own eyes."*
  - See (Visual)
- *"When I hear people talking about how good they are."*
  - Hear (Auditory)
- *"I would have to do it with them to fully know."*
  - Do (Kinesthetic)
- *"I like to read about how they perform at what they do"*
  - Read (Digital)

CONVINCER MODE
Automatic / number of times / chronological / consistent

This meta-program reveals the preference of how we become convinced after we have got information in our Convincer Channel. A preference for *Automatic* is a 'benefit of the doubt' preference whereas a preference for *Consistent* would need to be convinced in every instance. *Number of times* and period of time are self-explanatory. Here's a question to gain insight;

- *"How many times would you have to witness that to believe it?"*
- *"Until I see otherwise, I would assume it's true."*
  - Automatic
- *"Twice is enough to know it is true."*
  - Number of times
- *"I would assess their performance over the year"*
  - Chronological (aka. Period of time)
- *"Each time is different, so every time!"*
  - Consistent (aka. Never)

348

PRIMARY INTEREST FILTER
People / place / things / activity / information

This meta-program reveals the preference for where and what you put primary importance on in a situation. This shows up when you are asked to recall a favourite place. Here is a question to gain insight;

- *"Tell me about what you like about your favourite shop?"*
- *"The people there are so nice."*
  - People
- *"It is in such an inspiring place and the layout is great."*
  - Place
- *"They have the best clothes there."*
  - Things
- *"It's easy to shop there and the experience is perfect."*
  - Activity
- *"The level the information and detail they provide is great."*
  - Information

MANAGEMENT FILTER
Self / self & others / others

This meta-program reveals the preference of how we mostly direct our attention with respect to self and others. Namely, do you put yourself before others (Self), and vice versa (Others) or do you take into account the wider system? Here is a question to gain insight;

- *"What would you think if you took the last item on a shelf?"*
- *"Lucky me!*
  - Self Only
- *"There is probably someone in more need of this than me"*
  - Others
- *"It's not a problem as once I buy it, I can share it"*
  - Self and Others

WORK PREFERENCE FILTER
People / place / things / activity / information

This meta-program reveals the preference for what we find important about a situation in the context of work. It is similar to Primary Interest and yet the change in context can bring about a variance in preference. Here is a question to gain insight into a person's preference;

- **"Tell me about the last work situation you really enjoyed?"**
- *"It was when the whole team was last in"*
  - People
- *"It was in our old office"*
  - Place
- *"It was when we had better computers for the day"*
  - Things
- *"It was during the last project we were working on."*
  - Activity
- *"It was when we had a clear brief to work to."*
  - Information

Source Material & Further Learning for Meta-programs
(1988) Time Line Therapy & Basis of Personality, James & Woodsmall: Page 91

META-PROGRAMS AND BEHAVIOUR

Let's focus on four of the basic dichotomies in order to gain an understanding of the kinds of behaviour you will see in a person and how as an NLP Practitioner you can use this to aid instruction or task allocation effectively within teams based on people's preferences within certain meta-programs. The four meta-programs that are focused on here are the ones shared with the Myers Briggs Type Indicator (MBTI). If you are familiar with MBTI then you will notice the letters which represent the preference correlate to the four-letter code you get to describe a person's preference with MBTI.

- **External Behaviour**
    - o The source of energy is inside or outside of a person.
        - An *Introvert* (I) will have a preference for being;
            - Reflective
            - Inwardly focused
            - Think first
            - Focus on thoughts
        - An *Extrovert* (E) will have a preference for being;
            - Active
            - Outgoing
            - Prefers face-to-face interaction
            - Act first
- **Internal Processing**
    - o How a person likes to gain and process data.
        - A *Sensing* (S) person will have a preference for;
            - Data
            - Facts
            - Reality
            - Accuracy and precision
        - An *Intuition* (N) person will have a preference for;
            - Utilising hunches
            - Generalisations
            - Focusing on associations

- Meaning

- **Internal State**
  - o The state in which a person likes to make decisions.
    - A *Feeling* (F) person will have a preference for;
      - Personal opinion
      - Being Subjective
      - Sympathy
      - Appreciativeness
    - A *Thinking* (T) person will have a preference for;
      - Logic
      - Objectiveness
      - A bias towards impersonal
      - Binary analysis

- **Adjustment Response**
  - o How a person prefers to deal with the outside world.
    - A *Perceiving* (P) person will have a preference for being;
      - Flexible
      - Spontaneous
      - Reactive
      - Pending
    - A *Judging* (J) person will have a preference for being;
      - Organised
      - Planned
      - Decisive
      - Systematic

META-PROGRAMS AND COMMUNICATION

With these same four meta-programs that align with MBTI, we can begin to build some knowledge up about how people prefer to receive communication based on their meta-program preferences. The suggestions listed below provide a guide for effective communication so as an NLP Practitioner you work in a team environment and still have an impact on individuals operating from a resourceful state to get the best from them.

- **Extrovert (E)**
    - Speak with speed and brevity
    - Provide quick response
    - Be animated and energetic
    - Speaking loudly is accepted
    - Be enthusiastic

- **Introvert (I)**
    - Leave pauses for them to think
    - Don't break a silence too quickly
    - Be calm and considered
    - Speaking quietly is preferred
    - Communicate with text or email first

- **Judging (J)**
    - Be decisive
    - Be clear on the goals and outcomes with time frames
    - Avoid open-ended communication
    - Don't provide miscellaneous information
    - Allow an opportunity for them to advise

- **Perceiving (P)**
    - Be open-minded
    - Only provide structure when it is really needed
    - Be flexible
    - Be guided by them
    - Negotiate a path of action

INFLUENCING WITH META-PROGRAMS

To give you an idea of how large this topic can be and exactly how unique we all are, let's look few combinations that provide us with guidelines on how best to communicate with or present tasks to people based on a combination of preferences. Now imagine how many combinations there are with all the meta-programs you know from the section of the book!

- **Sensing (S) & Thinking (T)**
    o Be prepared in advance with facts
    o Bring proof of facts and relevant documentation
    o Start in a logical position and manner
    o Avoid vague details and miscellaneous information
    o Detachment does not mean they are disinterested

- **Sensing (S) & Feeling (F)**
    o Start with personalised introductions and personal interest
    o Be warned they will ask for personal details of you
    o Be sensitive to telling them they are wrong and hurting feelings
    o Go the extra mile as it will be appreciated
    o Be observant when it comes to non-verbal communication

- **Intuitive (N) & Feeling (F)**
    o Be interested in their vision
    o Be authentic
    o Be a problem solver and not a problem or issue creator
    o Be prepared to be asked about your own ideas
    o Pauses can insinuate there is a disagreement

- **Intuitive (N) & Thinking (T)**
    o Avoid setting or acknowledging rules
    o Allow for freedom of expression
    o Offer opportunities for them to be their unique-self
    o Get straight into business and don't chit-chat
    o Take into account broad trends rather than current details

BONUS PART TWO:
UTILISING VALUES

UTILISING VALUES

As values and beliefs are largely responsible for what a person puts effort into working to move towards or working to move away from, they are significant things for a person to understand if they have issues with motivation, procrastination or inner conflict across two or more contexts of life. *Values Elicitation* is an NLP technique that utilises the Meta Model to gain insight into a person's values. The process below follows a full coaching session so that you can see it in the context of being an NLP Practitioner. Be aware that there can be a lot of content to capture during this session so ensure that you have everything set up to enable you to document what your client is about to say.

VALUES ELICITATION

- **Be in rapport**
- **Identify a single life context.**
    - o For example; Work, Health, Relationships, Finances, Romance.
        - • See *Wheel of Life* for more.
- **Start the elicitation**
    - o *"In the context of (single life context), can you describe something that is significant, relevant, and important to you?"*
- **Obtain more and chunk down**
    - o *"Can you describe something else that is significant, relevant, and important to you in the context of (single life context)?"*
    - o *"What is important to you about that?"*
    - o *"What does that give you?"*
    - o *"What do you gain from having this?"*
        - • *You can repeat these types of questions several times*
- **When the client feels complete check for more unconscious values.**
    - o *"Can you recall a specific time when you were fully motivated in the context of (single life context)? As you remember this time what are you feeling? What is the very last thing you are feeling? Can you put a name or label to that feeling?"*
        - • Chunk down on this once you have something new.

At this stage, you will have a list of words that include all of the values your client has within a single context. The next step is to put these into some kind of order, a hierarchy to be exact.

VALUES HIERARCHY

Not all values are equal. Unconsciously we have our values arranged in a hierarchy of importance, with the most important one being referenced as a priority. This technique will illustrate this as well as enable a client to understand their own hierarchy of values contained within a single context.

- **With the list of values words (labels) written down ask the client to group together all the words that they feel represent the same thing and which word ultimately represents the whole group of words.**
    - o The additional benefit to doing this step is that the words that have been identified as meaning the same thing can be used as the words and language to construct the belief statement.
- **As a starting point ask the client to select the most important value.**
    - o *"From these values, if you could only select one, what would it be?"*
- **Now create the full hierarchy.**
    - o *"From the values remaining, if you could only select one, what would it be?"*
    - o Place the value words in a list in order of what gets selected
- **Check the hierarchy by comparing two adjoining values.**
    - o *"If they could have one but not the other how does that feel?"*
    - o The client will communicate which one is the most important.
- **Take the least important value of this pair and use that to compare with the next adjoining value.**
    - o Note that if one value gets swapped (is stated as more important) then you must revisit the value that immediately preceded that pair as a new adjoining pair.
        - It is possible to see a value jump up the list two or more spaces during this process.
- **Repeat the previous step until the full list is complete.**
- **With a fully completed hierarchy run through the entire list and calibrate for congruency.**

VALUES UTILISATION

With a known list of values, values utilisation can be used to create a meaningful resourceful state in a client by creating a compelling future paced proposition.

Below is a list of example values and how you would do fulfil this NLP technique for a client.

Example Values list on the life context of Work

- *Achievement*
- *Trustworthiness.*
- *Reliability*
- *Passion*
- *Creativity*

From this list of values create a utilisation statement that includes them all in the order they appear in the hierarchy.

- **Be in rapport**
- **Create an associated Future Pace utilisation for the client.**
  - o *"Imagine a moment sometime in the future in your business. You take a moment to look around, listen and acknowledge the feeling of **achievement** as you have built a company and team that fully demonstrates and has a reputation consisting of all of your personal work values. The **trustworthiness** of your team shows up in their relationships with you, each other and your clients. Your company is known for **reliability** often a differentiator for you winning new business. This coupled with your **passion** to provide your best **creative** work is also the reason clients stay with you for such a long time."*
- **Calibrate**
  - o *"As you hear this what is happening, what are you feeling?"*

CONFLICTING VALUES

TOWARDS VALUES AND AWAY FROM VALUES

As we have mentioned previously a Value is either something a person will work toward or away from. This can show up as wanting something or avoiding something, thinking something is right to have or wrong to have. Understanding the direction of each value in a hierarchy can be useful if a person communicates having a dilemma as an issue. This stuck state could be a result of indecisions caused by two values with opposing directions. In order to discover the directional motivation for a value a person is required to chunk up as opposed to chunking down. Here is a list of values a person could have and how you would do fulfil this NLP technique for a client.

Example of four Values within the life context of Relationships;

- *Love, Loyalty, Trustworthiness, Reliability, Loneliness*

- **Be in rapport**
- **Run down the hierarchy one at a time eliciting the direction of each value by chunking up.**
    - o *"In the context of (single life context), **why** is (Value) important to you?"*
    - o *Listen for towards and away language.*
        - *Model operators of necessity*
        - *Negative phrases*
- **With an answer, you may find you need to use the Meta Model to chunk down and investigate further if you need to.**
    - o For example, *"**What** about that is important to you"*

The result of this session could create a motivational hierarchy as follows;

- *Love (Towards)*
- *Loyalty (Towards)*
- *Trustworthiness (Towards).*
- *Reliability (Towards)*
- *Loneliness (Away from)*

BECOME AN NLP PRACTITIONER WITH NLP PRINCIPLES

MEANS VALUES AND END VALUES

There is one other aspect of the definition that we can attach to these values now that we have the list elicited with this level of detail. This is whether the value is a *Means Value* or an *Ends Value*. You will know when you have elicited an *Ends Value* as the person will state something along the lines of *'Because it just is important'* when being questioned. Ultimately the End Value will be describing a desired emotional state. A Means Value on the other hand is a value that will move you towards the End Value and the associated emotional state. Using the list already illustrated this could look something like this with *Love* (feeling *love*) being the desired emotional state.

- *Love (Towards) (End Value)*
- *Trustworthiness (Towards) (Means Value)*
- *Reliability (Towards) (Means Value)*
- *Loneliness (Away from) (Means Value)*

SIMULTANEOUS INCONGRUITY

With regards to helping a person be in a more resourceful state, the purpose of understanding the properties of a value in this much detail is to help identify two values that may be in conflict resulting in an unresourceful problem or stuck state. These two values may be occurring at the same time within two *parts* of a person (see Parts Integration) whether that is unconscious or conscious. This conflict is called *Simultaneous Incongruity*. A clue in identifying a *Simultaneous Incongruity* will be that a person's conscious communication through words (verbal language) will be incongruent with their unconscious non-verbal communication. An example of this might be that you hear a person say 'yes' and as they say the word, they are shaking their head from side to side, non-verbally communicating 'no'. Another example may be that they state a dilemma, *'On the one hand I want this and on the other hand I want that'*. This can occur when two values are pulling or pushing in the same direction and yet have different desired outcomes:

- *"I want the creative job and the money and yet I also want my freedom"*
  - *Towards/Towards*
- *"I don't want to be alone and yet I don't want to feel controlled by anyone"*
  - *Away/Away*

SEQUENTIAL INCONGRUITY

There may also be times when a person has two values from two parts that are working in opposing directions causing an issue for a person. In these instances where a person has the pull of a *towards* value and the push of an *away from* value happening it is called a *Sequential Incongruity*. A clue in identifying a *Sequential Incongruity* will be that a person's behaviour and desired motives can seemingly change from time to time. An example of this might be that you witness a person going to the gym and working out, stating that they want to be slim and fit and yet have an issue with overeating or eating foods they love that they know are hindering them from achieving their desired weight and level of fitness.

- *"I want to be fit and yet I don't want to stop eating unhealthy luxury food"*
  - *Towards/Away*

Source Material & Further Learning
(1976) The Structure of Magic, Vol. II, Bandler & Grinder: Page 29 (1981) Reframing, Bandler & Grinder: Page 179

REORDERING VALUES IN A HIERARCHY

PLEASE NOTE:
This technique uses Sub-Modalities (the very next section Sub-Modalities) which if you are working through this book as a training syllabus you may not be aware of yet. With this in mind, it may be worth reviewing that section before returning to this technique.

There may be a situation where a person wishes to reorder their hierarchy of values in a particular context of life. This may assist in resolving conflict or it may be that a client has identified that a particular value holds more energy than another and would therefore be resourceful for them to have it a higher level and priority to positively influence their behaviour. In order to be able to move a Value around we must first know how to distinguish between one and another.

Sub-Modalities are the key to being capable of reordering our values. Sub-Modalities are the subjective subdivisions of our modalities. They allow us to describe our sensory experiences in much greater detail and are responsible for the coding, order and therefore our meaning connected to experiences.

The NLP techniques used to change the order are called *Contrast Analysis* and *Mapping Across*. The full processes are described in the Sub-modalities section.

The technique described is an overview of what a full coaching session for a client would be like in the context of being an NLP Practitioner. It also assumes that you already have elicited the hierarchy of values and resolved any conflict with Part Integration for the client.

Here is a reference to other techniques used within this pattern:

- *Value Elicitation*
- *Parts Integration*
- *Eliciting Sub-modalities*
- *Contrast Analysis*
- *Mapping Across*

In the following example, we want to move Value A above Value B in the hierarchy.

MOVING A VALUE UP

- **Be in rapport**
- **Be in a Coach State**
- **Identify the issue**
- **Identify the Present State & the trigger.**
- **Identify Desired State**
- **Ecology Check.**
  - (+/+) *"If you have this, what would you have?*
  - (+/-) *"If you have this, what would you not have?*
  - (-/+) *"If you didn't have this, what would you have?*
  - (-/-) *"If you didn't have this, what would you not have?*
- **Break State**
- **Elicit Sub-Modalities of the Value wish to move up the hierarchy**
  - Value A
  - *"Go back to a moment where you were experiencing this."*
    - Associated
  - *"What image can you see?"*
  - *"What are you hearing?"*
  - *"What are you feeling?"*
- **Break State**
- **Elicit Sub-Modalities of the Value that is directly above this value in the hierarchy**
  - Value B
- **Break State**
- **Perform Contrast Analysis**
  - Find the differences, the Critical Sub-Modalities
- **Map Across the Sub-Modalities of Value B to Value A**
  - For example, *"Change the picture from colour to black & white"*
  - For example, *"Move the sensation from your chest to your gut"*
- **Break State**
- **Check the hierarchy by comparing the two adjoining values.**
  - *"If they could have one but not the other how does that feel?"*
  - Value A should now be above Value B

BONUS PART THREE: DISNEY STRATEGY

DISNEY CREATIVE STRATEGY

Staying with the work that Robert Dilts has published, with an understanding of perceptual positions we can look at the model he created whilst studying the work of Walt Disney.

Robert wanted to model the strategy Disney used to consistently transform and connect the creativity of dreams and fantasy with tangible organised business strategy via the medium of animated film, later resulting in the entertainment empire he had built through these films and in the physical place Disneyland itself.

The result of the modelling work was the Disney Strategy, a strategy that provides a structure for creativity.

The Disney Strategy relates to perceptual positions in that to work through it you need to create three positions, all positions possessing different characteristics and varied roles from different perspectives on the content being produced. These three positions are;

- 1st Position: The Dreamer
- 2nd Position: The Realist
- 3rd Position: The Spoiler (or Critic)

The Dreamer
The visionary creator: "I want to…"

This perspective is about creativity and possibility without the restraints of current reality. This position is about being a visionary with big ideas and a bigger picture without a care for the finer details. This position primarily uses a visual sensory representation to construct and communicate the ideas. However, Walt Disney himself being a 'dreamer' would often overlap and access Auditory Digital and Internal Kinesthetic sensory representations when constructing his ideas and concepts. A Dreamer is encouraged to be relaxed, have a symmetrical physiology and with their head up, look up and to the right (see eye accessing patterns).

The Realist
The organiser: "How do I…"

This perspective is primarily to observe the concepts and ideas provided by the Dreamer and split them up into sequential and manageable chunks to form a plan of action. This concept actually gave birth to the process of storyboarding where a collection of unorganised creative ideas is organised to present a logical plan and flow of a collection of images. This position primarily uses a kinesthetic sensory representation, considering how to make plans a reality. A Realist is encouraged to be relaxed, have a symmetrically centred physiology and with their head slightly facing down, looking either straight ahead or down and to the right.

The Spoiler
The Evaluating Critic: "Does it all actually work?"

This perspective is primarily to evaluate the ideas from the dreamer and work done by the realist against defined criteria to ensure a quality end result. The critic can be considered as negative and destructive and yet all they are doing is comparing the outcome to a defined set of criteria so it is equally possible for them to be positive when criteria are adhered to. This position primarily uses a digital sensory representation, considering logic and comparison by difference. A Spoiler is encouraged to have an angular posture and with their head facing down, looking down and to the left.

Disney Strategy Position Meta-Programs

From an NLP perspective, we can compare meta-programs and preferences across the three positions to understand how to perform a position effectively or similarly who to allocate one of the roles to if you have multiple people in a group part-taking in this strategy.

	Dreamer	Realist	Spoiler
Sensory Pref.	Visual	Kinesthetic	Digital
Direction Filter	Towards	Towards	Away From
Frame of Ref.	Internal	External	External
Time Orientation	Future	Present	Past & Future
Time Frame	Long	Short	Long & Short
Relationship Filter	Sameness	Sameness	Difference
Scope	Global	Detail	Detail

DISNEY CREATIVE STRATEGY TECHNIQUE

With an overall summary of the strategy and the roles within it explained we can run through how to use this strategy as an NLP Practitioner with a group of people (possibly in a work context) or alternatively with an individual wanting to create a general plan for a new idea or concept. In the process below it is assumed that you are working with an individual.

- **Identify something that requires a creative solution.**
    - o   Present State / Problem State
- **Desired State**
    - o   Defined Outcome
- **Break State**
- **Identify a Meta-position (Director's Chair) and set the three locations and positions to use as the three spatial anchors.**
    - o   *"Where you are now will be called the meta-position. Think of yourself being like a film director about to look on towards three members of your team, dissociated and detached from all they do and create for the vision that is your desired outcome. You hold the vision and the purpose of your outcome."*
    - o   *"Choose three locations in this environment to represent three roles."*
        - For example, three chairs or three circles on the floor.
    - o   *"The first location will be for the Dreamer role. Here you will be at your most creative, creating possibilities without constraint, thinking big."*
    - o   *"The second location will be for the Realist. Here you put some order to your ideas, organising them and creating an action plan."*
    - o   *"The third location will be for the Spoiler. Here you will judge your plan against success criteria, looking for problems, what is missing and undesirable consequences of the plan".*
        - You may need to move this 3rd position further away from the other two to benefit anchoring and association stages of this process.
- **Set up the process**
    - o   *"As you move from one position to the next you will act 'as if' you are a person with only the associated perspective and role that the position defines. You will see what they see and think how they think."*
- **Set Dreamer Spatial Anchor**

- o *"Step to position one. Close your eyes if necessary and think of a time when you felt you were being the most creative. Be there now and acknowledge the feeling of creative flow and inhibition, seeing what you see, and hear.*
- **Break State**
- **Set Realist Spatial Anchor**
  - o *"Step to position two. Close your eyes if necessary and think of a time when you were planning for something and actively making a plan of action. Be there now and acknowledge the feeling of being organised and fully prepared to take action, seeing what you see, hearing what you hear.*
- **Break State**
- **Set Spoiler (Critic) Spatial Anchor**
  - o *"Step to position three. Close your eyes if necessary and think of a time when, with positive intention, you were reviewing something and finding all the things wrong with it so you could make things better. Be there now and know you were giving constructive criticism to ensure undesirable outcomes would not happen, seeing what you see, hearing what you hear.*
- **Break State**
- **Become the Dreamer**
  - o *"With your desired outcome, step into the Dreamer position and become the Dreamer character that you are able to be."*
  - o *"Look up and to the right and allow yourself to think freely and unconstrained, visualise yourself achieving the outcome."*
    - Document the content presented
- **Become the Realist**
  - o *"With the ideas the Dreamer has created for you, step into the Realist position and become the Realist character that you are able to be."*
  - o *"Be straight and in alignment with your body, look straight ahead or down and to the right up allowing yourself to take all the Dreamer has presented and put in some kind of order so it flows and achieves the desired outcome.*
    - Document the content presented
- **Become the Spoiler**
  - o *"With the ideas the Dreamer has conceived and the plan the Realist has created for you, step into the Spoiler position and become the Spoiler character that you are able to be."*
  - o *"Look down and to the left allowing yourself to take all the content you*

have and find out what is wrong with it. What doesn't make sense, what is missing, meaning the success criteria of the desired outcome will not be achieved? What unwanted consequences will happen as a result of this plan."

- Document the content presented

- **As the Spoiler create questions for the Realist.**
  - Convert the content documented by the Spoiler into questions for the Realist to seek solutions.
    - Spoilers criticise the ideas and plan against success criteria and undesirable consequences and provide questions for the Realist to find alternative solutions.
    - There is no requirement to include the Dreamer unless more creativity is required.

- **Become the Realist**
  - *"With all the content and feedback presented back to you, step into the Realist position to become the Realist character that you are able to be."*
  - *"Look straight ahead or down and to the right up and allow yourself to find solutions to the questions presented to you by the Spoiler."*
    - Document the content presented

- **Repeat the Realist and Spoiler cycle at least three times.**
  - If the Realist cannot provide a solution allow the Realist to present a desired outcome to the Dreamer.
  - The Dreamer needs to be protected from the Spoiler so at no point is there direct communication between the two.

- **Break State**

- **Associate with the Meta-Position**
  - *"As you review the vision and purpose with all that you know now has anything changed, what are you seeing, feeling and thinking now?*
  - Calibrate

Source Material & Further Learning

(1991) Tools for Dreamers, Dilts
(1994) Strategies of Genius: Volume I, Dilts: Page 161

GETTING CERTIFIED

Get yourself or your teams certified with our NLP Principles™ Internationally Accredited Certification Courses.

You might be interested as an individual to gain a certification to further your career and credentials, or maybe you have aspirations to start your own coaching and consultancy company.

You might be a founder or leader within a business and would like your leadership, managers or workforce to have a greater awareness, knowledge and experience of practical application when it comes to utilising human behaviour to improve performance and generate more revenue.

The following pages present the syllabus for two of the business-related NLP certification courses you can achieve.

NLP DIPLOMA CERTIFICATION

No doubt you have read this book, now aware of the benefit and positive impact this content and knowledge can have on your own life and others around you. This section of the book is about how you can start your own journey to become an internationally certified NLP Practitioner and even maybe an NLP Master Practitioner!

A diploma in NLP is a great place to start if you want an introduction to NLP or if you are time poor yet want to start benefiting from implementing this content into your life whether that is personally or professionally.

To gain an internationally recognised NLP Diploma certification you will need to invest just 30 hours, over the course of a 4 days. The in-person training will with a registered and internationally accredited INLPTA NLP Trainer.

As a result of completing an INLPTA NLP Diploma you will have the ability to immediately demonstrate and implement new skills and attitudes as well as gain all the knowledge listed below in the course content.

The training course content of an INLPTA Diploma includes the following;

- **The History of Neuro-Linguistic Programming**

  The origins of NLP, the co-creators and the minds they modelled.

- **Presuppositions of NLP**

  Keys and principles behind personal development

- **The Three Legs of NLP**

  How to utilise the Outcome, Flexibility and Sensory Acuity model

- **The NLP Communication Model**

  How our perspective of the world is created and impact us.

- **Rapport**

  How to build and improve relationship skills.

- **Sensory Acuity**

  Fine tune your senses to understand reactions of others & yourself.

- **The Feedback Model**

  How to give and receive feedback positively.

- **Well-formed Outcomes**

  Ensure that what you think you want really is what you want.

- **An Introduction to Sub-modalities**

  Understanding how you think and make meaning of experiences.

- **Change of Perspective (New Behavior Generator)**

  Learn a simple tool for solving problems and generating creativity

- **Language**

  How to use positive language and have better negotiation skills.

- **Anchoring**

  Learn how to store and access particular states at will.

- **Introduction to Timelines**

  How you personally structure time and how to utilise the future.

To learn more and find out how to book yourself on to a course,

visit:
https://nlpprinciples.com/nlp-course/nlp-diploma

P.S. Proof of purchase of this book ensures you eligible for a discount on the NLP Principles™ training. Contact via the website for more details.

NLP PRACTITIONER CERTIFICATION

Becoming an NLP Practitioner is perfect if you are time poor yet want to start benefiting from implementing this content into your life whether that is personally or professionally.

To gain an internationally recognised NLP Practitioner certification you will need to invest 130 hours, over the course of a 15 days. The in-person training will with a registered and internationally accredited INLPTA NLP Trainer.

As a result of completing an INLPTA NLP Practitioner you will have the ability to immediately demonstrate your integration of self-evolving and ecological attitudes, proficiency in NLP skills and abilities, and will know the following NLP content at appropriate levels of frames, concepts, principles, processes, techniques, and distinctions:

- The Presuppositions of NLP
- The Legs of NLP
- The Present to Desired State Model
- Well Formedness Conditions for Outcomes
- State Management
- Rapport
- Pacing and Leading
- Calibration
- Sensory acuity
- 7+/-2
- Uptime/Downtime
- Representational system
  - Primary
  - Lead
- Reference
- Predicates
- Eye Patterns
- Synaesthesia
- Overlapping
- 4-tuple, 6-tuple

- Inventory
- Association and Dissociation
- Meta Model
- Deep and Shallow Metaphors
- Basic Inductions
  - Pacing and Leading
  - Overlapping
- Anchoring
  - Basic Anchoring
  - Stacking anchors
  - Collapsing anchors
  - Chaining anchors
  - Future Pacing
  - Change Personal History
  - Circle of Excellence
- Self-Editing
- Strategies
  - TOTEs
  - Well Formedness Conditions for Strategies
  - Eliciting, Calibrating, and Utilizing Strategies
  - Pattern Interrupts
- Sub-modalities
  - Analogue and Digital Sub-modalities
  - Critical and Driver Sub-modalities
- Swish Pattern
- Designer Swish
- Standard Belief Change (mapping across Sub-modalities)
- NLP Frames:
  - Outcome frame
  - Backtrack frame
  - Relevancy frame
  - As If frame
  - Open frame
  - Discovery frame
  - Contrast frame

- o Ecology frame
- o Agreement frame
- Secondary Gain
- Triple Descriptions
- Reframing
  - o Content/Context reframes
  - o 6 Step reframe
  - o Negotiating Between Parts
  - o Creating a New Part
- Simultaneous and Sequential Incongruity
- Visual Squash
- New Behaviour Generator
- Chunking and Sequencing
- Basic Timeline work
- In time - Through time
- Basic Modelling

To learn more and find out how to book yourself on to a course,

visit:
https://nlpprinciples.com/nlp-course/nlp-practitioner

P.S. Proof of purchase of this book ensures you eligible for a discount on the NLP Principles™ training. Contact via the website for more details.

NLP MASTER PRACTITIONER CERTIFICATION

Although this is an NLP Practitioner book, if becoming an NLP Master Practitioner is an ambition of yours here are the details of what the next level beyond Practitioner looks like.

To gain an internationally recognised NLP Master Practitioner certification you will need to have a recognised NLP Practitioner Certificate and then invest 130 hours, over the course of a 15 days. The in-person training will with a registered and internationally accredited INLPTA NLP Trainer.

To gain INLPTA NLP Master Practitioner certification you will have to successfully complete;

- Written assessment for intellectual integration
- Behavioural assessment for behavioural integration
- Case study documentation for Personal/Professional application

On completion you will have;

- Integration, mastery & elegance of all Practitioner Skills
- A high degree of integration of Master Practitioner Process Skills
- Conscious/Unconscious Embodiment of the Legs of NLP
- Conscious/Unconscious Embodiment of Presuppositions of NLP
- Conscious/Unconscious Multi-tracking:
    - o   Multi Layered Outcomes
    - o   Multi-Level Calibration Skills
    - o   Multi-Level Conscious/Unconscious Processing
- The ability to Be-At-Choice with Process of Identification
- The ability to Be-At-Choice with Process of Self Evaluation
- Precision Resourcefulness Through All Representational Systems
- Scope of Sensory Flexibility
- Perceptual Sorting Flexibility
- The Ability to Track One's Own Epistemological Processing
- The Ability to Track the Epistemology of Others

- Epistemological Flexibility
- The Ability to Track Logical Levels and Logical Typings
- The Ability to Process Learning from Achievement
- The Ability to Establish and Maintain Multiple levels of Rapport
- The Ability to Separate Process from Content About Process
- The Ability to Deliver Deliberate Multi-Level Communications
- Generalize and Contextualize Master Practitioner Content & Skills.

To learn more and find out how to book yourself on to a course,

visit:

https://nlpprinciples.com/nlp-course/nlp-master-practitioner

P.S. Proof of purchase of this book ensures you eligible for a discount on the NLP Principles™ training. Contact via the website for more details.

ABOUT INLPTA

'I seek to know, in order to serve'

In response to the growing need amongst NLP Trainers around the world for a unified accreditation body based on a consistency of quality in the accreditation standards, professional conduct and ethical applications of NLP technology, the International NLP Trainers Association (INLPTA) was formed in late 1993 by Wyatt Woodsmall (NLP Master Trainer and Master Modeller, USA), Marvin Oka (NLP Master Trainer, Australia), and Bert Feustel (NLP Master Trainer, Germany).

With trainers in over 50 countries on all five continents, including; the United States, United Kingdom, Germany, Canada, France, the Netherlands, Sweden, Slovenia, Turkey, Syria, Bahrain, the United Arab Emirates, Australia and New Zealand, INLPTA is an international cooperative association consisting of members that are NLP Trainers and NLP Master Trainers who have all agreed to abide by and uphold the high standards of quality, professionalism and ethics in their NLP accreditation trainings and the conduct of their NLP business.

INLPTA members passionately believe that NLP can play a significant role in contributing to the evolution of individuals, groups, communities, societies, nations, the world, and humankind. This leads to a focus and necessity of NLP being taught and learned within contextual frameworks of ecology and meta-ethics.

The mission of INLPTA is:

- to provide high-quality guidelines for NLP training
- to establish ethical guidelines for NLP use
- to promote professional usage of NLP in business
- to encourage NLP training to be compatible and develop with scientific principles to achieve broader acceptance.

To find out more about INLPTA visit:
https://www.inlpta.org

ABOUT ANLP

The Association of NLP (ANLP) are the global flagbearers for Professional NLP. In 2008, under the leadership of Karen Falconer (CEO from 2005 to present day (2022)) the ANLP became a Community Interest Company (CIC) after being founded in 1985. ANLP International CIC, as it is now known, has a primary purpose to serve as an umbrella organisation offering independent advice to NLP professional in a variety of sectors and backgrounds. It was awarded Best UK Community Interest Company 2020 at the 2020 UK Enterprise Awards in recognition of the high standards, operational excellence and continued service to members.

The ANLP's flagship publication Rapport (first published in 1985) is the leading NLP industry magazine and it accompanied by Acuity (first published in 2010), an anthology for shared findings and learnings and also the book The NLP Professional (originally published in 2011 and updated in 2022) authored by Karen Falconer. In 2017 ANLP took responsibility of the NLP Conference, and now hosts an international conference bringing together the international NLP community, supporting and celebrating excellent achievement and the positive impact NLP makes via the NLP Awards.

The mission of ANLP is to:

- have an international membership enabling a credible mandate to independently represent NLP Professionals in the global arena.
- promote and protect the reputation of NLP by:
  - encouraging professionalism and self-responsibility.
  - providing reassurance and a safety net for the public.
  - providing a self-regulatory framework for members.
  - promoting the positive power and flexibility of NLP.
  - promoting credible NLP Practitioners & Trainers.
- nurture and encourage individuals to be the best they can be by.
- develop internationally recognised accreditation & qualifications.
- encourage NLP research & further development of NLP models.

To find out more about ANLP visit:
https://anlp.org/

UNIFIED CODE OF ETHICS

In 2022 something fantastic happened in the world of NLP, the official launch of an NLP Unified Code of Ethics.

For the first time in history, the main globally recognised NLP Associations generatively collaborated as a group of professional bodies to
to develop a unified charter (effectively their code of ethics) enabling self-regulation and a standard of practice to adopt internationally.

As of 2023 (the date of this book being published), this has been adopted by;

- International NLP Trainers Association *(INLPTA)*
  https://www.inlpta.org

- ANLP International CIC *(ANLP)*
  https://anlp.org

- International Association for Neuro-Linguistic Programming *(IANLP)*
  https://www.ia-nlp.org

- International Association of NLP Institutes *(IN)*
  https://www.nlp-institutes.net

The Ethics.

A code of ethics has to do with responsibility.

They give us the necessary guidance to tell us how to treat others.

They are rules and boundaries standardising how to function and interact:

- as a human being with others
- as a business
- in society

All ethical behaviour and decisions are guided and evaluated by 3 principles:

- Flexibility, Diversity and Freedom
    - The principles of flexibility, diversity and freedom are about the variety and degrees of freedom of a system and/or person and/or model of the world.
    - The degree of freedom and diversity increases with increased choices, options and flexibility. It is better to increase them rather than decrease them.
    - The freedom of a system, a person, a society, a culture, or a model of the world ends where it starts to harm, discriminate against or restrict the freedom or diversity of others.
    - It is considered unethical if you do harm to others or discriminate or reduce their freedom or diversity.

- Ecology
    - The principle of ecology is an examination and consideration of consequences, interactions and effects on people, the system and
    - environment resulting from the communication, behaviour, decision or change.
    - It is considered unecological if the consequences and effects of your actions inflict more harm than good or have more negative effects, short-term or long-term, than before.

- Ethical Foundation Values
    - The principle of ethical foundation values means acting with honesty,
    - fairness, integrity, respect, responsibility and dignity towards others.
      It is considered unethical if you are dishonest, unfair, corrupt, disrespectful,
    - irresponsible or violate the dignity of others.

The Unified Code of Ethics

Based upon these principles, the Associations have agreed that a member;

- shall adhere to the three principles in teaching, certification, coaching or interacting with students or clients.

- shall only promote, advertise or offer ethical and ecological programs or events.

- shall only publish, advertise, distribute or post ethical and ecological information or statements online.

- shall not associate themselves, their NLP association or NLP with unethical and unecological practices or groups.

- will act ethically and ecologically towards other members, the NLP association, and other professional bodies and institutions and do their best to enhance the reputation of NLP and/or the NLP association.

- shall strive to improve the well-being and flexibility of their students, clients and society.

For the latest information on these ethics and to see all the latest associations that have combined to create and adopt these please visit https://www.unifiednlp.org

LEARN MORE ABOUT NLP PRINCIPLES™

There's a lot of noise in the world today, all trying to grab your attention in one way or another. Some of that noise is there with good intentions and yet unfortunately, and sadly, some of that noise has less ethical and ecological intentions. NLP Principles was formed based on the belief that people need to learn and understand more about humanistic psychology and in turn human behaviour so that they can be aware and educated on what they read, see, hear and experience in the world today. Whether that is via marketing from a business or via mass media and social media. By providing people with the fundamental and evolving knowledge base within the field of human behaviour science and psychology, we are passionate that individuals have the ability to positively influence themselves and others in an ethical way, whether that is by enhancing the own performance or the performance of a business. We have 5 values and beliefs that drive how we behave with each other and how we interact with customers, attendees and partners;

- **Trustworthy.** Be Reliable & Bring Integrity
- **Authentic.** Be Ethical & Bring Honesty
- **Progressive.** Be Inquisitive & Bring Excellence
- **Pragmatic.** Be Consistent & Bring Commitment
- **Positive.** Be Passionate & Bring Enjoyment

Our Mission
To provide a best-in-class service, by continuously gathering world-class knowledge and gain real-world experience taking action on what is learned. Our experience and expertise enable us to have authentic empathy with the ambitions and challenges people that are pulled towards our services bring. We encourage every person who passes through our training or services to share the knowledge share and create their very own positive impact to make a difference where it makes the difference.

What we do.
We offer best-in-class business consultancy and in-person training that focuses on evidence-based performance enhancement. Our services ranging from; masterclasses, workshops, NLP certification courses and coaching programmes, provide practical solutions with tangible results. If the content of this book or our mission resonates with you, please do get in touch.

Visit www.nlpprincples.com.

LEARN MORE ABOUT THE AUTHOR

Lee Groombridge is an experienced multi-business, start-up founder & CEO who turned to humanistic psychology and behavioural science due to a passion for providing business owners and high-performance individuals with premium, coaching, mentoring, training and consultancy, allowing both their businesses and themselves to optimise their thinking, performance and results.

After a successful career within the digital marketing and specialist magazine publishing industry, Lee was inspired to co-found a start-up. Ten years later armed with two decades of hands-on business operational and leadership experience and having scaled two to £1million+ turnover, including an online advertising agency that was eventually acquired, it was time for a change.

Combined with a life-long passion for personal development and being acutely aware from first-hand experience that there was a gap in the market for truly experienced business coaching, mentoring and training from people who have walked the walk, Lee focused his attention to the study of human behaviour and psychology to enable his knowledge and credibility to grow in this field.

Over the following years, Lee became; a certified Humanistic Linguistic Psychology Coach, a Professional Neuro-Linguistic Programming Master Practitioner, an Internationally Certified Neuro-Linguistic Programming Trainer and published four books on the topic of personal mindset and business performance enhancement.

Lee has also created a 12-week high-performance coaching programme for business owners and delivered leadership and management training programmes to large national multiple-million-pound, 4000+ staff organisations, while consulting for one of the largest business consultancies in Europe training coaches.

In 2022 Lee officially launched NLP Principles™ to provide business consultancy and training for businesses and individuals around the world, enabling them to apply human behaviour and psychology to enhance performance in sales, marketing, management and leadership as well as provide internationally accredited NLP certification courses so people can start their very own journey with Neuro-Linguistic Programming.

WHAT PEOPLE SAY

Here are a few words from people that have worked and trained with Lee and NLP Principles™. In order to give you a broader understanding of the positive impact NLP can have and do for you; they were also asked to mention what NLP means to them personally.

One of the most meaningful parts of the INLPTA Trainers Training was meeting Lee. It was a joy to connect with someone with such depth of knowledge on NLP as well as the practical application into real life contexts. NLP is the study of excellence and its effective application enables creating transformative and long-lasting change. The use of NLP principles, tools and techniques has transformed my personal and professional life and I believe it has enabled me to live my best life. Many people learn NLP theoretically, few have the capability to apply it and create new models of understanding and excellence. I find Lee is one of those rare individuals who can bridge the gap effectively. Lee is someone with a keen intelligence, observational capability and excellent humour supported by high integrity and professionalism.
Aliyah Mohyeddin NLP Master Trainer

Meeting Lee during an ANLP virtual conference and then training with him in-person during the month-long INLPTA training we were on in France, it's clear when you speak to Lee just how much he knows and how passionate he is to help others, providing in-depth, research backed NLP. I've worked with Lee on many occasions and his background in building successful businesses, alongside his canny ability to spot opportunities combined with personal journey and clear logical mind mean that you'll take so much from his book and NLP Principles approach. Like many NLP Trainers my personal experiences led me to want to help and support others. Using the principles, tools and philosophies of good, ethical NLP to create a space into which we reflect on our past and focus on what we'd like to have happen in the future. I can't recommend Lee highly enough as being a perfect guide and this book as a perfect companion for that journey.
Andy Coley, Award-Winning NLP Trainer & ANLP Ambassador

"I enjoyed many days and evenings studying, talking and laughing with Lee during the INLPTA Trainers Training. Lee is not only incredibly knowledgeable in the theory of NLP, but he has a unique ability of applying it to real-life settings providing a backdrop for real growth to take place. Having used many psychological approaches in my professional life, I can say with a high degree of confidence that NLP is singularly the most elegant performance psychology. Its applications are far reaching and has long-lasting outcomes."
Iain Adenis, INLPTA NLP Trainer, NLP Master Practitioner.

"The best part of my NLP trainer training was meeting Lee! His knowledge of NLP is incredible & he has a unique way of cutting through the fluff to convey the core message. Training alongside Lee, who has a rare combination of humour, support, skill & integrity, was a fabulous experience and one for which I will be eternally grateful. NLP changed my life! A life time of trying every diet available, losing weight and putting it back on with interest, led to barely existing. NLP helped me rewire my brain with more helpful thoughts and habits resulting in releasing 43kg at the time of writing this, smashing through limitation after limitation with no intention of stopping!"
Lou Laggan, NLP Master Practitioner, Mental Reconditioning Coach.

I got to know Lee very well during our NLP trainers training. He elegantly simplifies that which appears too complex and at times very complicated, making the application of NLP easy and accessible. His presence creates a massive impact both in the personal and professional context. He holds the space for personal growth organically and his incredibly humane, deeply connected sense of leadership combined with laser sharp business skills makes him one to watch and learn from. He has a talent in making things practical and simple in application, while retaining the rigour and thorough foundations of excellent NLP practice tailored to the needs of the situation. I believe NLP is the transformational "why" and "how" in practice, a life-changing way of life. NLP has allowed me to build a purpose-led, values driven and inspired way of living with authenticity. The book in your hand is a meaningful contribution to the unique journey with NLP, as a way of life."
Katalin Marton, Award winning-NLP Practitioner, NLP Master Practitioner & INLPTA NLP Trainer.

I've known Lee for a few years now right from when he started his NLP growth to becoming a certified Trainer. As one of his Trainers during both his Practitioner and Master Practitioner training, his joy at learning new aspects to both his own and other's behaviours and how to create an enabling environment for both his clients and customers was a pleasure to watch. He questioned many aspects of the learning so that he could gain a greater depth and breadth of understanding of the diversity of NLP and practiced it diligently to become both competent and flexible in its use.
Chris Menlove-Platt, NLP Trainer, Master Practitioner and Coach

Logical. Astute. Reflective. Immediate words that come to mind when I consider Lee and learning alongside him during my NLP Practitioner and Master Practitioner training. His insights continue to challenge my thinking and support my reflection to this day. Quite simply, NLP changed my life. I feel more empowered, observant and open-minded – if everybody had a smidge of this knowledge the world could be a very different place! I feel privileged to have played a little part in Lee's journey and want to say if you get the opportunity to work with him – do it!
Sarah Clarke, NLP Master Practitioner

I had the pleasure of co-training on Lee's NLP Practitioner and Master Practitioner courses. The quality of his work is fantastic, and it was always clear that he would take his knowledge to the highest possible level. Lee has a clear vision for taking NLP forward in the modern world and it will no doubt be awesome! NLP was life-changing for me and I know how much people will benefit from what he's doing.
Sam Dyer, Master Practitioner and Master Coach

I had the privilege of meeting Lee and getting to know him well at the INLPTA Trainers Training. He has a fascinating life story with many accomplishments and many more to come! This book fills a void in the NLP landscape and is exactly what I have been searching a long time for. I have found NLP to be the framework of choice in my coaching practice. It's a gamechanger when it comes powerful and lasting results.
Capt. Bo Goeran Peterson, CoachCaptain LLC, INLPTA NLP Trainer

Lee and I met whilst doing Trainers Training. Lee has the wonderful ability to see through 'the noise'. Whenever I was wrangling with a problem...overthinking things... he was able to help me see clearly and provide me with those light bulbs moments that made such a difference. My journey with NLP has had a hugely positive impact on my life. It helped me understand others by understanding myself and to get curious rather than make meaning of others behaviours.
Jayne Rolls, INLPTA NLP Trainer and NLP Coach

A GIFT FOR BUYING THIS BOOK

Remember at the very start of this book I mentioned that I had a gift for you due to the fact you purchased this book. Well, promises are promises and here it is…

As a thank you for investing your time and money please find below a 200% purchase contribution towards your first NLP Principles™ training or consultancy service.

By utilising this gift from us, you not only get fully reimbursed for the cost of this book, you also get a real-life monetary contribution towards your first training with us, meaning you've actually made money by buying this book!

200% MONEY BACK OFFER

This NLP Principles Gift Voucher entitles you to receive a contribution equal to 200% of the price you paid for this book towards a NLP Principles course, workshop or masterclass.

To receive your gift please follow these steps:

1. Visit **NLPPrinciples.com** and choose from our training courses.

2. Once you have made your choice, you can redeem this monetary gift by emailing **voucher@nlpprinciples.com** with the message stated below along with a copy of the book purchase receipt attached (so we know how much money to give you):

   TO: *Voucher@nlpprinciples.com*
   SUBJECT LINE: *"200% Book Voucher"*
   BODY: *I would like to put this money towards the following course…*
   ATTACHED: *'Become an NLP Practitioner' Book receipt.*

3. We will get back to you to confirm receipt of your email and with all the details you need to start your training with us.

REFERENCE SECTION

RECOMMENDED READING

This chronological bibliography is extended to include books considered essential reading by INLPTA or are recommend by the author.
Visit: nlpprinciples.com/nlp/nlp-best-books

Syntactic Structures
By Noam Chomsky
1957

Pragmatics of Human Communication
By Paul Watzlawick, Janet Beavin-Bavelas, Don D Jackson
1964

Steps to an Ecology of Mind
By Bateson
1973

Therapeutic Metaphors: Helping Others Through the Looking Glass
By David Gordon
1978.

The Structure of Magic, Vol. I.
By Richard Bandler & John Grinder
1975.

Patterns of The Hypnotic Techniques Of Milton H. Erickson, M.D.
Volume 1 & 2 By Richard Bandler, John Grinder
1975

The Structure of Magic, Vol. II.
By Richard Bandler & John Grinder
1976.

Frogs Into Princes
By Richard Bandler & John Grinder
1979.

NLP: Vol I. The Study Of The Structure Of Experience
By Dilts, Grinder, Bandler, Bandler, DeLozier
1980.

Reframing
By Richard Bandler & John Grinder
1981.

Trance-Formations
By Bandler and Grinder
1981

Using Your Brain for a Change
By Richard Bandler
1985.

Magic Demystified
By Lewis and Pucelik
1985

Turtles All The Way Down, Prerequisites to Personal Genius
By Judith De Lozier & John Grinder
1987.

Therapeutic Trances: The Cooperation Principle In Erickson Hypnotherapy By Stephen Gilligan
1987.

Ultra-Solutions
By Paul Watzlawick
1988

Time Line Therapy and The Basis of Personality
By Tad James & Wyatt Woodsmall
1988.

The New People Making
By Virginia Satir
1988.

Change Your Mind and Keep the Change
By Andreas and Andreas
1988

Insider's Guide to Sub-modalities
By Bandler and MacDonald
1989

Heart of the Mind
By Andreas and Andreas
1989

Changing Belief Systems with NLP
By Dilts
1990

Beliefs
by Dilts, Hallbolm, Smith
1990

Introducing Neuro-linguistic Programming
by O'Conner & Seymour
1990

Metaprograms
Wyatt Woodsmall
1990

Tools for Dreamers
By Robert Dilts & Todd Epstein
1991

Strategies of Genius: Volume I
By Robert Dilts & Todd Epstein
1994

Precision
By Grinder and McMaster
1994

The Enneagram and NLP
By Annie Linden and Murray Spalding
1994

Training Trances
By John Overdorf & Julie Silverthorn
1995.

The Minimalist Program
By Noam Chomsky
1995

The Patterns of Her Magic
By Steve Andreas
1999

People Pattern Power
By Marilyne Woodsmall & Wyatt Woodsmall
1998.

Coach to Awakener
By Robert Dilts
2003

Origins of Neuro Linguistic Programming
By Pucelik and Grinder
2013

How to succeed in Business with NLP Principles
by Lee Groombridge
2024

For easy access and links to get your hands on any of these books please visit: https://www.nlpprinciples.com

GLOSSARY OF NLP TERMS

This glossary of NLP terms presented in alphabetical order has been put together for you have a quick A-Z reference any time you need to quickly reference a term.

1st **Person** (Perspective)	A viewpoint of an experience that is viewing a situation out of your own eyes. Think of this to be like a first-person shooter video game. This is also referred to in some NLP techniques as the 1st Position.
2nd **Person** (Perspective)	A viewpoint of an experience that is viewing a situation out of someone else's eyes. Think of this as transporting into another person's body and seeing the situation from their perspective. This is also referred to in some NLP techniques as the 2nd Position.
3rd **Person** (Perspective)	A viewpoint of an experience where you are an onlooker or observer seeing yourself in that situation. Keeping with the video game analogy think of this to be like a third-person adventure game where the player has the freedom of motion with you looking from behind the main character.
Accessing Cues	Verbal and Non-Verbal signals that indicate which sensory representational system someone is accessing information from
Anchor	Naturally occurring sensory stimulus that consistently triggers a particular internal state and emotional response

Anchoring	The process of attaching an association of a sensory stimulus to an internal state to enable the set anchor to be fired in the future.
Analogue Sub-modalities	Modalities that are always present with continuous and infinite subjective subdivisions or subclassifications.
Associated (State)	A state of being able to connect to your own emotions associated with a sensory experience.
Auditory	The sensory modality that refers to the representational system of hearing.
Auditory Digital	This is the sensory modality that refers to the representational system Digital in the form of auditory language. Self-talk would be an example of internal auditory digital.
Behaviour	What a person is doing, what physical actions and what physiology a person has.
Belief	Generalised statements a person holds that they believe to be true. A belief can vary in strength between 0% to 100% certainty. A 50/50 strength could be considered as not being sure about the belief and below 50% being considered as doubt.

Break State	This is not a state in itself, it is a description of a change of state.
Calibration	This act of observing and measuring non-verbal communication as a cue for an internal state.
Capability	The strategies, internal processes and mental maps developed from past experiences that influence and direct specific behaviour a variety of environments.
Chaining Anchors	When the distance or variance in the degree of intensity between a current state and a desired state is too great or far apart, this technique creates intermediary anchors between the states so that smaller consecutive state changes can occur away from the initial state and towards the desired state.
Chunk	A group of bits of information
Chunking (Size)	Chunking size refers to breaking apart or combining existing chunk of information.
Chunking (Hierarchy of Ideas)	Language, concepts and ideas contain chunks of information that are interrelated and organized. *Chunking down* can be used to find more logical detailed information about the current chunk. *Chunking up* can gain more generalised categorical information about the chunk. *Chunking across or sideways* can provide abstract or alternate categories.

Circle of Excellence	A self-anchoring technique that enables a number of stacked resource anchors to be set to a spatial anchor.
Coaching	The role of facilitating change by meeting a person where they are in their model of the world, helping them define well-formed outcomes and by increasing flexibility of behaviour support them in their progress and achievement of the outcomes.
Congruence	Ultimately it means alignment or fitting together. This can be alignment of values, beliefs and behaviour for an individual as well as ecology alignment for an individual or a whole system.
Collapsing Anchor	The technique of dissolving the charge an unresourceful anchor. This may occur by overriding the charge of a unresourceful anchor with another anchor, which could in turn collapse them both.
Conscious Mind	A current awareness of thinking at any given moment that provides awakened purposeful control and direction. It excels at processing sequentially, logically and linearly, is capable of reasoning, setting targets and planning a path to achieving them.
Content	The story or event itself as it happens, from the world (territory) before your universal processes and internal filters create your perception (map).

Context	A particular setting such as; where, when, with whom, under what circumstance, what aspect of life that influences the interpretation of content.
Contrast Analysis	A method of comparing sub-modalities of two experiences to identify critical sub-modalities.
Critical Sub-modalities	A sub-modality that if changed will change something.
Cross-over Matching	You match one part of a person's physiology or behaviour with a different part of your physiology.
Deep Structure	Our pure unconscious sensory experience
Deletion (Filter)	An internal filter and universal model that ignores data from the territory.
Deletion (Transformation)	One of three unconscious automatic conversion processes. This one omits content from the deep structure resulting in the language used at the surface structure being deprived of information.
Derivation	A single instance of a deletion, generalisation, distortion that reverses an automatic conversion process (See Transformation) enabling the recovery of deep structure content that was deprived in the language used at the surface structure.

Desired State	This is a defined state that is more resourceful that the Present State. It contains the criteria for which the result of change is compared to in order to measure progress or be recognise the end. Hence why this is sometimes referred to as the End State
Desired Outcome	Something you specifically want that has some considered conditions and criteria containing components different or absent from what you currently have.
Digital (Modality)	The sensory modality that refers to the representational system of meaning via language. It is possible to have Auditory Digital (language we hear), Visual Digital (language or symbols we see) and Kinesthetic Digital (such a braille).
Digital Sub-modalities	Modalities that have binary subjective subdivisions or subclassifications that exist as an either/or with instantaneous change where both variations cannot co-exist.
Disney Strategy	A strategy providing a structure for creativity.
Dissociated (State)	A state where you are unable to experience or be connected to your own emotion of a sensory experience.
Distortion (Filter)	An internal filter and universal model that misrepresents data from the territory.

Distortion (Transformation)	One of three unconscious automatic conversion processes (See Transformations) that simplifies the deep structure content resulting in the language used at the surface structure being deprived of information.
Downtime	A state of having your focused awareness fully directed inside yourself, paying no attention to sensory experience from outside of you. Often in NLP this is referred to as a Hypnotic State.
Driver Sub-modality	The critical sub-modality has the most impact in changing something as once changed it pulls other sub-modalities to change automatically too.
Ecological	A study of consequence that evaluates the impact that will occur on the individual and the wider system during the progress towards an outcome and period of time that extends past the achievement of the outcome.
Elicit	The method of discovering information about another person's internal filters, state and strategies.
Emotion	Feelings associated or connected to behaviours.
Environment	The external settings and conditions that surround an individual.

Eye Accessing	Utilising eye movement or placement to help identify the representational system a person is using to access information.
Feedback	Method of observing or receiving information that can be compared against desired criteria to influence any required change of behaviour. Giving feedback is the act of communicating verbally and non-verbally your conscious and unconscious response to communication received.
Flexibility	Having the willingness to change and the ability to vary things such as behaviour, thinking or feelings.
Frame	The meaning we derive from context.
Future Pacing	This method of mental rehearsal is to enable a person to experience a situation in the future using all their senses and additional resources that they will have as a result of the desired outcome.
Generalisation (Filter)	An internal filter and universal model that groups a number of experiences with minor variances of data from the territory and represents them as the same or as a whole experience.
Generalisation (Transformation)	One of three unconscious automatic conversion processes that forms generalised rules for content from the deep structure resulting in the language used at the surface structure being deprived of information.

Gustatory	The sensory modality that refers to the representational system of tasting.
Hypnotic State	See Downtime
Identity	A defined perception that organises our values, beliefs, capabilities and behaviours into a single whole system.
In-Time	A preference for sorting and organising time where a person will generally experience their timeline running through their body with their future in front of them, past behind, and the now being associated inside of themselves.
Incongruence	Ultimately it means misalignment. This can be misalignment of values, beliefs and behaviour for an individual as well as ecology misalignment for an individual or a whole system.
Internal Dialogue	See Auditory Digital
Inventory	Conscious awareness and use of sensory acuity to be aware of your own internal sensory representation at a given time.
Kinesthetic	The sensory modality that refers to the representational system of feeling.

Lead Representational System	the sensory representational system for which a person prefers to access their internal representational information from
Leading	From a place of being in rapport and pacing, leading is to influence the options available to a person by providing direction towards a more resourceful state.
Leverage	Leading a person with a suggestion of what the next step can be when they are in a Stuck State.
Map	Our internal representation of the territory after the data has passed through our filters providing a perception unique to each individual.
Mapping Across	Adjusting elements or sub-modalities of a present context or state to match the properties of another. This is useful when wanting to change the meaning of an experience or utilising a resourceful state in another context or situation.
Matching	Where your physiology, words, voice tempo, voice tonality exactly matches what the other person is doing
Mentoring	The role of defining an issue or a goal a person has and then providing advice and required actions based on the Mentor's map of the world and past experiences.

Meta	A term with a Greek origin literally meaning to be above, beyond, or about something else.
Meta Mirror	Also known as the 4th Position, is a meta position from the perspective of a person looking onto the 3rd Position enabling a person to dissociate further from the advice provided by the 3rd position.
Meta Model	Meta Model is the linguistic process containing a list of recognisable patterns that enable elegant questioning to recover deleted components of a Surface Structure sentence to discover a Deep Structure sentence.
Meta Position	An associated position from the perspective of a person onlooking to a situation, seeing the world with you in it, holding an unbiased relationship between two people due to the dissociation from the situation therefore enabling independent reasoning. Also known as the Third Position or Observer
Metaphor	A story, parable or simile with an alternate sensory or contextual comparison that provide indirect communication about a desired subject or topic with a similar meaning.
Milton Model	The inverse of the Meta Model

Mind Read	Claiming to know what someone else is thinking or feeling without having any direct communication from them to validate.
Mirroring	Where your physiology matches the other person as though they are looking in a mirror.
Model (a Model)	A simplified representation or concept of the mechanics of an experience as a result of the process of deletion, generalization and distortion.
Model (an NLP Model)	A strategy that contains no Content only Process to repeatedly reproduce a particular excellent behaviour as the outcome
Model (to model)	To follow the steps of an NLP Model to reproduce the outcome.
Modelling	The process of capturing and coding the sensory representational system structure and repeatable strategy that produces a particular excellent behaviour as the outcome to enable the transfer of that outcome to others.
Neuro-logical Levels	A model that illustrates the different levels we experience the world and brings understanding to which level we should bring about change to depending on what level a person is being challenged on.

New Behaviour Generator	An NLP technique that provides a strategy to the enhance performance of an existing behaviour or capability via a visually constructed rehearsal.
NLP	Acronym for Neuro-Linguistic Programming
NLP Practitioner	A person that has the knowledge required within the NLP Practitioner syllabus and uses Neuro-Linguistic Programming techniques, models and methodology in a professional, ethical and ecological way.
Non-Verbal Communication	Communication without the use of verbal language that are conscious and unconscious changes in physiology and gestures. Also commonly known as body language
Olfactory	The sensory modality that refers to the representational system of smelling.
Overlapping	A form of pacing and leading that helps a person utilise another representational system different from the one they are currently using.
Pacing	Maintaining rapport with a person over a period of time by adapting and entering into their model of the world.

Parts	A metaphor for a part of you wanting one thing and another part of you wanting either the same thing or something different.
Parts Integration	An NLP technique can help resolve an issue related to incongruent values that are in conflict. These issues are commonly presented as dilemmas.
Pattern	Any aggregate of Content or Process that can be divided into individual parts and yet when aggregated the observer can guess with better than random success the next event, object or occurrence, thus reducing the probability of guessing wrong.
Pattern Interrupt	Is a trigger that interrupts a Pattern with the desired outcome being a state change.
Perceptual Position	A technique used to provide an insight into another person's perspective and understanding of a shared experience or situation.
Precision Model	A distilled version of the Meta Model with just five patterns, all presented in a way that is relevant to benefit a person in a business or project context.
Predicates	Sensory specific words

Present State	A state that is the starting point to advance from towards a more resourceful desired state.
Presupposition	A thing that is assumed to be true beforehand at the beginning of a course of action.
Primary Representational System	The sensory representational system for which a person prefers to take in and process information from the outside world.
Process	Process is not Content, rather it is how we deal with Content. It is how we create our internal representation (map) from the world (territory).
Problem State	A Present state that contains an issue. Also see Present State
Rapport	Process of establishing a relationship with another person that illustrates harmony, understanding, mutual trust and mutual confidence.
Reframing	A way to change a perception of an event therefore changing the meaning.
Reference Representational System	The sensory representational system that is used by a person within a particular strategy to detect whether they know and agree with information they have accessed via lead representational system.

Resource Anchor	An anchor that will enable a person to consciously and intentionally fire a resourceful state
Resourceful State	A state that provides choice and flexibility of behaviour towards a desired outcome resulting in positive or helpful emotions.
Resources	Anything that can help the progress or achievement of an outcome.
Sensory Acuity	The capability to use your senses to make accurate observations about ourselves and others
Sensory Representational System	A way we categorise, classify and process the sensory data from the territory to create a representation with a particular sense.
Spiritual	An awareness to the pattern that as individuals we are subsystems of a larger system that connects individuals beyond their identities.
State	The sum of conscious and unconscious thoughts or sensory feelings that a person is experiencing at a specific moment in time
Strategy	A series or sequence of conscious and unconscious behaviours and internal representations that we run in order to achieve a specific outcome.

Streamline	Process of identifying unnecessary or redundant steps in a strategy to achieve a desired outcome and either editing or removing them from a strategy.
Stuck State	An unresourceful state where the person experiences an inability to move due to confusion from a pattern interrupt or a lack of choice and flexibility due to no available strategies.
Sub-Modality	Subjective subdivisions or subclassifications of our sensory modalities allowing us to describe our external experiences in much greater detail enabling the coding, arranging, ordering and in turn creation of meaning connected to experiences.
Surface Structure	What we are consciously aware of and present linguistically as constructed sentences after derivations and transformations of deep structure.
Swish Pattern	A technique that utilises sub-modalities to change a state or behaviour to be more resourceful. A stage in the process contains saying the word 'Swish' hence the name.
Synaesthesia	When two or more representational systems overlap causing them to exist simultaneously.
Territory	The actual events as they are in external world outside of us before any processing of data via our universal models, internal filters, or perceptions are formed.

Through-Time	A preference for sorting and organising time where a person will generally experience their timeline outside of themselves with their future and past slightly in front of them going from side to side with the now being a spot just in front of where they physically are.
Time line	A line connecting two points in time; the past and the future, passing through the present that holds the sequence of memories from our experiences.
T.O.T.E. Model	[Acronym for Test, Operate, Test, Exit] Basic cybernetic principle for controlling processes adapted by Miller, Pribram, Galanter to thinking. This wellformedness condition for strategies is a 4-part sequence based on computer modelling and provides a dynamic feedback model allowing us to understand what works and what doesn't.
Trance	Hypnotic State with a very narrow focused awareness fully directed inside yourself, paying no attention to sensory experience from outside of you.
Transderivational Search (TDS)	Specifically rapid eye movement going from one eye pattern to another that occurs if a person has no reference representational system or is finding it hard to make meaning of information. It occurs due to the fact the unconscious mind is rapidly accessing and searching across multiple sensory representational systems as well as recalling and constructing the information that is present.

Transformation	The unconscious automatic conversion process of deletion, generalization or distortion of the deep structure that results in the language we use at the surface structure.
Unconscious Mind	The unconscious mind holds on to everything the conscious mind does not and refers to those things you have no awareness of in any given moment. It uses pictures, sounds, feelings, taste and smell as it's language and has a primary function to serve the conscious mind by helping achieve goals with automated actions and behaviour that maybe outside of your conscious control.
Unresourceful State	A non-resourceful state that provides no choice or lack of flexibility of behaviour resulting in negative or unhelpful emotions.
Uptime	A state of being fully present and having full focus and awareness directed outwards to the sensory experience and responding to it directly.
Values	Values are internal filters that mostly operate at an unconscious level, defining the positive intent behind all our behaviour.
Verbal Communication	The use of words to communicate information.

Visual	The sensory modality that refers to the representational system of seeing.
Visual Squash	An NLP technique of integrating parts that utilises visual anchors.
Well-Formed Outcome	An outcome that meets the well-formedness conditions.
Well-formedness Conditions	A specific set of conditions that enable an outcome to be more achievable.

INDEX

Internal Sensory Representational
  Systems, 134
Internal State [Meta-program], 343
In-Time, 301
Ivan Pavlov, 179

J

John Grinder, 56
Judgement [Meta Model], 226

K

Karen Falconer, 384
Kinesthetic [Predicates], 141
Kinesthetic [Sub-modalities], 278
Kinesthetic Anchoring, 184
Kinesthetic External, 134
Kinesthetic Internal, 134

L

Lack of referential index [Meta Model],
  225
Lack of referential index [Milton Model],
  240
Law of Requisite Variety, 65
Lead Representational System, 145
Leading, 155
Learning Ladder, 332
Leverage, 82
Limiting Belief, 292
Linguistic [Definition], 39
Linguistic Presuppositions, 202
Lost performative [Milton Model], 240

M

Management Filter [Meta-program], 349
Manipulation [Definition], 156
Mapping Across [Sub-modalities], 283
Matching, 153
Means Value, 362
Mentor [Role], 168
Mercedes Model, 256
Meta Mirror, 328
Meta Model, 217
Meta Model Patterns, 220
Meta Position, 325

Meta-meta Position, 328
Metaphors, 250
Meta-programs, 340
meta-programs [for communication],
  353
meta-programs [for influencing], 354
Methodology [Definition], 43
Milton Model, 236
Mind Reading, 151
Mind reading [Meta Model], 229
Mind reading [Milton Model], 241
Mirroring, 153
Modal Operator of Necessity and
  Possibility [Linguistic], 205
Modal operators of necessity [Meta
  Model], 222
Modal operators of necessity [Milton
  Model], 242
Modal operators of possibility [Milton
  Model], 242
Modal operators of possibility &
  impossibility [Meta Model], 222, 223
Model of Transformational Grammar,
  215
Modelling Period [Values], 100
Myers Briggs Type Indicator (aka
  MBTI), 351

N

Neuro [Definition], 39
Neurological Levels [Model], 102
New Behaviour Generator [Technique],
  163
NLP Diploma, 376
NLP Master Practitioner [Certification],
  381
NLP Practitioner [Certification], 378
NLP Principles [About], 388
Nominalisation [Meta Model], 227
Nominalisations [Milton Model], 242
Non-Verbal Accessing Cues, 143
Noun Blockbuster [Precision Model],
  232

O

Olfactory, 134
Olfactory [Sub-modalities], 278
Open Frame, 308

THE END?

THIS IS THE END OF *THIS* BOOK BUT AS YOU NOW KNOW...

THIS IS JUST THE VERY BEGINNING...

Where ever you are and whatever the reason for purchasing this book I sincerely hope that you have found value in content and that it has created enough curiosity to start your very own journey with NLP further.

Thank you for spending your time on this book. I truly hope that one day we can meet and I can thank you in person.

Lee Groombridge.

IF YOU LIKE THIS BOOK THEN…

…you'll no doubt LOVE these other books written by the same author,
Lee Groombridge.

HOW TO SUCCEED
IN BUSINESS
WITH NLP PRINCIPLES

A complete guide for the
practical application of NLP
to win in business and
progress your career

LUCID. THRIVE. PLAN.

How to get clear on what you
want, master your mindset and
reverse-engineer success.

GET RESILIENCE

7 Steps to a cool, calm and
collected you.

All are available from **Amazon** or to learn more contact us at **nlpprinciples.com**

One last thing from the author...

NLP Principles was formed with a mission to enhance business and personal performance via advanced learning and business consultancy in order to not only positively influence the recipients but also the other people around them.

If you have found this book useful, help us achieve our ambitious target of reaching 1 million people by 2030, by sharing this book with the people that matter to you and that you feel would enjoy or benefit from it.

If you would like to buy or gift multiple copies of this book, or any other NLP Principles book, to students, employees or colleagues please get in touch so that we can assist you with this.

Every small action to help make our work visible to those that need it counts, so if this book has provided you with great value in any way, **do something that is absolutely free and will take just a few seconds.** Please rate this book on the website from which you purchased it.

Thank you, and I leave you with this...

*"It really is possible for you
to create an infinite positive ripple effect
that empowers the masses and transforms the world.
All that is needed is a single moment,
a moment for YOU to make the first splash!"*

Lee Groombridge.

Printed in Great Britain
by Amazon

42979431R00238